WORLD SCOUTING

Further Praise for *World Scouting*

"Quite possibly the best discourse on World Scouting and non-formal education I have ever had the good fortune to read. Vallory's style, whilst uncompromising in its academic rigour, is highly readable for a reader who normally prefers 'doing' Scouting to studying it."

—John May, Vice-Chairman, World Scout Committee; Secretary General of the Duke of Edinburgh's International Award for Young People

"Written in a very exciting style that will make you want to keep reading till the end, this book revisits how Scouting started, showing its informal launching and its historical evolution throughout the twentieth century. The book analyzes Scouting's structure and recognition policy, its role in developing ideas of global citizenship and belonging, and the spirit of Scouting."

—World Scout Bureau

WORLD SCOUTING

EDUCATING FOR GLOBAL CITIZENSHIP

Eduard Vallory

First published in hardcover in 2012 by
PALGRAVE MACMILLAN®
in the United States—a division of St. Martin's Press LLC,
175 Fifth Avenue, New York, NY 10010.

Where this book is distributed in the UK, Europe and the rest of the World,
this is by Palgrave Macmillan, a division of Macmillan Publishers Limited,
registered in England, company number 785998, of Houndmills,
Basingstoke, Hampshire RG21 6XS.

Palgrave Macmillan is the global academic imprint of the above
companies and has companies and representatives throughout the world.

Palgrave® and Macmillan® are registered trademarks in the United
States, the United Kingdom, Europe and other countries.

ISBN: 978–1–137–35356–6

Library of Congress Cataloging-in-Publication Data

Vallory, Eduard.
  World scouting : educating for global citizenship / Eduard Vallory.
    p. cm.
  ISBN 978–0–230–34068–8
  1. Scouting (Youth activity) 2. Citizenship.
  3. Youth movements. 4. Service learning. I. Title.
  HS3269.V35 2012
  369.43—dc23   2011039848

A catalogue record of the book is available from the British Library.

Design by Integra Software Services

First PALGRAVE MACMILLAN paperback edition: May 2013

To all the friends I have made through scouting

Contents

LIST OF FIGURES

FOREWORD

DR. JOSEPH P. FARRELL

Professor emeritus, Ontario Institute for Studies in Education (University of Toronto)
Past President, Comparative and International Education Society

This is a *groundbreaking* and *unique* book. Those are words that can seldom be used honestly in referring to a new book. In this case they are well justified. Vallory's work begins to fill a huge gap in the published literatures regarding (1) comparative education, (2) nonformal education, and (3) citizenship/moral education. The subject of study is world scouting, which is a curiously *unexplored* phenomenon. This is curious because it is the largest nonformal youth education movement in the world, currently enrolling approximately 30 million young people in 166 nations covering virtually all of the major cultural/religious/faith/cosmological traditions of the world, which has been in existence, and steadily growing, for more than a century. It also, in 1981, was the first organization to receive a newly established UNESCO Prize for Peace Education.

In spite of its size and reach and international recognition, the published academic literature on world scouting is scanty, to put it mildly. There are some local accounts or histories, and a few scholarly articles or books, mostly dealing with the early history of the movement, all of which the author cites. But it is a quite tiny list considering the history, global reach, and size of the scouting movement. I have often wondered why this is so. I suspect it is related to a kind of intellectual snobbishness, which looks down on scouting as "not serious," as a recreational activity for comfortable, middle-class youngsters in well-off nations. (In reality about two-thirds of the world membership is from poor segments of poor nations.) One has popular stereotypes of young boys in a short-pants uniform helping old ladies across the street. One hears or reads in popular discourse statements such as "We can't be boy scouts about this," meaning implicitly that we can't be ineffectual do-gooders, but have to be serious people of action. And so on. There is also, I suspect from long work in faculties of education, a kind of self-imposed blindness to any sorts of major learning activity that takes place outside of the formal school system. In any event, the ignorance is there.

I have read this book from a particular background, as do we all. I have been a graduate professor of Comparative and International Education since 1968, now formally retired but still working away! For 15 of those years I was also a professor of Adult Education. In addition, I have been connected with scouting both locally and at the world level, since 1948, when I first joined Cub Scouts in the United States. Since then I have served as a scout troop leader in various locations in the United States, in Latin America, and in Canada, from 1958 to 1997, when I "retired" from frontline leadership to work in more background support activities. Moreover, from 1985 through 1996 I served as a member of the International Relations Committee of Scouts Canada, which is the formal linkage between Scouts Canada and the world scout movement. From these multiple and overlapping standpoints I make the following observations.

This is a masterful book on the history of world scouting. Vallory has managed to capture the main features of the worldwide spread of this voluntary educational movement over a century, through the course of two World Wars, many smaller conflicts, the "cold war" and its aftermath, and the eras of European colonization of much of the world, and then decolonization and the establishment of myriad new nations, all in a relatively brief text. Vallory is excellent at pulling together the various strands of a very complicated history covering just over a century, in a manner that is readable and clear. He highlights and outlines the main tendencies and tensions without getting dragged down in endless details, but does offer telling "details" at just the right point to illustrate the main story that he is developing. And the Notes are quite helpful in guiding the reader who may have a great interest in some particular detail to a deeper level of literature. Now, to the gaps the book begins to fill.

In the *comparative and international education* literature there is virtually nothing about scouting, except as a brief mention while discussing something else. Almost all scholars in this field study "formal" schooling. Those few who study nonformal education study it only in relation to adults or older youth. Almost exactly three decades ago, in 1981, Thomas LaBelle in his presidential address to the Comparative and International Education Society urged comparative educators to turn their attention to the study of nonformal education of children and youth, arguing that it is much more widespread and much more important to the overall development of young people than is commonly assumed by educational researchers. As he noted then: "educators might be better off looking at schools as only one locus for education, as many youngsters and parents apparently do."[1] A colleague, Vandra Masemann, and I attempted a response to that call by organizing a panel at the 1990 meeting of the same society on nonformal youth movements across cultures, dealing mainly with scouting.[2] And now, along comes Dr. Vallory!

This work is a monumental contribution to the ongoing debates in comparative and international education, and other social science and educational fields as well, over issues such as "globalization" and "localization" or cross-cultural institutional transfer. (See, for example, the most widely used basic textbook in comparative education, now going into its fourth edition, whose title is *Comparative Education: The Dialectic of the Global and the Local*.)[3] Scouting, as Vallory tells the story, is an excellent lens through which to view these complex issues. It is the most widespread youth educational movement in the world. It is also entirely *voluntary*. Young people, and their leaders, join and stay only because they *want to*. What is it that attracts some 30 million young people to become involved and stay involved in this program across almost all of our world? What is the "magic" here? How has this movement managed to spread, over the course of a century, literally around the world, adapting to vastly different cultures and histories and spiritual traditions, while maintaining a core identity, a common set of basic values and beliefs, teaching and learning practices and methods, and what amounts to a core curriculum? And all of the spreading and adopting/adapting was done with no impetus from some central organization or authority. There is in this story no corps of "missionaries," out to spread the "good news" of scouting; no educational reform "implementers"; nor a cadre of "change agents." There has been no international agency or donor promoting it. It is rather a story of voluntary adoption and adaptation, a worldwide century-long process of innovation diffusion. The world organization has mainly one key function: "recognition," which gives a national association the right to legitimately use the word (or label) "scouting." It thus protects the "identity" of world scouting. Moreover, as Vallory amply demonstrates, "scouting" is everywhere "local" yet everywhere "global," always identifiably "scouting." For students of comparative and international education there is much of great value here to ponder over and learn from.

Adult Education scholars, who study nonformal education extensively, do so almost exclusively in relation to adults, especially with respect to literacy learning, community development, health learning, and such. In a sense in this they are "staying within their franchise," but there is something lost here. The "method" of scouting, as discussed in this book, is quite properly carefully distinguished from the pedagogical methods of formal schooling. When I began my 15-year stint in a department of

Adult Education (how I got there is a rather picaresque tale of academic administrative misadventure, but that's another story for another time) I quickly noted that my new colleagues almost never used the word "education" in their professional discourse. The words of choice were "learning" and its "facilitation." One did not "educate" adults; one facilitated their learning. They had a new word to distinguish what they did while working with adults: "andragogy," as opposed to "pedagogy," which was for children. But it quickly became apparent to me that what my new colleagues in adult education called "andragogy" was actually a rather accurate description of the "method" of scouting that I had been routinely practicing as a scout leader for decades. I came to wryly refer to the scouting method as "andragogy for smaller people." Or perhaps andragogy is the scouting method for larger people? What these ruminations, stimulated by reading Vallory's book, lead me to is that we need to be very careful about what we think we mean by such traditional distinctions as school versus adult education; formal versus nonformal education; adult versus child education.

The heart of this book, as the title indicates, is the role of world scouting in *Educating for Global Citizenship*. There is a huge literature that has developed over decades on "citizenship education," which sometimes overlaps strongly with "moral education," in the formal schools. That portion of such literature which is not hortatory is for the most part rather dismal reading in terms of the possibilities of the formal schools, as we have them, being able to produce any sort of learning conducive to living in and contributing to democratic polities. How does one learn democracy in an institution that is fundamentally undemocratic? In the early 1970s a colleague and I conducted a massive study on student participation in decision making in high schools in the Province of Ontario. We had thousands of questionnaires, hundreds of interviews, many (what we would now call) focus groups, and observations. Our conclusion was that there was precious little student participation, and that which existed was counterproductive to the supposed learning objectives: that is, students who were actively involved in decision-making processes in school were more cynical regarding the broader democratic processes in their societies than those not involved, and the longer and deeper their involvement, the more cynical their beliefs about the broader society became. That is, they were learning that democratic institutions were (their words) a "sham" or a "con game" to disguise the fact that the "real power" was exercised by those "who already had it and wouldn't let it go." Not likely the intended learning outcome![4] Nothing I have read about formal schools and citizenship education over the ensuing 35 or so years has changed that conclusion.

Scouting is quite the opposite. A well-run scout troop is a small, well-functioning democracy; this is fundamental to the scout "method." Scouting does not "teach" democratic citizenship; it simply provides through its basic "method" opportunities for young people to "learn" democratic citizenship. That is, as adult educators would say, it "enables" or "facilitates" learning, rather than trying to didactically "teach." In a series of small essays published in the journal *Curriculum Inquiry*, I have provided examples and analyses of how this "method" works out, on the basis of my own experience.[5] Vallory brings these very local experiences and meditations to a global stage. The idea of "citizenship education" clearly has very different meanings and connotations depending upon the sort of society in which one lives: democratic, totalitarian, tightly controlled, loosely controlled, theocratic, non-deist, and on and on. Given its global scope it is obvious that world scouting exists and thrives in all such societies, and develops within them (among its members at least) as well a consciousness of "belonging" or "citizenship" in a global community. It is in discussing how this came about, how scouting could develop, implant, and maintain its vision of global citizenship across such varied cultural/historical terrain that Vallory's work really stands out. This is ultimately a story of subtle international diplomacy at one level with local level work at another level. (Again, the "global" and the "local.") It is a very complex and conflict-ridden tale that is very well told in this book, and well worth pondering for anyone who is seriously interested in trying to find ways through which the varied people of this planet can learn to live together peacefully.

Since this book is the first systematic scholarly study of the vast terrain of world scouting, there are many questions that beg for further study. But that is a function of a *groundbreaking* work such as this. Now that the ground has been broken there are myriad furrows to plow, and fields to sow and harvest. That is for the future. Here it is enough to have begun, and done so very well indeed.

ACKNOWLEDGMENTS

The research behind this book was made possible by the help and support of a long list of people and institutions in one way or another, and I would not like to begin without first thanking some of them.

First and foremost, I would like to thank Fitzwilliam College of the University of Cambridge for its generosity in awarding me the position of Batista i Roca Fellow for two academic years (2004–2006). That position enabled me to conduct my research in excellent conditions within a stimulating academic environment that gave me a direct insight into the English liberal tradition that led to the birth of scouting 100 years ago. Incidentally, it was a happy coincidence that this fellowship was endowed with a donation to the College by Prof. Josep M. Batista i Roca himself, who was also the founder of Catalan scouting almost a century ago.

This research is the product of the perseverance in the face of skepticism of those who questioned the suitability of "scouting" as a research topic, but also of the encouragement, unwavering support, and friendship of Dr. Jacques Moreillon, a support that has indeed been an honor for me. I would not have discovered so much about the scout movement or have had access to all the previously undisclosed documents and information I have used were it not for him. I am particularly grateful to him for allowing me to work on his dense and rich "Secretary General Monthly Reports," drawn up over the 16 years during which he served as Secretary General of WOSM. My gratitude for support, friendship, and enriching discussions also extends to Lesley Bulman-Lever, Chief Executive of WAGGGS until 2006.

The academic rigor with which I have tried to produce this research is largely the result of the intellectual ambition and intense academic work I experienced during my graduate studies at the University of Chicago, under the stimulating guidance of Prof. Carles Boix, combined with the encouragement and sense of challenge conveyed to me by Prof. Andreu Mas-Colell. I was not the first, nor will I be the last researcher to receive many comments belittling the interest in scouting as a topic of study. But over and above my conviction, the support and help I have received from professors Andreu Mas-Colell, Montserrat Guibernau, Josep Picó, and Imma Tubella contributed to my persistence: my indebtedness to them. My acknowledgment goes also to Prof. Joseph Farrell for his encouragement on turning the research into a book and for his stimulating Foreword.

In world scouting, I was privileged to have profound conversations on the research topic with many people, among them the aforementioned Jacques Moreillon and Lesley Bulman-Lever, as well as the late Malek Gabr, Mateo Jover, Laszlo Nagy, Eduardo Missoni, Heather Roy, Camilla Lindquist, Barbara Calvi, Mario Díaz, Miquel Essomba, and Raül Adroher. Thanks to them all I was able to grasp the wealth and enormous complexity that lies behind the apparent simplicity of scouting. Particularly, thanks to Mark Clayton and Joshua A. Kirby, I better understood US scouting. Likewise, thanks to Luc Panissod I was given access to all original WOSM censuses and was able to solve issues in the data validation phase. I am also grateful for the help of several other professionals of the World Scout Bureau, the World Bureau of WAGGGS, and the Scout Association UK, some of them already friends, that I don't have the space to quote here.

I must thank Rachael Merola for her contribution in adapting the research and the Catalan book into this English version, particularly on some sensitive sections, a gratitude that also extends to Sara Yamaka and Jodi Neufeld. I also thank Montse Vergara and Jesica Aracil for their work on the statistical part of the research, and Laura Cozma for her assistance on the statistical graphs of this book.

The research this book summarizes was conducted in parallel to the commemoration of the centenary of scouting worldwide. Three academic events I participated in contributed indirectly to make this book what it is today. First, the symposium organized in Barcelona in summer 2007 by the Institut d'Estudis Catalans (the Catalan Academia), whose support three years later led to my book in Catalan, *L'escoltisme mundial* (2010), which is the precedent of this present work. Second, the World Scientific Congress on Scouting held in Geneva in late 2007, where I met Prof. Fernando Reimers, who increased my knowledge on global citizenship education. And finally, the symposium "Scouting: A Centennial History" held at the Johns Hopkins University (Baltimore) in 2008, where I interacted with many researchers on scouting worldwide, and which originated the book *Scouting Frontiers* (2009).

I cannot list here all the people I have met through scouting whom I would like to thank. If scouting is a life experience, I have been extremely rich in experiences and in people to share them with. Let me just thank all the people I worked with in Escoltes Catalans and in the Catalan

Federation, and from there in the world community of scouting, to build a better society and a better world.

In the course of my research I also discovered just how lucky I am to have a loving environment of family and close friends. It is to them that I owe the smile I wake up with every morning.

INTRODUCTION

A falling tree makes more noise than a growing forest

African Proverb

IF YOU WERE TO ASK SOMEONE on the streets of Mexico DF for the description of scouting, it is unlikely to include Asia, World War II, colonialism, or the United Nations. It might include a neighborhood scout unit or memories of being a cub scout as a child. But scouting is the neighborhood and also the world: the local group in London's East End and the training of those who would lead the processes of decolonization; the boys and girls camps in the Pyrenees and the brotherhoods of youths in countries and communities at war; the social implication in Harlem and the community development programs in Indonesia.

Thus, few people know that scouting is a movement particularly strong in developing and emerging countries, that it is one of the strongest association realities in Arab countries, and that when it was formalized in 1920, world scouting had national associations in over 50 percent of the world's independent countries—a percentage that has not dropped since and has actually increased to a current figure of 83 percent, while the number of independent countries increased from 63 (1922) to 194 (2008). It is likewise unperceived that former scouts constitute the main parliamentarian intergroup in the British House of Commons and in the Parliament of Korea. It is mostly unknown that scouting has been forbidden by totalitarian regimes, and it is still forbidden in communist countries. And not only this—even fewer people know that more than two-thirds of all current and former NASA astronauts have been involved in boy and girl scouting, among them 20 of the 24 men who traveled to the moon, including 11 of the 12 moonwalkers. Neil Armstrong, the first human who walked on the moon, had a Scout Badge with him in that historical moment.

Actually, scouting is today the largest youth educational movement in the world, comprising 30 million children and youth of around 165 countries of the five continents. Its purpose is to contribute to the self-development of young people in achieving their full physical, intellectual, social, and spiritual potentials as individuals, as responsible citizens, and as members of their local, national, and international communities. And it does so as a movement of volunteers operating through a world-wide network of local groups, belonging to national scout associations and to two world organizations—the World Organization of the Scout Movement (WOSM) and the World Association of Girl Guides and Girl Scouts (WAGGGS)—both based on the same principles and founded by the same person, Robert Baden-Powell. Although both world organizations and their members have differences in their traditions and approaches (starting with the names: boy scouts, girl guides, girl scouts, scouts), in this book "scouting" refers to the movement gathered by the two world organizations, as will be explained later.

Scouting is a movement that many people are vaguely familiar with, relating it mainly to recreational activities that have no social impact other than the fact that they keep the boys and girls busy. That is the consequence of one of the greatest strengths of the scout movement, which is also one of its worst weaknesses: the deeply intuitive nature of its educational action. For young people, scouting is about enjoying, not about learning. And that is why they become scouts. But, at the same time, this is a weakness because most scholars and professionals see only the recreational aspect of scouting, unable to perceive the strong educational impact of this movement.

One of scouting's many fascinating attributes is its ability to make deep roots in disparate societies. That is why we the Catalans are convinced that scouting is a product of our way of life, just as the American, Korean, French, or Egyptian are convinced of the same. Precisely because of this deep identification with scouting in each of the societies where it is present, there has been no study to date of the world movement of scouting as a whole.

As Dr. Laszlo Nagy explained in his important 1967 Report on World Scouting, "many misunderstandings, as well as many differences of appreciation, arise from the fact that some observers concentrate their whole attention on one kind of Scouting only, the one they see, know, like and practice." The reason for this is the strong local grounding of the scout movement, which confused the part with the whole. Thus, we find a great many studies on scouting that focus on the movement's presence in a particular society. There is research on early British scouting, US scouting, Catalan scouting, Belgian scouting, Indian scouting, African scouting, et cetera, with a large volume of literature in many languages, convinced that they are dealing with what scouting "is." (In the social sciences, this is known as "methodological nationalism," that is, confusing a society with the global framework of analysis.) And yet, with the exception of Nagy's Report on World Scouting—which analyzed the basic principles and problems with unity and with global organization in WOSM—there have been no known studies on world scouting as a whole, as a voluntary movement of global dimensions that has educated millions of individuals to become responsible citizens during the twentieth century. This tangential approach has prevented the study of world scouting as a whole up to this point. The book you have in your hands is therefore the summary of the first research on scouting at a global level.

The doctoral research that this book now summarizes was completed in 2007 under the title "Global Citizenship Education: Study of the Ideological Bases, Historical Development, International Dimension, and Values and Practices of World Scouting." That research and this book condense four years of research and nearly two decades of scouting leadership in Catalonia, in Europe, and internationally. Given the absence of literature that examines scouting at the global level, the first step in conducting this study was to reset the foundations in four large blocks. First, a historical analysis that would show that scouting as a world movement has existed as a subject since 1920, therefore separating its eventual consolidation from earlier controversies. Second, an in-depth study of the movement's ideological coherence through the evolution of its positions and legal framework: definition, purpose, principles, method, organization, operation, educational impact, and recognition policy. Third, an unprecedented statistical study of WOSM census from 1924 to 2004, subjecting all data to computer analysis for the first time: the new data is segmented by country, corrected when needed, and the newly created databases are a resource for future research. The fourth and final piece of the project's foundation is some case studies that analyze the consistency between principles at the global level and practices at the local level on the topics related with global citizenship.

The academic analysis was possible through a combination of the experience as an insider of the movement with the intensive bibliographical compilation and analysis of academic studies on scouting and of many historical and current world scout documents. I also interviewed key-informants, processed original statistical data, and analyzed several projects and initiatives as case studies. It is necessary to point out that most of the material used in this research were not only original sources but also material that had been kept unknown to most researchers until now, such as most of the statistics of the World Scout Bureau since 1920s, the essential Nagy Report of 1967, and the Monthly Reports of the WOSM Secretary General between 1988 and 2004. This access to and analysis of previously undisclosed sources gives the research a particular academic significance.

Throughout this book I have used the terms "scouting," "scouts," and "scout associations" generically to describe the activities of associations that would find themselves in membership of WOSM and/or WAGGGS and that together constitute the scout movement. Where possible and wherever information was readily available from either organization, I have tried to show the specificities of policy, action, and orientation of both organizations concerned with scouting/guiding worldwide.

This research seeks to respond with data to those who would dismiss the potential of the scout movement, unaware of its unconventional nature and its enormous influence. As the historian Tim Parsons explains, "there is a broad perception that Scouting is a relatively inconsequential institution that is not worthy of serious academic investigation. Friends and acquaintances often responded with wry chuckles or bemused looks when I explained that my next project was going to be a study of African boy scouts during the colonial era." The first challenge of my research, therefore, was to prove that scouting as a world movement, as a research subject traditionally underrated by or foreign to the scientific community is potentially very useful for studying the contradictions in the contemporary development of the concepts of citizenship and education, from the basis of national loyalty to the complexity of a globalized world and in increasingly multicultural societies.

Clichés, rather than scientific analyses, have been the main source for opinions on the scout movement. It is often said that scouting was founded by a British colonial army officer, but nobody stops to ask why it enjoys such great prestige nowadays in the former colonies in Africa and Asia, or why it had supporters like Mahatma Gandhi or Nelson Mandela. Attention is paid to its patriotic content, while ignoring the many cases of armed conflict between communities in diverse countries where scouting has acted as a bridge. It is said that the scout sense of global belonging is not extraordinary because this happens with many religious organizations too; however, no one realizes the potential conflicts that may arise in a movement that deals with citizenship education, national involvement, global commitment, and world understanding while bringing together individuals representing a very wide spectrum of national identities, religious beliefs, and cultural traditions.

The resilience of scouting is such that the late Malek Gabr suggested that I begin my research by asking the question, "Why has the scout movement not yet disappeared?" How is it that a movement run by volunteers from all over the world that aims to educate citizens by combining the sense of national belonging with global belonging and that interacts with religious beliefs, cultural identities, and government institutions can continue to recruit millions of voluntary people who want to further its aim of educating new generations to become responsible citizens of their countries and of the world?

The research this book is founded on is the fruit both of intellectual curiosity and of personal experience as a scout. Indeed, I have experienced the magic of the campfires and the value of friendship, service, adventure, and excitement. I know the indescribable sensation of returning home and leaving my mates after an international exchange. I have been part of some scout groups with very different social profiles, both as a youth and as a leader; I have been International Commissioner of Catalan scouting; and I have participated in several European and World Conferences of WOSM and of WAGGGS.

I carried all this baggage with me when several years ago I decided to focus my doctoral research in Political Science on world scouting, thinking in terms of the wise African proverb that says: "A falling tree makes more noise than a growing forest." This is what this book deals with: an educational movement growing around the world, slow and silent but powerful.

The strength of this growing forest is hidden in a certain magic that permeates the scout movement—the magic of the contagious excitement that it transmits, the joy in the shining eyes of the boys and girls singing on an outing, or returning from a development project in Africa. It is a magic that has lasted for decades, and that this book attempts to explain.

ONE HUNDRED YEARS OF TRANSFORMING THE FUTURE

I pray that every home in India may have children like Scouts and Guides

Mahātmā **Gandhi**, promoter of Indian independence and advocate of nonviolence

THE BEGINNINGS OF THE SCOUT MOVEMENT can be found in 1907, when Robert Baden-Powell, a renowned lieutenant general in the British Army who had just turned 50, started writing a book that would transform the lives of millions of people around the world: *Scouting for Boys.* The journey that scouting has taken since that time as a worldwide educational movement is long, and deserves thoughtful, piece-by-piece explanation.

To do so, we should explore, first, how the scout proposal appeared since 1907, the context surrounding its emergence, and the major transformations it underwent in just the following 15 years, crucial to the understanding of the foundations of scouting (i.e., both *boy* scouting and *girl* scouting or *guiding*) as a world movement. Once the preliminaries of the movement are explained, we will lay out the formalization of world scouting as an organization in 1920, as well as its development under the leadership of its founder, Robert Baden-Powell, and of his wife, Olave Baden-Powell. Moreover, we will scan the stage of its globalization and the updating of its international role in the 1960s. To be aware of the enormous presence of scouting worldwide, we will finally have a glance at some original, never-published census data outlining the evolution of the movement throughout this history and also some quantitative figures about the world movement at the beginning of the new millennium.

1. THE PRECEDENTS OF WORLD SCOUTING (1907–1920)

Though British scouting began to take root in the first decade of the twentieth century, the world movement as such did not exist until 1920, with the formalization of a worldwide organization leaded by Baden-Powell himself. For the sake of clarity, it would be useful to divide the period before the formalization of world scouting in 1920 into three phases. The first regards the sequence of events and ideas that led Robert Baden-Powell to publish *Scouting for Boys* in 1908, and the path that led from the publication of this book to the creation of two British associations: the Boy Scouts Association (1909) and the Girl Guides Association (1910). The second phase is longer and covers the sporadic international growth process—under the moral authority of Baden-Powell—simultaneously with the creation of the two British associations, the development and maturing of the ideological discourse of Scouting, and the strengthening of its relationship with progressive educational movements. Finally, the third phase, which forms the ideological and international basis for the scout movement, stretches from World War I to the creation of the Boy Scouts International Bureau (BSIB, which later became WOSM) in 1920 and of the World Association of Girl Guides and Girl Scouts (WAGGGS) in 1928.

1.1. AN IDEA, A BOOK, AND HOW THEY CAME ABOUT

Scouting is, above all else, the fruit of a brilliant idea of a man named Robert Baden-Powell: the ensemble of his technical knowledge, resurgent patriotism, and childlike dreams and hopes, which he, like in the work *Peter Pan,* would never give up. It is unanimously agreed that the catalyst for the birth of scouting was Baden-Powell's book *Scouting for Boys: A Handbook for Instruction in Good Citizenship.* The author had risen to popularity in Britain after successfully commanding the defense of the South African border town of Mafeking in 1899 during the Second Boer War.[1]

The editor of *Scouting for Boys* was the newspaper magnate C. Arthur Pearson, of *The Daily Express,* who recognized the commercial potential of the book and published it in six fortnightly installments beginning in January 1908, and after its success, as a book in May of the same year along with a magazine, *The Scout.* The book became an immediate best seller: after the first four editions were printed in the first year and were received with great enthusiasm, there were more than 60,000 additional copies published in the second year.

What brought Baden-Powell to write this book, which would influence the lives of millions of boys and girls around the world? In 1899, the same year as the siege of Mafeking, Baden-Powell published the book *Aids to Scouting for NCOs and Men,* a military training manual in which he recalled his experiences training young soldiers and emphasized the importance of outdoor games and activities in character development. Though intended for a military public, the book contributed to Baden-Powell's rising popularity with both young people and students. William Smith, founder and leader of the Boys' Brigade, a British youth movement with military and Christian overtones, asked him to make an adaptation of the book for adolescent boys.

A first foray into what the book would look like in practice took place in August 1907, when Baden-Powell brought together 20 adolescent boys from various social classes to live together for ten days in an encampment in the small island of Brownsea, in Poole Harbour (South England), where they cooked their own food, played games, learned skills, and listened to the fanciful and exotic stories that Baden-Powell told. This date is generally considered the beginning of scouting. In January of the following year, *Scouting for Boys* was published, and in April *The Scout,* the magazine for boys, which printed an impressive 110,000 copies each week in its first year.

Despite the growing informal following, *Scouting for Boys* was not therefore intended to spur the creation of an organization or a movement of any sort. In fact, an analysis of the first edition of the book (1908) recently edited by Elleke Boehmer shows how it was "a fragmentary, porous, non-cohesive mishmash of other texts," many of which were his, while others were not—such as the notes and experiences regarding Native-Americans' heritage, which were taken from Ernest T. Seton,[2] an early ecologist and educator who initiated the League of Woodcraft Indians youth program in 1902. The mixture resulted tremendously suggestive: packed with exotic tales (from Africa and India), games, theatrical works, and secret signs and symbols and written in a style to stimulate adolescent minds, the book combines entertainment with moral lessons, as though it were a game.

A game that did, in fact, offer a convenient outline for character development for adolescents in their leisure time, ready to be adopted by existing British youth organizations like the Boys' Brigade or the Young Men's Christian Association (YMCA),[3] or directly by civic groups. In fact, the book began with a letter intended for adults, explaining that the scout system is "applicable to existing organisations such as schools, boys' brigades, cadet corps, etc., or can supply a simple organisation of its own where these do not exist."[4]

Part of the reason for the success of the book is that it was the "right time" for such an idea. Society was just beginning to recognize adolescence as one of the life stages of humans, and there was a greater understanding of the unique needs of boys during this time of life. In addition, with the industrialization of the western world, children of this age group were in school during the day, rather than working, and fewer of them participated in apprenticeships. Declining birth rates and an increased standard of living also contributed to an increased value placed on children's well-being and character development. The ideological background to Baden-Powell's initiative came from the social and political tensions in England following the Victorian age, and it also included assumptions like that industrialization was undermining the traditional notions of good conduct and leading to the moral and physical degeneration of the lower classes in the British Empire, as well as the fear for the possible decline of the Empire.[5] Given the underlying threat of German invasion and his conviction that British youths were not prepared to defend the nation, Baden-Powell believed that he could propose a model to complement the education received by adolescents at school from an overtly patriotic point of view; a model that would shape their character and teach them initiative and useful skills by means of open-air activities, games, and observation, in a popular, motivating format.

Thus, the first edition of *Scouting for Boys* is a bit of a hodge-podge of previous works and materials from different sources, with no clear doctrinal strategy. According to Allan Warren, a historian of the scout movement, "Baden-Powell, no systematic thinker or critic, picked up and dropped social and political concerns as he went along."[6] Indeed, there are constant contradictions: the book seeks the complicity of parents, the school, and the church, while criticizing parental laziness, the inconsistency of schools, and the biblical teachings of the church. Furthermore, the model endeavors to shape autonomous individuals, but proposes doing so through obedience and self-discipline. Overall, the book's emphasis is on the development of the individual's character and the moral influence of the small group—quite the opposite of impersonal training for the masses. It would not be until later that the book, and the scout movement, would develop an ideological consistency.

In fact, the book offered an imaginary element of self-identification to its adolescent readers: the feeling of being part of a grand game of sorts. Just like a game, *Scouting for Boys* explained who the "scouts" were— fictional explorers, rather than members of an educational movement— and described how they dressed and behaved. One of the various stories, or "campfire yarns," of the book says that "Scouts, all the world over, have unwritten laws which bind them just as much as if they had been printed in black and white. They come down to us from old times....

The following are the rules which apply to boy scouts, and which you swear to obey when you take your oath as a scout, so it is as well that you should know all about them."[7]

The story goes on telling that these behavioral guidelines (or "rules") were collected and written down in the "Scout Law," which, it explains, the scout accepted when he took the "Scout Oath": "Before he becomes a scout a boy must take the scout's oath, thus: 'On my honour I promise that: 1. I will do my duty to God and the King. 2. I will do my best to help others, whatever it costs me. 3. I know the scout law, and will obey it.' "[8]

Following that text of the first edition in 1908, we could see that the book outlined a so-called Scout Law to be followed by scouts around the world—though boy scouts did not yet exist in that moment:

1. A Scout's honour is to be trusted. 2. A Scout is loyal to the King, and to his officers, and to his country, and to his employers. 3. A Scout's duty is to be useful and to help others. 4. A Scout is a friend to all and a brother to every other Scout, no matter to what social class the other belongs. 5. A Scout is courteous. 6. A Scout is a friend to animals. 7. A Scout obeys orders of his patrol leader or scoutmaster without question. 8. A Scout smiles and sings under all circumstances. 9. A Scout is thrifty.[9]

These values—like those of medieval knights—allowed the readers to bring the rich world of fantasy of the book into real life, and constituted a universal and positive code of conduct (being these "laws" are positive injunctions). Boys engaged and identified with the material in the book, applying the novel principles of this new idea called "scouting" in their daily lives.

The "Scout Law" and the "Scout Oath" would come about shortly after the principles of scouting were identified. In the original edition of the book, however, the Scout Oath does not contain the solemn and official tone that differentiates it from the other elements used to identify scouts. In fact, after it has explained the Oath, the story continues in an epic and fantastical tone to describe the Scout's Salute and the secret signs that those "scouts" used.[10] Baden Powell's description of the Scout Law ("Scouts, all the world over, have unwritten laws . . .") is clearly only part of the story, since he is not referring to the Boy Scouts (which did not yet exist); instead, he blends fiction and intention with an "unwritten law" accepted by scouts all over the world (referring to the explorers, the characters in the story). When, later on, the scout movement was formalized, these elements—the Law, the Oath, the Salute, and the Badge—would become part of the symbolism of scouting.

Moreover, the references to *God* and the *King* in the text of the Oath and the Law must be read in the context of Britain at that time: a religious society with no hegemonistic church that, at the end of the eighteenth century, had established the independence of its parliament from the monarchy—thus creating a democratic structure: "If the service which was required of the boys was for God, it was for the God of a multi-confessional and tolerant society; if loyalty to the King was asked for, it was faithfulness to a monarch who reigned rather than governed."[11]

Therefore, although the original intention of Robert Baden-Powell was not to create a widespread movement, the extraordinary reception of the book make also the idea of "scouting" to succeed in such a way that it surprised even its author. Groups of self-identified *scouts* soon appeared throughout Britain, clamoring for guidance and a more cohesive identity. But what did it mean to be *"considered a scout"*? It was simply to follow the conduct and ethics outlined in *Scouting for Boys*. And it seemed that this was done all around. One should bear in mind that the clever intervention of Pearson, the publisher, supplied the book with a commercial appeal, where it was advertised—when the scout movement did not yet exist—giving a postal address, that "Scout's Badges, Medals, Patrol Flags, and Crests, Tracking Irons, and such articles of scouts' equipment, can be obtained at low rates on application here."[12]

In September 1909, 21 months after the book was published, Pearson sponsored a rally at London's Crystal Palace, spotting a burgeoning business opportunity in doing so. To the surprise of its organizers, headed by Baden-Powell, 11,000 self-identified "scouts" adolescents turned up at the rally.[13] Baden-Powell described this spontaneous following in an interview in 1937:

> Boys were writing to me telling me how they had started Patrols and Troops and had got men to come and act as their Scoutmasters. So we had to start a Headquarters office in a tiny room to deal with correspondence and supply equipment. . . . In that year, 1909, I arranged to have a meeting of the would-be Scouts at the Crystal Palace on a certain day. And when I got there, my wig, there were a lot of them. Rain was threatening, so we mustered them inside the Palace and arranged a March Past and counted them as they entered at one door and went out at the other. There were 11,000 of them—11,000, who had taken it up of their own accord! That is why I say that one didn't see the start: Scouting started itself.[14]

Certainly, this description does not mention the initial link between the book on scouting and the militaristic Boys' Brigade, with which Baden-Powell had already severed ties.[15] In fact, ever since the London rally in 1909, Baden-Powell had been working to set up an organization for scouting, with the continued financial support of the book's publisher, the support of the ruling class in Britain, and the territorial help of the ecumenical YMCA,[16] which hoped that the scouts would become its members once they reached adulthood.[17]

There are probably three reasons as to why scouting took off so quickly. First, its historical opportunity: the idea came about with emerging concepts of "adolescence" and "leisure time," increasing rates of school attendance for boys in that age group, and a preference for "the country life" over life in industrial cities.[18] Second, the project was thoroughly supported by institutions with social and political authority in Great Britain, that is, the monarchy, the army, the school, and the church— a support that would be replicated in many other countries. And last, the heterogeneous and relatively ambiguous model of citizenship espoused in *Scouting for Boys* easily gained a wide public acceptance as well as paved the way for the later international expansion of the movement.

It was the ambiguity and heterogeneity of the ideals that help to explain the wide social support for early scouting. That is the reason why, as Laszlo Nagy—the first scholar to do a research on world scouting—indicates, we should not be surprised that the movement has been accused of being too pro-military by some and pacifistic by others; that many have regarded scouting as overly religious, while churches have criticized its lack of religious content (only two of the 300 pages of *Scouting for Boys* discuss religion); or that Britain's Labour Party accused it of promoting values that helped to keep the Conservatives in power, while the Tories attacked it for its socialist overtones.[19] The initial adaptability of the early scout movement to the purposes of diverse organizations and bodies of thought was a double-edged sword, simultaneously a boon to its spread and a target of criticism for having largely undefined core values.

1.2. Scouting in Britain and Its Spontaneous Internationalization

Just three months after the Crystal Palace rally, in December 1909, the Boy Scouts Association was set up with an astonishing 108,000 members and Baden-Powell himself as Chairman. A year later, in 1910, the UK Girl Guides Association was created by Robert Baden-Powell, with 6,000 members, chaired by Baden-Powell's sister Agnes.[20]

Many believe—and Baden-Powell himself has said—that he decided to create a parallel organization for girls when he saw that some girls had come to the Crystal Palace rally, who, as the boys, considered themselves scouts.[21] Nevertheless, earlier documents of Baden-Powell explicitly indicate the contrary: that girls could also be scouts. In his "Boy Scouts Scheme" of 1907, the first pamphlet outlining the scouting project, he wrote that it was the basis "for an attractive organization and valuable training for girls," and in an article in 1908 he said: "I think girls can get just as much healthy fun out of Scouting as boys can...and prove themselves good Scouts in a very short time."[22] Tim Jeal, British biographer of Baden-Powell, argues that the idea of a separate organization came later, due to pressures from the social establishment that thought it inappropriate for girls to carry out activities that were supposed to be "masculine."

It is in August 1909, therefore, that Baden-Powell decided to adapt a version of *Scouting for Boys* for girls, a move that would lead to the eventual creation of a separate organization. That same year, his book *Yarns for Boy Scouts* already suggested that girls, and society in general, could benefit from girls following the principles of scouting, albeit with a "slightly modified" system of training, and added: "I am forced to this suggestion by the fact that already some thousands of girls have registered themselves as 'Boy Scouts'!."[23] In effect, the girl "scouts" were in fact provisionally registered in the Boy Scouts' census until 1910, when the female association was established. In November 1909, Baden-Powell published *The Scheme for Girl Guides*,[24] which finally adapted scouting for girls, and adopted the term "Guiding"[25] for the female version of the movement.

In 1909, Baden-Powell was knighted by King Edward VII, and the following year, encouraged by this, he retired from the military in order to dedicate himself exclusively to scouting.[26] In its formalization as a British association, the combination of the Scout Law and Oath outlined in *Scouting for Boys* became the main ideological reference for scouting. Indeed, the methodology of scouting, developed for adolescents, offered shared values through its "Law," and voluntary commitment to these values through its "Oath," the key to self-education through which youth purposefully turned into voluntary members of the scout movement.

It is interesting to note that the code of conduct outlined in the Scout Law is a social code that benefits others rather than the person who adopts the Law. It is a set of rules stated in positive terms, with duties instead of rights, designed to produce better neighbors and hence better citizens,[27] with a series of principles that would later become essential for maintaining the ideological unity of the movement. Precisely because of the growing importance of these principles after the movement's formalization, Baden-Powell and the British association made a series of gradual changes to the text of the *Scout Law,* the first of which, in 1911, was to add a tenth point with moralizing overtones: "10. A Scout is pure in thought, in word and in deed."[28]

Though the code of conduct emerged early on, the educational ideology of scouting was formed after the movement had already begun, during a prewar time when the influence and presence of the military in UK society was growing and getting further away from these militarizing influences.[29] This is why, in parallel to the progressive education movements' development, scouting presents itself as a movement for citizenship training, essentially educational, which includes patriotic elements and religious references. Hence, the educational feature of scouting was particularly highlighted by its promoters in the years prior to 1914, in reaction to the accusations of the movement being militaristic. And, in fact, the deepening of scouting on its own educational method focused on the *individual* and on the full development of his/her potential set it apart from the military's method of education *en masse*.

Moreover, it was around this time—between 1911 and 1914—that England received the influence of the modern ideas of the Italian feminist and educator Maria Montessori and her "learning by doing" philosophy—very similar to the method that scouting was intuitively developing. The ideological connections between scouting and the progressive education movement were noticed by many of Baden-Powell's contemporaries.[30] Back in 1914, Baden-Powell remarked in a text that "Montessori has proved that by encouraging a child in its natural desires, instead of instructing it in what you think it ought to do, you can educate it on a far more solid and far-reaching base."[31]

In 1916, seven years after the creation of the Boy Scouts Association in Britain, Baden-Powell responded to the demand to extend *scouting* to the preadolescent age range by creating a version of the book with a mood set around Rudyard Kipling's *The Jungle Book*,[32] calling the boys "Wolf Cubs" or "Cub Scouts," just as the book character Mowgli's friends are called. In 1922, the scouting concept was extended upward to the postadolescent age range, calling the older kids "Senior Scouts" or "Rovers,"[33] while "Scouts" remained the term used for those aged 12–15. Although they initially had a certain degree of autonomy, these ranges eventually became sections[34] or age groups within the same movement. The scout movement as a whole took its name from the original adolescent group.

Regarding the female association, where the same age adaptations as in the male association were made, Baden-Powell designated his 52-year-old sister, Agnes, to manage it. In 1912, the two published *How Girls Can Help to Build up the Empire*,[35] a supposed feminized version of *Scouting for Boys* that never really took off. Additionally, there was a constant clash between the ideas of Agnes, who believed that girls should be refined, and those of her brother.[36] The separation of boys and girls into different organizations created a tendency to avoid working with the opposite sex. A few years later, Rose Kerr, a historian of guiding/girl scouting, made the criticism that some girl guide leaders appeared "to have been preternaturally sensitive on the subject of boy scouts and girl guides breathing the same air."[37]

In 1912, Robert Baden-Powell, 55, married Olave Saint Claire Soames, who was 23 years old at the time.[38] Two years later, in January 1914, the first edition of the *Girl Guides Gazette,* the official British girl guiding magazine, appeared. Olave quickly replaced Baden-Powell's sister Agnes at the head of the girl guides: she was much younger, more active and sporty, and her ideas were closer to those of her husband, who wrote at the time that "girls must be partners and comrades rather than dolls."[39] In 1915, Robert Baden-Powell became Chairman of the Girl Guides Association, and in 1918, Olave became the new Chief Guide. Later on, she would become the real world leader.[40] Also in 1918, Robert Baden-Powell published *Girl Guiding: The Official Handbook,*[41] to replace the poorly received book published with his sister in 1912.

If Baden-Powell had not intended to create an organization in the United Kingdom when he first published *Scouting for Boys,* much less was he thinking to do so on an international scale. However, just as it had spread across England, scouting, and to a lesser degree, female scouting, immediately began quickly expanding to the rest of the British Empire and to the entire world. Actually, the many beliefs and characteristics contained in the original concept of scouting and the various ways in which it could be interpreted also help explain how a product designed to revitalize the British Empire could have such an immediate, successful reception in Chilean, French, Malaysian, and Japanese societies, to name a few.

Nonetheless, both in Britain and abroad, the propagation of the scout movement was helped by public institutions, due to its civic values, its focus on building citizenship, and its will to community service. Scouting first spread throughout the British Empire (Ireland, Canada, Australia, New Zealand, Zimbabwe, South Africa, and India, between 1908 and 1909), which, in the 1920s, had a population of 500 million people, close to a quarter of the world population, and stretched 37 million kilometers, a quarter of the earth's land surface. The movement also spread to many other countries worldwide such as Chile, Denmark, the United States, and Russia (1909); Brazil, France, Finland, Germany,[42] Greece, and Holland (1910); Belgium, Estonia, Norway, Sweden, Malaysia, and Singapore (1911)... The untrammeled growth of the scout movement in both name and number went hand-in-hand with the spread of the book *Scouting for Boys:* by the end of the 1920s, two decades after it was first published in London, it had already been published in 26 countries—not including editions already printed in the British Empire—making it the fourth best-selling book of the twentieth century.

Baden-Powell was an iconic figure for the associations that adopted the scout method worldwide, and even though the prevailing Chairman of British scouting did not actively seek the expansion of *scouting,* he did maintain close contact with promoters of the movement abroad, traveling often to give talks and attend conferences. This is documented in his 1913 book, *Boy Scouts beyond the Seas,* in which Baden-Powell describes his trips to visit scouts in the United States, Japan, Norway, Sweden, Denmark, Holland, Belgium, and the British dependencies of India, South Africa, Australia, and New Zealand[43] and that shows how he maintained close contact with the international emergence of the movement.

This inadvertent international expansion was given a cautious welcome in London. According to Laszlo Nagy, Baden-Powell himself proposed that the association not accept applications to join from outside the British jurisdiction. Alternatively, in the October 1911 edition of the *Scout Headquarters Gazette,* he suggested the idea of setting up a foreign affairs department to maintain contact with scouts throughout the world. It marked the dawn of a movement with international ties, but not yet a world organization.

As Mario Sica explains, Baden-Powell did not regard the international proliferation of scouting as simple coincidence, as though it were the mere spread of an institution with a social purpose. In fact, he refused to patent the term for the exclusive use of British scouting and gradually abandoned the idea of producing "citizens of the Empire" in favor of a more international discourse. The movement also evolved in this direction because Baden-Powell had traveled to many countries—and continued to do so—with a liberal vision that represented a stark contrast to the expansionist nationalism of continental Europe at that time.

The extensive territorial limits of the British Empire contributed to the growing awareness of the scout movement worldwide. In the summer of 1913, the first "international" scout camp was organized near Birmingham, with an attendance of 30,000, most of whom came from British territories, though some also hailed from European countries and the United States. However, the world was on the brink of a great war and tension was in the air. In Australia, New Zealand, Canada, and South Africa, compulsory military training was introduced in schools, generally in the form of cadet corps, and it seemed only a matter of time before Britain did the same. It is known that Baden-Powell tried to convince authorities that scouting could be a good form of indirect preparation for this type of training, to avoid a potential takeover of the movement. His case was backed by the fact that many of those in charge of the British organizations and their Scoutmasters and leaders were also soldiers. This is a key issue in the scholarly historical controversy regarding the military origins of the early British scouting.[44]

When war finally broke out, the process of defining scouting was in full swing and the movement was still learning how to run itself. The structural and ideological bases of the movement were still too weak to sustain its new, unwieldy size. With origins that lay in romantic tales of frontier pioneers, World War I was a reality check for the scout movement that rocked its foundations.[45]

1.3. PEACE AND THE IDEAL OF THE LEAGUE OF NATIONS

As Nagy explains, in the summer of 1914, millions of young men from all sides went to war believing that they were fighting for a noble cause and a better world. Amidst the patriotic and nationalist fervor, there was no room for nuances. In Great Britain, around 150,000 of the young men mobilized for the war were or had been scouts, and 10,000 of these died. Many were scout leaders. Many others, boys and girls scouts, carried out auxiliary tasks and services.

But this was not the only setback for the new movement—the war would have a profound effect on the emerging links between organizations following *Scouting for Boys*. For example, in 1911 in Germany, later the enemy of the British, 80,000 Germans considered themselves scouts. By the time war broke out, *Scouting for Boys* had already been translated into German and close contact had been established between the British scouting and the German associations that were using the scout method.[46]

It seemed clear that, after such a bloody conflict between countries, the international aspirations of scouting would be reduced to ashes. And yet, once the war was over, the movement did not wane; on the contrary, its numbers increased—Great Britain had almost 200,000 boy scouts, and just a few years later, almost half a million girl guides—and it had a presence in 30 or so countries. Boys in British scouting were mainly from the middle to lower-middle classes, rather than the lower class.

World War I and the international expansion of scouting and the possibilities that it offered are two of the main reasons why Baden-Powell changed the register from citizens of the Empire to the ideal of citizens of the world.[47] The war showed him the firsthand effects of a full-scale conflict on young people. The vision of a soldier trying to maintain the stability of the Empire was transformed into that of a civil activist committed to avoiding another armed conflict by firmly distancing scouting from nationalist tendencies with expansionist ambitions.[48]

In a 1917 text on "Scouting as a Peace Agent" he wrote:

> Nations disillusioned by war are seeking something better than pieces of paper produced by unscrupulous statesmen. They are proposing war reparations and indemnities but beyond these material obligations it is surely possible *to encourage the feelings and emotions of peoples as the best hope of permanent peace.* The Scout Movement on its relatively small scale has taken root among the youth of all civilized countries and is still growing. It is not too much to hope that in the years to come, with increasing numbers joining this fraternity in the coming generations, they will unite in personal friendship and mutual understanding such as never before and thus find a solution to these horrendous international conflicts.[49]

The ideas of peace as a contribution to one's country and an early internationalism also crop up in Baden-Powell's first book written specifically for scout leaders (educators): *Aids to Scoutmastership,*[50] published in 1919. In this work, he told Scoutmasters that "our aim in making boys into good citizens is partly for the benefit of the country, that it may have a virile trusty race of citizens whose amity and sense of 'playing the game' will keep it united internally and at peace with its neighbours abroad."[51] Similarly, in each and every of the first ten editions of *Scouting for Boys,* until 1922, the social and cultural references of the text were increasingly open and global, so that Great Britain was no longer the clear center of the scouting world, though the book remained the official point of the UK Boy Scouts Association.

Baden-Powell had planned to organize an international meeting in 1918, the tenth anniversary of the movement, with a series of clear aims that he explained in 1916: "to make our ideals and methods more widely known abroad; to promote the spirit of brotherhood among the rising generation throughout the world, thereby giving the spirit that is necessary to make the League of Nations a living force."[52]

The League of Nations was an idea put forward by the British government that the US President, the Democrat Woodrow Wilson, adopted in 1918, including it as the final point of the "14 points" for world peace in the postwar period: "A General Association of Nations must be formed under specific covenants for the purpose of affording mutual guarantees of political independence and territorial integrity to great and small States alike."

This was the first time that the idea of an international organization of countries had been put forward to replace war as a way of resolving conflicts. The League of Nations was eventually established at the Paris

Peace Conference in 1919, under the Treaty of Versailles "to develop cooperation among nations and to guarantee them peace and security." It was composed of 40 countries, though the US Congress ultimately vetoed the government's motion to join. The League of Nation's first years were very unstable, particularly because of the growth of expansionist Nazism in Germany, fascism in Italy, and imperialism in Japan, as well as the civil war in Spain. Despite this shaky trajectory, the League of Nations started many initiatives, such as the launching of the International Labour Organization and the International Criminal Court, the first steps for setting an important precedent for the idea of peace as a political objective and laying the ideological foundations of what in 1945 would become the United Nations Organization.

Great Britain created a civic organization, called the League of Nations Union, in support of the ideals espoused by the League of Nations. Various texts and speeches by Baden-Powell from the time when people began to discuss "the League" reveal his awareness that the scout movement could help to create a public mind frame that would encourage the existence of a supranational organization with peace—and governance—as its basic political aim. This is clearly demonstrated in a 1919 letter from Baden-Powell to the Mayor of London, one of the men behind the Union, in which he said:

> I need scarcely say how, in common with most people, I am anxious to do anything to make the League a living force.
>
> [...]. Through the Boy Scout and Girl Guide Movement we have already instituted [...] the training of young citizens of the different countries to think in terms of peace and good will towards each other, so that the League of Nations shall, in the next generation, be *a bond between peoples rather than a pact between Governments.*
>
> We have now over a million young members in the different civilised countries, all working under the same Scout Law and ideals, looking on each other as brother and sister members, and in a great number of cases interchanging letters and visits.
>
> Next year will see a great International Conference of these boys and girls in London.
>
> So I hope that our aims and doings will commend themselves as all in the direction in which your society is moving.[53]

This was, therefore, the ideal behind the project of the international scout meeting, the "great International Conference" he refers to in the letter, which had to be postponed originally because of the war.

2. THE HISTORICAL DEVELOPMENT OF SCOUTING WORLDWIDE

2.1. THE PERIOD UNDER THE LEADERSHIP OF ROBERT BADEN-POWELL

Before 1920, scouting could not be considered an international movement, but a British initiative with a clear leadership replicated in other countries. Notwithstanding, in the summer of 1920, the organization of the international encounter wished by Baden-Powell was the definitive move to transform scouting into a worldwide movement.

It should be noted at this point that the aims and ideology of Baden-Powell had evolved significantly since 1908. First, there was the link to the progressive education discourse, particularly in relation to the teaching methods of Maria Montessori, and the rejection of the military tradition. Second, an increased emphasis on the need to develop critical thinking skills, clarifying the educational role of obedience.[54] Third, a clear international commitment, linked to the ideals embodied by the League of Nations, which was partly the result of the international scout network that was materializing. Last, and closely related to the previous point, was the scout movement's steadfast commitment to peace stemming from the profound impact of World War I.

Although these elements constituted the foundations for the formalization of world scouting, many countries continued to set up associations based on the early British model. This meant that there was an ambiguous tension in many countries between the early British scouting model of 1909—connected to the military sector and based more on discipline with various levels of nationalism—and the evolved model that Baden-Powell promoted in 1920—civic, socially committed with an emphasis on the education of the individual, internationally oriented, and focused on working toward peace. The paradox is that both visions were based on texts written by Baden-Powell!

The international scout meeting originally planned for 1918 was finally held in London in August 1920, with 8,000 scouts from 21 independent countries and 12 British territories. It was the First International Jamboree, an event that has since been held regularly and has become an icon of the movement. The Jamboree originated as a copy of the Olympic Games (which had been resumed in London in 1908), with a variety of sports. However, it soon became apparent that these competitions encouraged national rivalries instead of universal fraternity, so they were replaced by activities of artistic expression, such as singing and acting (Baden-Powell loved to act), and technical activities based on the cooperation of participants.[55]

It was at the first Jamboree that Robert Baden-Powell was appointed Chief Scout of the World by acclamation, an honorific title that only he has held since then. Although the Jamboree was essentially an adolescent gathering, the First International Scout Conference was held there in the presence of 33 scout associations from diverse countries and it was agreed to create a world body, the Boy Scouts International Bureau (BSIB).[56] In that same year, 1920, the permanent secretariat was set up, and two years later, the organization was legally established in Paris.[57] Scouting now had a million members worldwide.

Therefore, the new international scout organization established a permanent secretariat (the *Bureau*)[58] along with an *International Conference* (a governing body formed by the national associations, each of which had six votes) and an *International Committee* (an executive body formed by individuals elected by the Conference). This bears some resemblance to the structure adopted by the League of Nations a year earlier. The Treaty of Versailles had established that the League of Nations would have a secretariat, an Assembly (a governing body composed of all member countries with one vote per country), and a Board (an executive body formed by four countries that would be permanent members and four that would be nonpermanent members).

Despite this organizational formalization, Baden-Powell stressed from the outset that the sense of "movement" was to be maintained, which meant that more importance was placed on principles and method than on the organization itself. If that was important at the national level, even more so internationally, where while a set of standard principles determining scout recognition was being established, great measures were also being taken to avoid the tendency of a potential centralizing and controlling world organization. As the BSIB Director pointed out in 1922, "[the international organization] possesses no executive authority whatever and in no way controls the different Scout Organizations which constitute its members."[59] That meant that the world organization was in charge to democratically establish the ideological framework of scouting, but had no capacity whatsoever to decide how an association should be run or which decisions it should take.

Meanwhile, female scouting was headed in a similar direction. In 1919, an International Council for Guiding was set up on the initiative of Olave Baden-Powell, Chief Guide of British guiding since 1918 and wife of its founder. Though the Council lacked a legal structure, it held its first conference in England in 1920. At the Fourth International Conference in 1926, steps were taken to formalize the organization, and in 1927, the International Bureau (the permanent secretariat) was finally established.

WAGGGS[60] was established on the suggestion of Robert Baden-Powell at the Fifth International Conference of Girl Guides (Hungary, 1928). Delegates from 26 countries were present at the conference and the association was given a similar organizational structure to that of the international scout organization: a permanent secretariat (the Bureau), an elected International Committee with nine members (the executive body), and a plenary International Conference of national associations (the governing body). Robert and Olave Baden-Powell were registered as nonvoting members of the International Committee. In 1930, Olave was elected World Chief Guide, the equivalent of her husband's title in male scouting. By 1931, female scouting had a million members around the world, though mainly in English-speaking countries.[61]

The ideals of peace and international fraternity—traditionally called "world brotherhood" in the movement—have been a constant in scouting ever since it was internationally formalized. An official document from 1922 explains that the world organization was affiliated to the International Peace Bureau, the oldest peace organization in the world.[62] Baden-Powell himself was the keynote speaker of the Third International Conference of Moral Education held in 1922 in Geneva, with the conference "Education in Love in Place of Fear."

Baden-Powell's enthusiastic commitment to the League of Nations as a way of securing world peace is evidenced by various statements he made. Just after the 1920 Jamboree, when it was agreed to set up the international organization, Baden-Powell published an article in *The Scout* explaining the structure and aims of the League of Nations. In it, he lamented the absence of the United States but expressed his conviction that it would end up becoming a member. He also openly encouraged scout groups to work together to promote the League of Nations Union: "probably a local branch exists in your town; if so, you should ask the secretary if you can help him in any way, such as distributing handbills for meetings."[63]

Mario Sica explains that during the first few years of world scouting, Baden-Powell attempted to make the organization into a sort of League of Nations youth movement but came up against the staunch opposition of the Committee of the Council, the executive body of the UK Boy Scouts Association, which considered the British League of Nations Union to be a "political organization." In fact, some of the Committee members who did not want the link with the League of Nations had even opposed the organization of the International Jamboree in 1920. These tensions came as no surprise; dissidence between the ideals of the movement and the interests of some of its "stakeholders" had been a constant throughout scouting history.

The creation of the two world organizations led to the establishment of an official "international recognition system" for scouting, which became all the more necessary when, for example, in 1923, the League of Nations assembly encouraged governments to facilitate the mobility of "recognized associations" of scouts: the Austrian government said that it did not know what "recognized association" meant in the context of the resolution.[64] After the formalization of the movement, it would be a democratically operated international organization (the BSIB or WAGGGS) that would officially approve the membership of national associations.

The establishment of an approval system was timely because scouting had simply grown too big to allow imitations to use its "brand" for other purposes. In 1924, for example, the BSIB rejected German associations' request for international scout recognition on the grounds of dispersion of associations—there were too many disorganized groups adhering only partly or not at all to the scout method.[65] The refusal was also due—at least in part—to the fact that "the German movement was too pro-military, too nationalistic and overly expansionist in the wrong directions since it was attempting to absorb Austrian Scouting."[66] Therefore, no German "scouting" obtained international recognition until the fall of Nazi totalitarianism.[67]

With the new world organizations, although the "word" of Baden-Powell still held authority, it was gradually being replaced by democratic agreements reached in the world conferences. Nonetheless, Baden-Powell held on to his moral authority. His writing, speeches, and even the modifications made to subsequent editions of *Scouting for Boys* reflect the evolution of his thought, particularly after World War I. While in 1908 he said, " You belong to the Great British Empire, one of the greatest empires that has ever existed in the world,"[68] by 1921 he was warning of the perils of excessive national pride, pointing out that " [t]he world-wide crash of war has roughly shaken us all and made us awake to the newer order of things. No longer is one nation better than another."[69]

The world conference agreements can be discerned through the "resolutions," which are the official stances adopted by the organization. In the Second International Scout Conference resolutions (Paris, 1922) there are clear signs of the move toward establishing common standards: the Conference established that scouting membership must be voluntary, not obligatory; it emphasizes the need for unity within the movement and cautions against the fragmenting of associations within the same country. This last point clearly demonstrates that the world organization, from very early on, attempted to ensure that each country had just one association, based on the British model. However, the existence of three distinct "scout" associations in France in 1920—one secular *(laïque)*, one

Protestant, and one Catholic— resulted in the creation of a federation of associations rather than one single national association. This federation model was spread in Catholic countries by the church and also in French colonies.

This set of common standards was also useful to ensure that scout leaders were on the same page. The standards were a foundation of the curriculum at the newly established training school for Scoutmasters by the Boy Scouts Association (UK) at Gilwell Park, near London. In 1922, with the launch of the BSIB, this school became the world reference for the approved training of Scoutmasters and trainers of Scoutmasters, also making it possible to control the international ideological unity of the movement until the late 1960s.[70]

In the uneasy calm of the interwar period, the dual condition of national/international of the scout movement was undeniable. At its third meeting, held in Denmark in 1924, the International Scout Conference passed the "Principles of Scouting" resolution, which established that scouting "is a movement of national, international and universal character, the object of which is to endow each separate nation and the whole world with a youth which is physically, morally and spiritually strong." At the same time, in order to silence criticisms—principally from the Catholic Church—that it was lacking in religious content, the resolution reiterated its commitment to promote religious beliefs, although forbidding "any kind of sectarian propaganda at mixed gatherings."[71] The resolution contains the two key elements that scouting has repeatedly emphasized, as well as their counterweights: national identity balanced out by internationalism, and individual faith balanced out by acceptance of religious plurality. Scouting, therefore, did not wanted to become a strictly secular movement[72] without national identities. On the contrary, it was a movement committed to the spiritual dimension of the individual and giving a role to religion,[73] a movement where dialogue between religions was possible and where national identities were the way forward, not the impediment, to build what we now know as global citizenship.

Therefore, in just over ten years, scouting had undergone critical changes—it had transformed from a training idea based on the experiences of a senior military man to a thriving British youth movement, and from this to an organized international movement composed of national scout associations determined to stamp out exclusionary nationalist tendencies among its members. On this, the same 1924 International Scout Conference that refused to recognize German associations pointed out "[t]hat there should be no discrimination as to admission to membership of fellow subjects or citizens for any reason of race, creed or politics' as a condition for recognition."[74] Although it wished to increase membership, the world organization was determined to have as its unalterable foundation the recognition of scout brotherhood, regardless of race, creed, or class. This condition was established with the full knowledge that public institutions in many countries with scouting discriminated on grounds of race, creed, or ideology, including the United States, where racial segregation would not be abolished until 1954.

In the second half of the 1920s and throughout the 1930s, the structural bases to internationally organize scouting finally came together. A look at the balance between national identity and global belonging in the scout movement, and the tendency of associations to accept the established order, helps explain how this structured internationalization was possible. For example, many delegates came to the 1926 conference with messages of support and encouragement from their respective governments, signed by the relevant Minister or Secretary of State of countries like Denmark, Finland, France, the United Kingdom, Hungary, Iraq, Japan, Poland, Romania, Siam, Spain, and Yugoslavia.

These were the years of the Great Depression, which began in 1929 and mainly affected the United States, Europe, and the British Empire; the period also witnessed expansionist nationalism take root in Germany, Italy, and Japan, and the decline of European colonialism in general and the fragmentation of the British Empire in particular.[75] Against this backdrop, world scouting tried to set down a series of rules that would stabilize the operation of the new international organization. During these years, it dealt gradually with the tasks of defining a "national" association, the limits of patriotism, the regional scope of associations, and the role of national minorities, and later on, of displaced groups.

However, the rise of fascism, and its accompanying aggressive nationalism, was a threat to the ideological stability of the scout movement. The regenerative discourses of Benito Mussolini and Adolf Hitler, who were initially somewhat admired in many western countries during the 1920s,[76] spoke out against political corruption and the decline of their respective countries, overlapping with part of the discourse of scouting: values such as duty, discipline, and self-sacrifice; suspicion of industrialization; rejection of Soviet communism; love for one's country and culture; the importance of physical exercise; the romantic invocation of explorers... Furthermore, at that stage, when world scouting was only just starting to develop its structure, unrecognized self-styled "scout" associations existed in many countries, interpreting *scouting* as they saw fit.[77] As a result, the international organization ruled that it would have to approve the text of the "Oath" and the "Law" of each country to make the acceptance of shared values more explicit, with the additional obligation of notifying the international organization of any changes. Associations were also encouraged to legally protect uniforms and identify signs of fraudulent use.[78]

In countries with totalitarian regimes, though, the situation was more complicated than the straightforward fraudulent copying of the scout appearance. In 1917, when the Soviet Union was established, there were 50,000 scouts in Russia. In 1922, the scout movement was banned and replaced by the Young Pioneer movement, which was controlled by the Communist Party and where former scouts with Bolshevik sympathies collaborated.[79] In turn, many Russian scouts went into exile, setting up a Russian scout association headquartered in France, internationally recognized by the BSIB from 1928 to 1945.[80] In Italy, the fascist youth organization *Balilla* absorbed existing scouting associations in 1927 under the direction of Mussolini. In the early 1930s, the Nazis also outlawed self-styled "scout" associations, none of which were internationally recognized, and gradually incorporated their members into the *Hitler-Jugend* (Hitler Youth).[81] To summarize, in the Axis countries, the regimes banned scouting (Italy after 1922, Germany after 1933, and Japan after 1941, together with fascist Spain after 1939) and replaced it with indoctrinating official youth movements controlled by them that imitated the scouts in appearance. The same occurred in the Soviet Union after 1922 and in the occupied Baltic States and in the Soviet republics as they were formed, with the single exception of Poland.[82]

The brazen imitation of the scout image and activities by fascist and communist regimes took place at a time when awareness of the scouting "brand" was still emerging in many countries, and this led to a confusion that still exists today regarding the scout movement's alleged proto-fascist past,[83] while in reality what happened was the opposite: the Nazis even copied the uniforms and neckerchiefs of scouting and made unsuccessful arrangements for the *Hitler-Jugend* to be internationally recognized as German scouting.[84]

The comparison between scouting and official youth movements that pushed the discourse of national loyalty and acceptance of the status quo to its very limits forced Baden-Powell to further clarify the ambiguities that had come about around the time of establishment of the international organization. Nagy explains that, in his meeting with Mussolini in 1933, Baden-Powell rejected the claim that the *Balilla* was an improved version of scouting, arguing that "the Balilla was an official instead of a voluntary organization; that it aimed at partisan nationalism instead of wider international good feeling; that it was purely physical, without any spiritual balance; and that it developed mass discipline instead of individual character."[85]

In order to dispel doubts about the internationalist commitment of scouting, in contrast to the nationalist hyperfocus of fascist regimes, the 1937 International Scout Conference, held at the Hague in the Netherlands, officially modified one of the points of the Scout Law, adding references to brotherhood between countries: "A Scout is a friend to all, and a brother to every other Scout, no matter to what *country,* class, or creed the other may belong."[86] It also approved a very explicit resolution on "Patriotism," declaring that the International Committee

> be requested to do all that it can to ensure that Scouting and Rovering in all countries, while fostering true patriotism, are genuinely kept within the limits of international cooperation and friendship, irrespective of creed and race, as has always been outlined by the Chief Scout. Thus, any steps to the militarization of Scouting or the introduction of political aims, which might cause misunderstanding and thus handicap our work for peace and goodwill among nations and individuals should be entirely avoided in our programs.[87]

In that same year, 28,000 scouts had congregated for the Fifth International Jamboree, which took place in Holland. It was preceded by the one in Hungary in 1933, with 25,000 participants; England in 1929, with 50,000 participants; and Denmark in 1924, with 4,500 participants. Seventeen years had passed since the First International Jamboree, when the BSIB was set up. To all intents and purposes, the International Jamboree had become the practical representation of the international nature of the movement: adolescents from all over the world coming together to share the principles of scouting.

In July 1939, the Tenth International Scout Conference was held in Edinburgh. Shortly afterward, war broke out and international activity was paralyzed. In most of the countries that took part in World War II, whether actively or passively, scouting played a role in the organized resistance to state oppression, both in the countries that were occupied and in those of the attackers. Only 3 of the 17 European countries with recognized scouting had remained neutral. Neutrality took on a new dimension—and not only in scouting: refusing to take a stance in front of crimes against humanity could never again be accepted.

Scouting was banned not only by fascist regimes, but also by the countries they occupied. In spite of this, many of these countries experienced organized resistance at a local level. Hilary St. George Saunders found various examples of scout resistance in occupied countries such as Czechoslovakia, Poland, Denmark, Norway, Luxemburg, Holland, Belgium, France, Greece, Yugoslavia, Hungary, Philippines, and Burma. He also highlights scouting's contribution to resistance against outside aggressors in China, Formosa, and Thailand, and to the internal resistance against regimes in Germany, Italy, and Japan. In contrast, while the Catalan scouting association rebelled against its illegalization by bringing the movement underground, in the rest of Spain, Spanish scouting accepted the suspension of activities under Franco.[88]

Meanwhile, the Chief Scout of the World, Robert Baden-Powell, retired from scouting in 1937 and lived the last years of his life in Nyeri, Kenya, where he died peacefully and was buried in 1941. In his last years he felt that World War II was somehow a failure of the scout movement, unable to preserve the peace values of the League of Nations among the countries. In the six years of international conflict during World War II, while the scout movement was being persecuted in the occupied countries, the BSIB was paralyzed and there was no external coordination for associations. The death of the founder and inspiration of the scout movement occurred at the height of the war, in the midst of a social crisis, mass population movements, and the imposed paralysis of the international scout structure. Everything suggested that scouting was caught in a downward spiral, with most associations prohibited, shut down, or severely weakened.

But this tumultuous time did not extinguish the scout movement. The International Committee met in London in November 1945,[89] where two important agreements were reached. First, the foreseen International Jamboree and Conference, which were supposed to be held in 1941, were planned: they would take place in 1947 in France. Second, the organizational decision was made to separate the BSIB from the headquarters of the UK Boy Scouts Association and was carried out that same month. This decision signals a continued awareness that the scout movement needed to keep its international focus and global expansion in order to survive.

Among the 17 European countries where recognized scouting existed, only three had been neutrals during the war. However, as the work began on the reconstruction of the international movement, it was clear that it had gained newfound strength despite the destruction wrought by World War II: at the start of the war, male scouting had just over 3.3 million members, while the 1947 census revealed that it had 4.4 million members in 43 countries, despite the demise of 11 associations. Comparing the censuses of 1939 and 1947 (in thousands) reveals that male scouting doubled in Argentina (from 5 to 10), Denmark (18 to 36), France (94 to 211), and Sweden (23 to 51), and tripled in Belgium (17 to 53), Greece (12 to 41), Holland (36 to 116), and Czechoslovakia (20 to 67). In India, membership increased from 285 to 414, in China, from 315 to 570 (in 1941),[90] while Britain's membership of 600 was maintained.

However, almost half of the total 4.4 million members were from the male scouting organization of the United States, which had grown from 1,200,000 members in 1939 to 2,000,000 in 1947.[91]

Eventually, the reasons for scouting's enormous success in the United States could include the fact that since the beginning the Boy Scouts of America (BSA) had adapted the British model, added several innovations, and produced a form of scouting suited to the US context.[92] Tying in with the original idea that Baden-Powell had before the UK Boy Scouts Association was established, the US association did not carry out activities directly. Instead, they were carried out by sponsoring institutions with an interest in children's welfare, such as churches, schools, trade unions, parents' associations, and Rotary Clubs, as well as by voluntary firemen, and the BSA would provide them with everything they needed. The BSA was also responsible for professionalizing scouting management and using academic research to inform the growth of the association.[93]

The international stage following World War II was in stark contrast to the one that had followed the 1914–1918 war: while the defeated were not humiliated, the world was divided into two camps. An international organization, the United Nations, was set up with similar political principles to the League of Nations,[94] but with a stronger moral message following the defeat of fascism. Both the United States and the Soviet Union signed the UN Charter together with 49 other countries. The United Nations is structured around a General Assembly (its governing body) in which all member countries have the right to vote, a permanent secretariat, and a Security Council (its executive body), which has five permanent members (the countries that won the war: the United States, the Soviet Union later the Russian federation, the United Kingdom, France, and China) with the right to veto and a further ten members elected by the General Assembly for a two-year mandate.

The creation of the UN Security Council composed of permanent members introduced the notion that not all countries were equal. To accept the legitimacy of the United Nations was to accept the greater say of countries with greater military power, albeit within a framework of common principles that were reinforced three years later when the UN General Assembly proclaimed the Universal Declaration of Human Rights,

> as a common standard of achievement for all peoples and all nations, to the end that every individual and every organ of society, keeping this Declaration constantly in mind, shall strive by teaching and education to promote respect for these rights and freedoms and by progressive measures, national and international, to secure their universal and effective recognition and

observance, both among the peoples of Member States themselves and among the peoples of territories under their jurisdiction.[95]

This new framework also conditioned what was came to be known as the "Cold War," based on the tension between the capitalist countries that reconstructed Western Europe, led by the United States, and the communist countries, led by the Soviet Union. At the 1945 Yalta Conference, the Allies agreed to respect the status quo of the countries that had ended up under Soviet influence. The division in Central Europe was the clearest, including in Germany.

In this new state of the world, scouting was outlawed in the countries annexed to the Soviet Union, together with others in the socialist sphere of influence: Poland, Romania, Hungary, and Bulgaria, and later on, North Korea, Czechoslovakia, China, and Cuba.[96] But the international scout movement continued to grow with new, recognized associations, not only Federal Germany (recognized in 1950), but many countries outside Europe, largely as a result of decolonization. While in 1922, just 9 of the 31 scout associations were non-European, by 1955 only 18 of the 56 recognized associations were European.

2.2. The Globalization of Scouting

The founding of the United Nations Organization and the subsequent Universal Declaration of Human Rights ushered in a new era for scouting. The renewed strength of world scouting after World War II coincided with these two international initiatives, both of which were in line with the ideology that the scout movement had adopted when it was set up in 1920. The principle of equality between countries and their right to sovereignty as a prerequisite for peace, so important in the founding of world scouting, had now reached new heights and paved the way for decolonization. In 1949, the International Scout Conference passed a resolution affirming: "We rededicate ourselves to the principles of liberty and the freedom of peoples and nations. We believe that the cause of peace and understanding can effectively be served by encouraging the spirit of world brotherhood amongst the youth of the world through Scouting."[97]

This concept of world scouting as a tool for constructing peace comes to the forefront once again alongside the new world institutions, as indicated in another resolution of 1955: "The Conference as the central world body of our Movement expresses the conviction that World Scouting in the existing general international atmosphere can play a most important part by preparing good citizens for tomorrow with all the right ideas of a constructive mutual understanding among all nations and towards lasting peace."[98]

It was during the 1950s that the International Scout Conferences were held outside Europe for the first time (Canada, 1955; India, 1959; and Mexico, 1967; and in girl scouting/guiding: Brazil, 1957, and Japan, 1966), together with the Jamborees held in Canada in 1955 and the Philippines in 1959. The headquarters of the BSIB were also moved from London to Ottawa, Canada, in 1958, and then finally to Geneva, Switzerland, in 1968. Also around this time, different "regions" and regional bureaus were set up rather unsystematically in various Arabic, European, African, Inter-American, and Asia-Pacific regions of the world. The International Bureau and Committee also became increasingly multicultural and multiracial: the first Asian member of the International Scout Committee was elected in 1931, followed by the first Arabic member in 1951 and the first African in 1961.[99]

Scouting also played a vital role in the processes of decolonizing and nation building. The in-depth study of Timothy H. Parsons on the role of the scout movement in British colonial Africa reveals the two faces of the movement outside Europe: its early days as a means of social control of the colony, introduced and managed by the colonial authorities, and its subsequent use by the colonized societies, first as a way to achieve greater equality[100] and form troops, then as a form of social protest, and finally as an instrument for national construction during decolonization.[101] At the 1959 International Scout Conference in New Delhi, Pandit Nehru, then Indian Primer Minister and leader of the nonaligned countries, recognized the importance of scouting and its excellent potential for third world countries in his welcome address.[102]

In the 1960s, scouting's mixed coeducational model began to take off in many countries that had until then separated boys and girls. In France, however, that was just one of the most important changes that were carried out. The social-democrat argument that schools, instead of reproducing social systems, should work to transform society provoked radical changes to the education system and gave a boost to French scouting, particularly to the *laïque* association, Éclaireurs de France. In this way, the *Éclaireurs* began to incorporate a nonauthoritarian educational approach, placing more importance on the group—the so-called social dynamic—than the individual. This was marked by a reform that went so far as to affect symbolic elements: converting the Scout Promise into a simple, explicit commitment (giving it a more informal tone), cutting out uniforms (leaving only the scarf and the shirt), et cetera.

At the same time, the Catholic Scouts de France adopted a new "enterprise" approach to scouting, in which the members of the troop work together toward a goal, substituting the patrol approach, in which a group of scouts have individually assigned duties and roles. This allowed more informal and variable groups of scouts to form. Additionally, Scouts de

France divided the old branch of scouting into two groups: preadoles-
cents (*rangers,* a term coming from the World War II heroes called *raiders*)
and adolescents *(pioneers)*. All of these changes strongly affected French
scouting, and its influence spread to many other associations as well.

Although the scout movement spread across the world very early on,
its operations and planning capacities were far from those needed by
a world organization. True globalization required a solid strategic base,
so the Ford Foundation (which aims to "strengthen democratic values, reduce poverty and injustice, promote international cooperation and
advance human achievement") decided to fund a study to help scouting with this challenge. In 1965 the Ford Foundation commissioned
the Graduate Institute of International Studies in Geneva to study the
situation of the then male scouting worldwide. The head of research
at the Institute, Dr. Laszlo Nagy, a former Hungarian scout exiled in
Switzerland, was chosen to prepare the report, which was published two
years later as the "Report on World Scouting."[103] One of its conclusions was the suggestion that the "director" figure of the World Bureau
be replaced by a "secretary general" with more executive powers. It was
this position that the BSIB offered to the principal researcher of the
study, Laszlo Nagy, making him the Bureau's first Secretary General
in 1968.

WOSM today is far different from what it was back then. When Laszlo
Nagy wrote his report on the state of world scouting, the BSIB had eight
million scouts, one-third of the current census; mostly male; in 86 countries, whereas today that number has doubled; there was no worldwide
regional system: just two or three executives in Ottawa; no coordinated
adult training system or common youth program; a faltering fee system;
no contact with the non-scout world; and no development project.[104]
Something similar happened with WAGGGS.

Given these unmet needs, a plan for the future was devised between
1969 and 1971 that professionalized the permanent structure; legalized
the international scout organization in the eyes of the Swiss authorities;
created the Bureau divisions of foreign relations, communication, and
research; and set up a committee of operations for quality and growth,
headed by the former President and CEO of IBM. The International
Conference held in Japan in 1971 approved the incorporation of community development into the scout program: in 1972 the first world seminar
was held on this issue in Cotonou (now Benin), and 1973 saw the first
world seminar on the environment, held in Sweden.

Around this time, new forms of scouting that could be adapted to
contexts such as that of rural Africa were also being explored. The
term "international" was replaced with "world," and at the World Scout
Conference of 1973 (Kenya), in the framework of wider constitutional

reforms, the name "Boy Scouts International Bureau" was changed to the "World Organization of the Scout Movement" (WOSM). At the 1977 conference, the fundamental principles of the constitutional text were reworked.[105] This was also the year of Olave Baden-Powell's death, who beyond her role as Chief Guide of the World had become an icon for male and female scouting.

One of the most important changes in the scout movement as a whole in the 1960s was the tendency in several countries, particularly European, to break the separation between boys and girls in scout activities and to embrace coeducation, through the rapprochement of male and female scout associations. As a result, some WOSM and WAGGGS member associations were gradually merged or joined to create new associations with dual membership—though these new associations continued to pay boys' and girls' fees to WOSM and to WAGGGS, respectively. Notable changes to the WOSM Constitution in 1977 included a new definition that did away with the words "boy" and "adolescent" and kept only "young people," on the pretext that the latter term included the other two, though it was a move that clearly opened the door to the progressive entry of girls in many countries.[106]

Despite the vitality of the movement, membership in industrialized countries began to dwindle. According to Nagy, Secretary General of WOSM at the time, the reasons for this drop included inadequate leadership, failure to adapt programs to modern requirements, an uncertain economic atmosphere, a drop in the birth rate, and the rise of dissident factions. However, the decline in membership in Europe and the United States was offset by a spectacular increase in membership in developing countries. In 1968, industrialized countries accounted for three-quarters of the world membership, and over half of all members hailed from English-speaking countries. But by the mid-1970s, industrialized countries had become the minority and Asia alone accounted for half of the world scout population. This naturally had repercussions on the content of educational programs.[107] The 1980s also saw the entry of microstates as members, which sparked an interesting debate on states as subjects of the world organization. The debate ended with the agreement that, like it happened in the United Nations, rights would not depend on size, though voting rights would be restricted in some cases when population was excessively small.[108]

It was in this context of a steady growth in international prestige that UNESCO awarded WOSM the first *Prize for Peace Education* in 1981. The prize came after years of collaboration between world scouting and UN agencies. The participation of NGOs in the United Nations has been the norm since its founding in 1945. World scouting has been active in this context, and both WOSM and WAGGGS have been members of the United Nations Economic and Social Council since it was created in 1947. The growing influence of these NGOs on issues on the international agenda, such as civil rights, the environment, and peace and development cooperation, also afforded them greater political involvement in supra-state decisions on matters that nonetheless affected state policies. This meant that individuals who did not represent state governments—such as representatives of WOSM and WAGGGS—could take part in international debates. In 1972, *The New York Times* reported that during the UN Conference on the Human Environment, in Stockholm, a representative of WOSM, on behalf of WOSM, WAGGGS, and nine other organizations, made an appeal to end "the deliberate destruction of the environment by warfare," and added that "the United States Government's disgraceful war of ecocide in Indochina and similar wars in other parts of the world should have been dealt with by this conference." [109] The traditional apolitical stance of the scout movement was being replaced by nonpartisan political activism.

In 1982, scouting celebrated the seventy-fifth anniversary of its founding, reaffirming its strategy of social presence and growth in membership, and in 1988, WOSM appointed Dr. Jacques Moreillon, former Director General of the International Committee of the Red Cross, as Secretary General. That same year, the World Scout Conference approved the "Towards a Strategy for Scouting" project, a strategic plan covering the following ten years that would bring the movement at the cutting edge and develop it both worldwide and in individual countries. But the international stage was about to undergo a very important transformation. In 1985, Mikhail Gorbachev was elected General Secretary of the Communist Party of the Soviet Union. Four years later, the Berlin wall fell and the Soviet Union and the communist regimes of its countries of influence quickly began to fall apart. The division of the world into two sides had suddenly disappeared.

Scouting had been seen by communist countries as a capitalist tool "for deceiving, oppressing and exploiting young people," and had been outlawed and prosecuted as a result.[110] The new situation in these countries after the prohibition was lifted led to an astonishing resurgence of scouting, especially considering that it had been banned for 40 years; scout associations were quickly set up in Russia, Czechoslovakia, Poland, Hungary, Yugoslavia (and the countries it was later divided into), the Ukraine, Armenia,[111] Albania, Estonia, and Lithuania, all of which were swiftly given international recognition.[112] The resurgence of scouting in Eastern Europe came as a surprise and was the first time since WOSM had extended membership to girls that new possibilities for rapid territorial growth had been discovered. In just a few years, 23 new countries[113] joined world scouting: either WOSM, WAGGGS, or both at the same time.

This process raised a certain rivalry between the two world organizations for the recognition and membership of the new associations. In this context, the gender issue lost importance and the pressure on the two world organizations—WOSM and WAGGGS—to increase membership became a more significant concern. Actually, the 1990s were marked by the strategic update of the two world organizations, as well as by the attempt to merge them by many European associations, mainly members of both organizations. As part of this process, a joint scout and guide region was set up in Europe in 1995, with just one committee and one bureau, though it broke down three years later.

Despite its huge impact throughout the twentieth century, scouting as a world phenomenon was still a mainly unresearched subject for the academic community. An exception was the research *La jeunesse et ses mouvements: Influence sur l'évolution des sociétés aux XIXe et XXe siècles*— edited by Denise Fauvel-Rouif, published in 1992 by the CNRS, and prepared by the Commission Internationale d'Histoire des Mouvements Sociaux et des Structures Sociaux. Possibly the broadest study in this field, it includes scouting in its analysis of various countries and also has a chapter exclusively on "Scouting Action in Peace Education"—written by Laszlo Nagy—the only chapter on a specific youth organization as a "movement of interest to every continent."[114]

In the late 1990s, scouting in Asian countries became increasingly linked to schools through voluntary but recognized extracurricular activities, which has led to spectacular growth. Indonesia is an extraordinary example of this: by linking scouting and public schooling, it reached 8.9 million members (2003), almost 30 percent of the WOSM total. Notwithstanding, only around 10 percent of these members in Indonesia are proper scouts: the rest are children who participate in extracurricular activities organized by the scout association. That is why, in the figures shown in the following sections, Indonesia will be treated in a different way.

In 1997, the cautious international public stance of the two world organizations gave way to a new formula more akin to advocacy: the alliance of the CEOs of four large youth organizations (WOSM, WAGGGS, YMCA, and YWCA[115]), of the Red Cross[116] (as a major humanitarian movement that focused on young people), and of the International Award Association (a worldwide youth program). In 2000, the alliance was joined by the CEO of the International Youth Foundation, the largest international foundation aimed at young people. World scouting used this alliance as a platform for articulating its position on long-term policies affecting the world. These stances were communicated as "declarations" by the top executives of the organizations that championed its causes, rather than through agreements reached at world conferences or by committees.

The first declaration made by this alliance (1997) was to raise awareness of nonformal education, a concept that had already been defined by UNESCO, and to ask governments to extend their educational policies beyond school; the second (1999), to request long-term national youth policies; the third (2001), to promote empowerment for girls in the twenty-first century; the fourth (2003), to promote an initiative for all of Africa to unite against HIV/AIDS, which has since been put into practice, and the fifth (2005), to encourage the participation of young people in decision-making processes.[117]

These declarations show the increasing awareness of the two organizations of world scouting on social problems that affect all children and young people, one more step in the long process of updating and adaptation to new realities of the movement. Some other changes and controversies happened in the movement and in the world organizations in the first decade of 2000, but they are too close to be considered part of history yet, and we need some more perspective of time to be able to analyze them.

3. Evolution of the WOSM Censuses (1924–2004)

A deeper understanding of the world evolution of the scout movement can be attained through examination of the annual censuses undertaken by WOSM[118] between 1924, when it published its first membership census, and 2004. The statistical research this book contains is based on collating the available censuses, processing them by computer, and checking possible errors. The original censuses were published by the World Scout Bureau, or—as was the case in the 1930s—by the Scout Association (UK). Copies were kept in the archives, sometimes with corrections to the published versions. This census data was used in my research to create the "WOSM Census Data Set, 1924–2004." Although the database deals with the countries[119] individually, the statistics in this section of the book examine world scouting by continental regions.

There is a great deal of data available on the scout movement, thanks to consistent efforts to gather statistics on membership. The censuses were broken down by age range from 1968 onward, which was used to generate a second new database: "WOSM Ages-based Census Data Set, 1968–2004," where the sections were organized into three population ranges

(5–9, 10–14, 15–19) and the continental regions of the United Nations Demographic Yearbook.[120]

Finally, data taken from reports submitted by the World Bureau at its respective conferences allow an accurate measure of country participation in world scout conferences. This data is available in a third new database: "Data Set of International and World Scout Conferences, 1924–2002."

Contrasting the changes in the number of member countries with the emergence of independent countries (figure 1.1) reveals a parallel evolution between the increase in the number of WOSM member countries and the emergence of new independent countries: while in 1922 there were 63 independent countries around the world, of which 36 (50.7%) had recognized scout associations, in 1937 this figure had risen to 67 percent (52 countries). Following a gap during World War II, there was a constant increase in the emergence of new independent countries from 1959 onward, initially because of decolonization and subsequently because of the fall of the communist regimes. By 2004, 78 percent of independent countries had recognized scout associations. In summary,

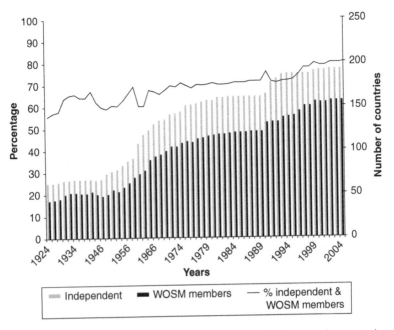

Figure 1.1 Evolution of independent countries and WOSM member countries, 1924–2004

Source: WOSM Census Data Set, 1924–2004.

in 82 years, the number of independent countries increased from 63 to 192 and the number of WOSM national scout associations rose from 36 to 154. This steady growth rate has been experienced by all continental regions.

Comparing the growth in member countries with the total number of members in WOSM (figure 1.2) reveals a constant increase up until the mid-1970s, when WOSM's membership leveled off. However, because the analysis uses raw data that has not been adjusted for changes in the world population (no data for all countries were available), it is unknown how much of this increase is explained by the increase in world population. Nonetheless, the data reveals a steady increase in the membership of WOSM, from 1.3 million in 1924 to almost 14 million in 1974.

After this date, the figure oscillates between 14 and 18 million, up to 22.7 million in 2004. The rise and fall in membership—to the tune of 6 million people—between 1996 and 2002 can be attributed to the substantial variations in the 1990s caused by change of criteria in Indonesia, the Philippines, and the United States censuses, that included children and youth who participated in scout activities without being "actual"

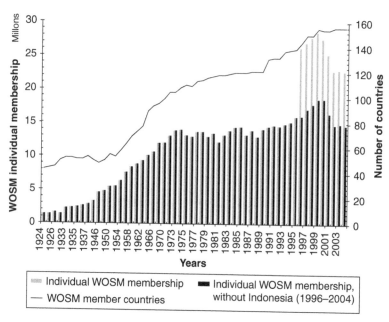

Figure 1.2 Changes in the number of individual members and of WOSM member countries

Source: WOSM Census Data Set, 1924–2004.

scouts. Whereas after few years the Philippines and the United States returned to the data criteria from 1995, Indonesia continued to count non-scouts. In particular, in 1995, Indonesia reported a membership—gathered since 1982—of 2.29 million members, which by 1996 exceeded 10.1 million with the new criteria, and which in the following six years would slowly shrink to 8 million members. To avoid noise in understanding the data evolution worldwide, therefore, some graphs do not include Indonesia after 1996.

Breaking this information down by continental regions (figure 1.3) reveals that the increase in membership worldwide is brought about mainly by increases in Asia and North America, with insignificant increases in other regions, and with European membership in particular dropping toward the end of the 1990s, though Africa shows a slight increase that has remained constant since the 1970s. (The curve between 1996 and 2002 in North America and Asia has been explained in the previous figure.) Overall, the census data shows that while Europe and North America initially represented the majority of WOSM membership, Asia took over from Europe after the 1960s and joined North America as one of the two regions with the highest proportion of the total census.

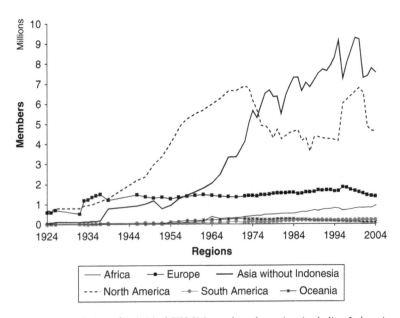

Figure 1.3   Evolution of individual WOSM members, by region (excluding Indonesia after 1996)

Source: WOSM Census Data Set, 1924–2004.

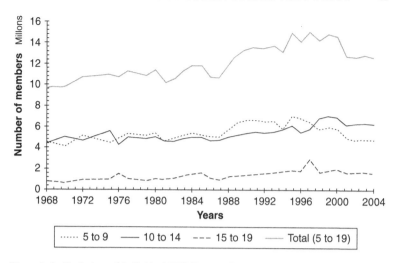

Figure 1.4   Evolution of individual WOSM members, by age, 1968–2004 (excluding Indonesia after 1996)

Source: WOSM Ages-based Census Data Set, 1968–2004.

Moreover, breaking down the census data after 1968 into the three age ranges (child, 5–9; adolescent, 10–14; youth, 15–19), we see (figure 1.4) that the distribution has not varied significantly. Over the course of 36 years, the adolescent and child age ranges remain quite equal; in fact, the child age range was slightly ahead until the late 1990s, when the adolescent age range overtook it. Meanwhile, youth has always been the minority age group.

A further analysis by continental regions outside the figure shows that while this trend holds true in Asia, South America, and Oceania, the other regions of the world have different distributions among the age ranges. In Africa, where the adolescent range is by far the biggest age group—and growing—the child and youth ranges have always been very much head to head. In Europe, the child age range was similar to the adolescent range until the late 1980s, when it became even stronger. In North America, the child range was the largest age group until 1999, when the adolescent range took over as the largest.

The last graph (figure 1.5) analyzes the participation of national scout associations in world scout conferences, the largest governing body of WOSM. The relevance of this analysis lies in that it reveals whether or not western countries were the majority in democratically defining the profile of the movement. The analysis shows, first, that the number of countries attending conferences increases in parallel with the increase in

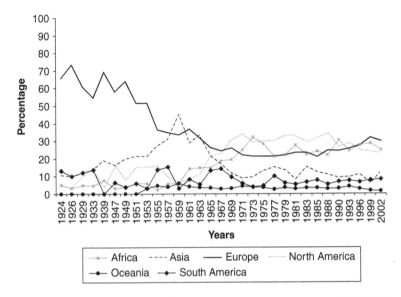

Figure 1.5   Share of countries attending world scout conferences, by region (1924–2002)
Source: Data Set of International and World Scout Conferences, 1924–2002

member countries, and second, that an important change has taken place in the proportions of continental regions. Because country participation in conferences has been very irregular, few trends are evident; one possible reason for the inconsistent attendance could be the geographical location of the conferences, allowing for increased participation of countries from the region in which the conference was organized. In any case, the data reveal that European countries composed the clear majority at world scout conferences until the 1950s. In the 1950s, Asia caught up with Europe, and Africa followed its example in the 1970s. Since then, scout associations from these three continental regions have had the biggest numerical weight at world scout conferences.

4. WORLD SCOUTING IN THE TWENTY-FIRST CENTURY: SOME NUMBERS

Whereas the previous section has shown a historical evolution, this section tries to reveal the current presence of world scouting using the latest available data on the world organizations WOSM and WAGGGS in the moment when the research was done (2006). Just as the historical data previously presented, the statistical analysis of world scouting today is based on the sum of the WOSM and WAGGGS censuses of 2003 for all countries, a census data that was used in my research to create another new database: the "World Scouting 2003 Data Set," which combines the scout censuses with population data from the United Nations for three age ranges (5–9, 10–14, 15–19) for all countries.[121]

Though the database examines individual countries by year, the results presented include data aggregated by continental regions. The list of member countries is a certain figure given that it was verified every three years at the world conferences. Nevertheless, even though the censuses are the only existing count of the number of scouts worldwide, their accuracy is disputable, given that it is based on the voluntary report of member associations, and is also linked to the payment of dues. This last fact could suggest that the real numbers might actually be larger than those reported by the censuses.

The definition of individual "members" is not always the same, and particularly some countries with a very high number of members in the census, like Indonesia and the United States, have "associated members"—children who participate in the extracurricular activities organized by scouts. By this measure, Indonesia alone has 7.2 million "members"; as previously explained, we will count it separated from the rest to avoid confusion. Additionally, the three age ranges (child, adolescent, and youth) analyzed in this study are not totally homologous across scout associations—for that reason, the age ranges are approximate.[122] Finally, analysis by gender is complicated by the fact that gender is considered additional information in the WOSM census, and therefore was not supplied by all countries, making an accurate breakdown of gender by age group impossible.

A first step in analyzing the global dimension of a movement like scouting is to understand whether its presence extends to the majority of countries, and if so, whether it has a uniform presence across continents, or it is found only in a few countries outside the western world. We could state that scouting has a large presence globally as well as on every continent. Scouting has national associations in 13 of the 15 most populous countries in the world;[123] in fact, the two remaining most populous countries where it is not present are the People's Republic of China and Vietnam, where it is outlawed (not including Hong Kong or Taiwan, which together sum 215,000 members). Scouting is officially present in 68 of the 80 countries and territories with over ten million inhabitants.[124] In order of population (2005), of these 80 countries, scouting is only not officially present in the People's Republic of China, Vietnam, Iran, Myanmar, Afghanistan, Iraq, Uzbekistan, North Korea, Syria, Kazakhstan, Mali, and Cuba.[125] Moreover, the majority of independent countries where scouting is not present, with the one big exception of China, are microstates.

Taking a broader look, scouting is officially present in 83 percent of all independent countries, a proportion that does not go below 73 percent on any continent with the single exception of Oceania, where due to the large number of microstates just 38.5 percent of the total independent countries have scout associations. WOSM has a larger geographic presence than WAGGGS on every continent, but the presence of the two organizations is complementary. Regarding the proportion of the 165 national associations of scouting (figure 1.6), Africa is the region with the highest number and it accounts for almost 28 percent of member countries. It is followed by Europe and Asia, with 24.2 percent and 23.0 percent, respectively, and after that North America with 13.9 percent. South America and Oceania have 7.3 percent and 3.6 percent of the total country representation, respectively. These numbers, which do not vary substantially between WOSM and WAGGGS, have important implications for the decision-making powers within world scouting: since it is the national associations that have voting rights at the world conference, countries in Africa and Asia represent more than half of the total country votes (figure 1.7).

Not counting educators and scout leaders, scouting has 26.7 million members. Of the 20 million belonging to WOSM, 7.2 million are

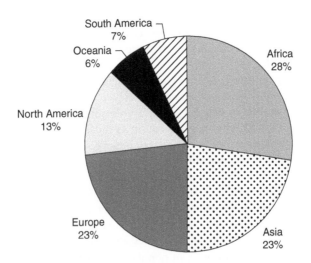

Figure 1.6 Share of WOSM and/or WAGGGS member countries by region in 2003 (n = 175)

Source: World Scouting 2003 Data Set.

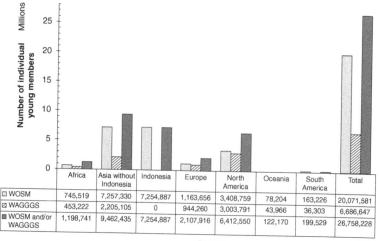

	Africa	Asia without Indonesia	Indonesia	Europe	North America	Oceania	South America	Total
□ WOSM	745,519	7,257,330	7,254,887	1,163,656	3,408,759	78,204	163,226	20,071,581
▨ WAGGGS	453,222	2,205,105	0	944,260	3,003,791	43,966	36,303	6,686,647
▦ WOSM and/or WAGGGS	1,198,741	9,462,435	7,254,887	2,107,916	6,412,550	122,170	199,529	26,758,228

Regions

Figure 1.7   Number of young WOSM and/or WAGGGS individuals by regions and overall, 2003

Source: World Scouting 2003 Data Set.

part of the Indonesian WOSM association (counting both the "associated" and the actual scouts). However, regardless of whether Indonesia is counted in the census, Asia is the region with the most members, followed by North America, Europe, and Africa—though with WAGGGS, North America occupies the first place. Neither South America nor Oceania has more than 200,000 members. Although, in general, WOSM has substantially more members worldwide than WAGGGS, the numbers are fairly equal in both North America and Europe—it is in the other regions that we see much higher membership of WOSM than of WAGGGS.

Scouting was created as an educational movement aimed at adolescents, although it was extended shortly afterward to the youth and preadolescent age groups. This has had a lasting impact on how scouting is done, because a movement that is aimed at a narrow age range does not have the same ability to carry out citizenship education as a movement that includes a wider range of young people. Analyzing the age ranges (figure 1.8) reveals that youth between the ages of 10 and 14 have the greatest representation (12.1 million) in scouting, followed by children aged 5–9 years (10.8 million), while only 3.8 million members are between the ages of 15 and 19.

Continental regions with more developing and emerging countries have more girls and boys between the ages of 10 and 14, whereas

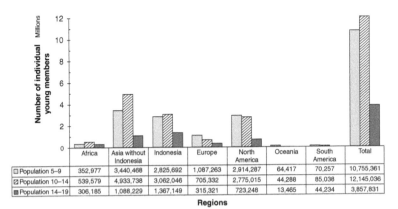

	Africa	Asia without Indonesia	Indonesia	Europe	North America	Oceania	South America	Total
▢ Population 5–9	352,977	3,440,468	2,825,692	1,087,263	2,914,287	64,417	70,257	10,755,361
▨ Population 10–14	539,579	4,933,738	3,062,046	705,332	2,775,015	44,288	85,038	12,145,036
▥ Population 14–19	306,185	1,088,229	1,367,149	315,321	723,248	13,465	44,234	3,857,831

Regions

Figure 1.8   World scouting census by regions according to member age, 2003
Source: World Scouting 2003 Data Set.

continents with industrialized countries (North America, Europe, and Oceania) have more boys and girls aged 5–9. On all continents, the youth age range (15–19) is the smallest, although in Africa this figure is very close to the child range. When in the database we compared the scout census data with the UN population data for 15–19-year-olds, we found that the densities in the adolescent and child ranges were highest in the aggregate. On a worldwide scale, 200 adolescents (ages 10–14) and 177 children (ages 5–9) per 10,000 are scouts. In some regions, densities are higher: in North America, 688 children and 669 adolescents per 10,000 are scouts, and in Europe and Oceania 262 and 241 children per 10,000 are scouts, respectively. Adolescents have a density of 197 in Asia, 175 in Oceania, and 143 in Europe. The youth age range (15–19) is low around the world, as demonstrated by the 83 per 10,000 in North America and 62 per 10,000 in Europe.

By comparing the number of scouts within each age group with the country's total population aged 5–19, we avoid the mistake of comparing members with the total population of each country, since the most relevant statistic is the density within the age range that could potentially participate in scouting: the youth age group. For that reason, the UN population data of youth aged 5–19 in every country is compared with the census of every national scout association. The density is expressed as the number of scouts per 10,000 youths aged 5–19.

Comparison of the census data with the population data (figure 1.9) reveals that 146 of every 10,000 young people (5–19 years old) belong to scouting (particularly, 202 adolescents, 166 children, and 63 youth), of

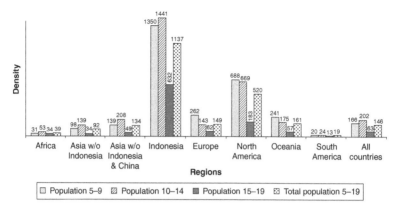

Figure 1.9   World scouting density by age group and region, 2003
Source: World Scouting 2003 Data Set.

which 110 are members of WOSM and 36 are members of WAGGGS. When breaking down the data, we eliminated two important sources of bias in the figures from Asia: Indonesia and China. The first group, "Asia without Indonesia," does not count the Indonesia (both the youth census and the scout census); the reason is that, as I have mentioned, Indonesian scouting counts young people who only participate in school extracurricular activities, besides proper scouts; so if we counted them it would seem that there were more members in this country than any other country in the world, having a density of 1,137 Scouts for every 10,000 young people. The second group, "Asia without Indonesia and China," avoids not only the bias from Indonesia, but also the weight of the population of the People's Republic of China, due to the fact that China, the most heavily populated country in the world with one- fifth of the world's population, still outlaws scouting, and that influences the calculation of the scout density of the region.

If we break down the data by geographical region, excluding Indonesia, we see that North America is the region with the most scouts per 10,000 young inhabitants, with the high number of 520, even higher when talking about 5–9 and 10–14 age groups (688 and 669, respectively). It is followed in order of density by Oceania—the continent with the least members—and Europe, with 161 and 149, respectively, which also rise over mid-200 for population 5–9. It is worth noting that without Indonesia, Asia has a density of 92, and without taking China's population into account, this number increases to 134. Africa and South America are the continents with the lowest density of scouts (39 and 19, respectively).

There is then a difference between number of countries, number of individual members, and densities: Oceania has few individual members and few countries, but has a higher density than Europe. Africa is the continent with more countries, but it has a low density.

Nevertheless, again, when comparing with the real population censuses, the continents with most developing and emerging countries have the highest density in the adolescent age group, whereas the continents with most industrial countries have the highest density in the children age group.

If we compare separately the scout densities of the two world organizations, we see that WOSM has a higher scout density than WAGGGS, and that this is consistent across regions. Nonetheless, North America and Europe differ in that the two organizations have a fairly similar number of individual members. The clearest differences are to be found in Asia, even excluding Indonesia, and in Oceania (figure 1.10).

The combined analysis of WOSM and WAGGGS shows that despite a numeric difference between the two organizations, the percentage of boys and girls reached by scouting as a whole is close to 50 percent on three continents: North America, Oceania, and Europe, and on two others, Africa and South America, the percentage is very close—53.8 percent and 57.2 percent are boys, respectively. This balance is due to the fact that

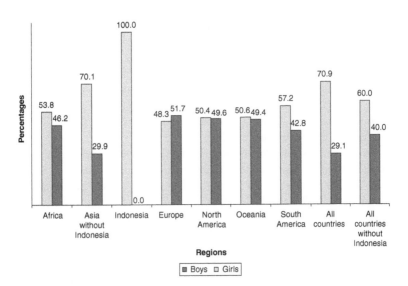

Figure 1.10   Share of boys/girls in world scouting (WOSM and/or WAGGGS), 2003
Source: World Scouting 2003 Data Set.

although WAGGGS is smaller than WOSM, several WOSM associations include girls among their members. Only in Asia is the percentage disproportionate, where 70 percent of scouting individual members are boys and 30 percent are girls, not counting Indonesia, which on the WOSM census does not declare to have female members—though it most certainly has.

In summary, these figures show that scouting is present in the vast majority of countries, and on all five continents, and that Africa and Asia together represent the majority of countries, meaning that they have the most weight in the democratic decision-making processes of the world conferences. We also see that membership is substantially higher in WOSM than in WAGGGS, though the numbers in Europe and North America are fairly equal. A comparison of the number of boys and girls belonging to scouting with the total population aged 5–19 reveals that 170 of every 10,000 youths belong to scout associations worldwide—even with scouting being banned in the country that has one-fifth of the world's population. By age range, the adolescent group (10–14 years) is the largest around the world, despite the fact that in western countries there are slightly more children (aged 5–9) than adolescents. With regard to gender, it is important to emphasize that there are fairly equal numbers of boys and girls in scouting in most parts of the world, with the exception of Asia, which could be due to inaccuracies in the census data since numerous WOSM associations may not specify numbers of boys and girls, as is the case in Indonesia.

CHAPTER 2

AN IDEAL, A MOVEMENT, AN ORGANIZATION

The Scout movement is a world leader in youth education, and has particular relevance to the needs of youth in Africa and in the emerging democracies around the globe.

Nelson R. Mandela, President of South Africa (1994–99), Patron of the South African Scout Association

ONCE THE ACTUAL BEGINNINGS OF THE SCOUT MOVEMENT in England are known, we can better understand what Baden-Powell meant when he said: "First I had an idea. Then I saw an ideal. Now we have a Movement, and if some of you don't watch out we shall end up just an organization."[1] Because actually, scouting is first and foremost an idea: that through games and adventure, adolescents can take responsibility, develop their potentials, and internalize the societal values of coexistence that form the basis of citizenship. Since its British beginnings, that idea took shape both through its shared principles and through its educational methodology, which is at once very intuitive and easy to carry out by those who practice it. As a result, the idea was transformed into an ideal of living, and that ideal into an organized educational movement.

But the balance between the ideal of living, the movement of volunteers, and the institutional organization is a difficult one, especially when shared by millions of people around the world. A first challenge is simply figuring out what all those calling themselves *scouts* have in common. Second, finding an operational system that is neither too rigid nor too diffuse. And finally, guaranteeing that groups with values and objectives that clash with or oppose those of the scout movement aren't able to utilize the scout name or identity for their operations. These three points of scouting—its essential characteristics, its organizational structure, and its recognition policy—form the axes on which its ideological consistency is founded, as much now as it was when it was first formalized on a world scale in 1920.

Even so, the educational design of the scout movement is profoundly intuitive: it does not require many *explanations,* but rather *life experiences.* This is sometimes forgotten when nearly all emphasis is placed on pedagogical preparation, something common in continental Europe. The sociologist Mateo Jover, former Deputy Secretary General of WOSM for Prospective Studies, pointed out a few years ago in Barcelona that thanks to this intuitive pedagogy, in a mostly illiterate town in Indonesia, an illiterate carpenter made a very good scout leader.

Precisely for this reason, if we want to acquire an in-depth understanding of how scouting functions and know its three axes, we will have to explore each one in turn; that is just what we will do in this chapter.

We will start dealing with the essential characteristics of scouting, which result from the sum of the movement's principles (purpose, values, and educational method) and from its definition of itself as an organization (taking the World Organization of the Scout Movement [WOSM] and the World Association of Girl Guides and Girl Scouts [WAGGGS] together). Given that scouting is a global movement that encompasses a broad social, cultural, and linguistic diversity, it is fundamental that its basic principles are defined as accurately as is possible, so that everyone understands them in the same way.

Then, we will analyze the highly intuitive profile of scouting as an educational movement, showing the difference between the apparently hierarchical model of its organizational and decision-making systems and the network dynamic that actually characterizes the movement and its way of functioning in the world, and also explaining the educational impact of scouting.

Subsequently, we will look at the structure and function of the scout organization, from the local level to the global, showing as well the role of associations and federations, and the existence of two different world organizations. And finally, we will get to know world scouting's policy for recognition, which is to say, the established procedure by which it determines who does and who does not form part of the organization, in order to avoid the use of the word "scouting" (and "guiding") by those who act contrary to the ideals of the scout movement.

Let me emphasize once again that we refer to the scout movement as including mixed associations, girls' associations, and boys' associations, all assembled in the two world organizations—WOSM and WAGGGS. The history covered in the previous chapter shows how scouting, although in some cases separated by gender, is in fact one movement. If we know that in the first quarter of the twentieth century Robert Baden-Powell constituted separate scouting entities for boys and girls, with the same principles, purpose, and method, and presided over by himself at the British and global levels, we also know that in practice he gave no importance to this separation, as is voiced in the preface to the 1919 book directed at scout leaders (educators), *Aids to Scoutmastership:* "The term 'Scouting' has come to mean a system of training in citizenship, through games, for boys and girls.... The training is needed for both sexes, and is imparted through the Boy Scouts and Girl Guides Movements. The principles are the same for both. It is only in the details that they vary."[2]

For the general public of most countries, *scouting* means the same thing, regardless of whether or not boys and girls belong to different associations, as Laszlo Nagy explains.[3] Actually, it is often seen by society as one movement with two organizations, and a single term has been used in many countries to cover both genders: *scout* in English (even if saying "boy scouts" or "girl scouts"), also adopted by many other languages— *escolta* in Catalan; *éclaireur* in French; *escoteiro* in Portuguese; *pfadfinder* in German; etcetera This does not mean that the two world organizations are identical, nor the corresponding national associations, as we will see. It simply means that when speaking about world scouting as a global educational movement, the elements that this movement has in common worldwide are more relevant than the differences due to the history and traditions of each scout association on its own country.

1. ESSENTIAL CHARACTERISTICS OF SCOUTING

The basic elements on which scouting is founded are, on the one hand, its definition, and on the other, its purpose, principles, and method, together called the *fundamentals*. But this has not always been the case. Since the formalization of world scouting in 1920, both WOSM and WAGGGS established that their basic principles would be those expressed in the text of the *Promise* and *Law*.

In 1977, however, the World Scout Conference modified the WOSM Constitution by incorporating a clear definition of the purpose, principles, and method[4] as a modern formulation of the *fundamentals*. The establishing of these three elements follows the structure of Chapter 1 of the UN Charter, which explains the organization's purposes and principles. The three elements of scouting's *fundamentals* cover why it exists *(purpose)*; what the ethical rules that govern its existence are *(principles)*; and how it will achieve its purpose *(educational method)*.

While the *fundamentals* (purpose, principles, and method) cover the ideological elements of the scout movement, the definition covers its characteristics as an organization. The elements of the definition are as important as the *fundamentals* in determining what scouting is and what it is not. Government control, lack of independence, partisanship, obligation, and discrimination have all been reason enough to suspend the recognition of a scout association by the world organization.

Let's then take a look at the *essential characteristics* of scouting, which is the expression used to refer to the sum of its elements (definition, on the one hand, and purpose, principles, and method on the other), laid out in the Constitutions of the two world organizations. We must keep in mind that if the scout movement takes many forms as it adapts to the social context of each country, these essential characteristics are the common denominator that allows discussion of a single subject at a global level, since all member organizations must fulfill these characteristics.

1.1. DEFINITION (*WHAT IT IS*)

Scouting is an educational movement for and of young people, self-governed; independent and nonpartisan; voluntary; and open to all regardless of origin, nationality, race, or creed on the basis of shared purpose, principles, and method. The movement is institutionally organized into two international organizations: WOSM and WAGGGS.[5]

The definition of scouting has eight elements—movement, educational, institutionally organized, self-governed, independent and nonpartisan, for and of young people, based on voluntary membership, and open to all; taken together[6] these describe scouting in all its complexity and set it apart from other civil society organizations in both individual countries and on a global scale.

A Movement...
Scouting is defined first and foremost as a movement. Robert Baden-Powell's early writings indicate a certain reluctance to formalize it into an organization,[7] a reluctance that somehow remained even after the creation of the British associations and later the world organizations. Although Baden-Powell's hatred of bureaucracy held him back in the formalization of the movement, he realized that coordination and the establishment of standards were the key to ensuring that the reputation scouting was earning was not used to promote under that name corrupt, or worse still, damaging programs.[8]

The expression *scout movement*—and its synonym *scouting*—is therefore used to define what is involved in the *activity* carried out by millions of boys and girls around the world with a set of shared values: organized educational activities that lead into a common purpose. This distinction between *movement* and *organization,* as we will see later, is very significant because it shows that scouting could ideally exist without the need for an organization, as was the case in many countries before the world organization was created. The distinction also underlines the fact that the organization exists to serve the movement, not the other way around.

The combination of "movement" and "organization" gives scouting a particular strength, lending it the flexibility of a movement while affording it the security and consistence of an organization. As a movement, every scout group has significant leeway when it comes to adapting the directives of the world and national organizations at a local level. Similarly, as an organization, scouting maintains its essential characteristics over time, having also the democratic procedures to update them.

... Which is Educational...

Scouting is, fundamentally, an educational movement that helps youth develop their potential as individuals and as citizens. The recreational activities carried out in scouting are a means to an educational end, and not in themselves an end. This means that scouting should not be regarded as a recreational movement or a leisure activity, but as an educational movement acting in young people's leisure time.

The educational potential of scouting, complementary of school and family, was already recognized by new pedagogical movements before it was internationally formalized. In 1917, the Dean of the prestigious Teachers College of Columbia University wrote in the academic article "Scouting and Education": "I declare the Boy Scout movement to be the most significant educational contribution of our times."[9]

Scouting adopts UNESCO's Delors Report definition of education: "a life long process which enables the continuous development of a person's capabilities as an individual and as a member of society."[10] UNESCO identifies three types of education: the most known, *formal education,* is the hierarchically structured, chronologically graded educational system running from school to university. Removing intentionality we find the second type, *informal education,* the process whereby individuals acquire attitudes, values, skills, and knowledge from daily experience, such as from family, friends, peer groups, the media, and other influences and factors in the person's environment.

The third type, *nonformal education,* takes the form of "organized educational activity outside the established formal system that is intended to serve an identifiable public with concrete learning objectives."[11] Though it is not as rule governed as school, and it does not have the same officiality, it does have educational purposes and directives. Scouting falls under the category of nonformal education, and serves as a complement to the education provided by the formal and informal sectors. In this way, scouting has a distinct role to play—not as a substitute for the education provided at school or at home, but as an additional strong influence on the development of the young members of scouting.

...Institutionally Organized...

Scouting can be described as a "movement of volunteers operating through a worldwide network of local groups belonging to national scout organizations."[12] First and foremost, scouting is a movement; but to guarantee unity and coherence to values in its activities worldwide, it is *institutionally organized* at a global, national, and local level.

Indeed, some consistency is needed for an educational movement that gathers millions of people from more than 160 countries worldwide, with enormous flexibility and ability to adapt to very distinct social and cultural contexts. Ensuring this dynamic fluidity requires an institutional referent to democratically establish what are the minimum standards that in every moment of history and for the entire world define what is scouting. This is one of the primary purposes of the world organization as well as of each national scout association.

This specific, internationally defined identity is protected by a strict admissions system for scout associations (recognition policy) with a double filter: the World Bureau checks that prospective associations meet the criteria, and they have to be accepted by the democratic vote of national scout associations at the world conference.[13]

...Self-governed...

Scouting is an institutionally organized *self-governed* educational movement, which means that it has full liberty to formulate and enact its own policies. The adaptability of the movement to different countries and social contexts requires clear educational grounds and a common identity established at the world level. Scouting can only fully accomplish its purpose if its different identity is guaranteed through self-governance, avoiding third party interference.

For this reason, the scout movement, at all levels—the group on a local level, the association at the national level, and the organization at the world level—must be able to decide and direct its own future. The movement must also have full capacity in making decisions affecting it, remaining autonomous from private institutions—associations, churches, congregations—as well as from public and government institutions.

Self-governance does not mean isolation: the scout movement grew everywhere thanks to the already existing organizations welcoming scout groups, be it mountain clubs, churches, schools, or other entities. *Self-governing* signifies that the purpose and principles of the movement must always be prioritized over the bodies that host them. These hosting organizations can't affect the work and the priorities of the activities of scouting—and this is not always well received by the bodies that support scout groups.

...Independent and Nonpartisan...

The scout movement is not only autonomous in the sense that it is self-governing and establishes its own goals, but it is also *ideologically independent*. This independence is relevant when being referred to religious denominations, political ideologies and government institutions, as well as to political parties: for this reason, the scout movement is *independent* of any other institution and *nonpartisan*, the later signifying that neither scouting nor its educational activities can be used as a means of any kind for achieving political power.[14]

The scout movement itself is a social reality and its aim is to help young people to develop as responsible individuals, as citizens, and as members of society. This civic education cannot take place in a vacuum, and the movement must be able to defend the values it stands for and to create the best possible conditions for the type of education it proposes.[15]

Therefore, nonpartisanship does not prevent the movement from taking a public stance on issues related to its educational objectives, on the basis of its principles, as long as the taking public instance is not mixed up and used to help a political party in its struggle for power or used in partisan politics, which the scout movement must transcend. What scouting seeks in defining itself as nonpartisan is a differentiation between the shared interests with its respective society and the specific interests of political parties and ideologies.

...for and of Young People...

If scouting was initially a movement designed essentially for adolescents (12–16 years), its rapid expansion to include other age ranges made it a movement *for young people*. In general, scouting targets boys and girls beginning around ages 6 or 8 until the ages 18 or 21, depending on the country.[16] Scouting does not work well for much younger children in making them understand the concept of personal commitment to a shared code of conduct or in developing leadership skills.[17]

On the other hand, the world organizations have clarified that scouting is not only a movement *for* young people managed by adults only; it is also a movement *of* young people, supported by adults.[18] The roles that youth play in the decision-making process have resulted in a number of different practices depending on the association and the diversity of sociocultural factors in every country, as well as the size of scout associations (some with millions of members).

Though in some European countries scout activities are run mainly by people under 30, in many other countries few young people hold leadership positions in either local scout groups or national associations. This also tends to be the case in the regional (continental) and world committees of both WOSM and WAGGGS, though this is changing due to initiatives begun in the mid-1990s by the two world organizations designed to strengthen and expand democratic decision making within the world organizations.[19]

... Based on Voluntary Membership ...

The scout movement is based on the voluntary, open, and unpaid commitment of its members, and on their free adherence to its principles: in scouting, each person decides when to become a member or when to leave—children, adolescents, and adults, who serve as leaders. This is how the scout movement began: with people freely ready to commit themselves to shared values and to behave in accordance with them.

That voluntary nature of individuals' participation in scouting is important because it differentiates it both from the formal educational system and from extracurricular educational services, as well as from government-driven organizations with compulsory membership in some authoritarian regimes. Moreover, the voluntary adherence to scout principles is a fundamental tool of its educational method, because it is in that free and voluntary adherence where the power of self-education in scouting lies.

When talking about adult participation in the movement—as scout leaders (educators) or in the organization—that *voluntary* character also means that they do their tasks "of their own accord, freely and willingly, without being paid for their services or time."[20] This also has an influence on the way these adults democratically participate in decision-making processes and commit at the different levels: local group, national association, world organization.

... Open to Everybody

Scouting is an educational movement open to everybody, regardless of origin, race, creed, or socioeconomic status,[21] an openness that has been part of its identity since its inception.[22] Nevertheless, in different moments of history the legal framework of some countries have built boundaries to the aim of scouting to include everybody willing to be a member and to freely adopt its principles. That is why scouting has had to deal with discrimination under particular legal frameworks. In South Africa, for example, until the end of apartheid, scouting was not allowed multiracial units, although different single-race units formed part of a common association from the start.[23] Similarly, until racial segregation in education was abolished in 1954 in the United States, the Boy Scouts of America (BSA) was a racially segregated organization. Concerning gender, in some countries joint activities involving boys and girls are still prohibited, either legally or morally—many Islamic official interpretations consider *haraam* (forbidden by the faith) the free mixing of boys and girls, or even to touch any non-Mahram (immediate relatives) person of the opposite gender. In these cases, the separation of the movement in gender-based associations or sub-associations is not an option.[24]

Religious beliefs and sexual orientation in many countries have also legal limits and punishments that in some cases even include the death penalty. As a result, openness to agnostics or homosexuals, which is the norm in European WOSM and WAGGGS associations, might be today legally impossible in these countries.[25]

1.2. PURPOSE (*WHY IT DOES EXIST*) AND PRINCIPLES (*VALUES ON WHICH IT IS BASED*)

The *raison d'être* of a movement is reflected in *its purpose*. And the purpose of the scout movement is to contribute to the self-development of young people in achieving their full physical, intellectual, social, and spiritual potentials as individuals, as responsible citizens, and as members of their local, national, and international communities.[26]

One of the main elements of this purpose is the educational identity of scouting, as well as the will of its educational action to integrally cover the several dimensions of a human being. The educational purpose of scouting complements, rather than substitutes, the duties carried out by other social institutions. The educational work of the scout movement is especially relevant in everything that requires learning for the action and from the action. In this way, scouting complements the difficulty of schools in teaching some of the basic general competencies, or even the metadisciplinary ones (those not linked to any discipline or subject), especially those involving autonomy and personal initiative, as well as in interaction with social and physical environments—which is where scouting works best.

Clearly, the direct goal of scouting is education. Social transformation is a consequence, not a purpose. Its commitment to leave the world better that it was found is an indirect result of improving individuals (educational aim), creating responsible citizens. Scouting's citizenship education pursues that, on the basis of its shared values, individuals develop the ability to define what society should be like, and as responsible citizens, make it a reality. This means that, besides the principles that outline its shared values, scouting does not provide its members specification on how to improve society; instead, its option is to allow them to freely develop their awareness within the freedom framework of the scout group, from the consciousness of the rights and duties that they are committed to as members of their city, country, and the world.

However, the shared principles of the scout movement involve a substantial commitment to inclusion, peace, understanding, and dialogue between cultures, and to solidarity. These broad values of coexistence will be highlighted when speaking about the role that scouting plays in global citizenship education. Scouting is an educational movement, forming the character of individuals and maximizing their leadership potential. Leadership skills, however, are meaningless without purpose: instead, the leadership that scouting promotes among its millions of members is committed to creating a better world based on those values of coexistence.

Finally, a word about the different reference to gender that WOSM and WAGGGS make in their wording of the movement's purpose. To WOSM, the purpose of the movement is to "contribute to the development of young people," while WAGGGS says that it is "to provide girls and young women with opportunities" for personal development. This difference shows the two formulas used to develop the maximum potential of youth without gender inequality: doing it together or separately—and in each one of the two world organizations there are associations that have followed one model or the other.

So, while in the last two decades WAGGGS has opted to focus exclusively on females' education, WOSM has opted for coeducation and drafted an official policy regarding gender within scouting, declaring its commitment "to maintain the principles of equal opportunity and equality in cooperation between women and men, both within the scout movement and in society in general."[27]

Whereas the purpose of a movement explains why it does exist, *the principles* express in which values the movement is based. The educational action of scouting for girls and boys is based on a values system that is expressed methodologically through a social code *(Scout Law)* and the free adoption of it as a guideline for conduct *(Scout Promise)*. But for the scout movement as a whole, these values are expressed in three principles that refer to the spiritual, social, and personal dimensions. These principles represent the model of society and lifestyle that all scouts share.[28]

In the previous chapter we saw that the "Scout Law" and the "Scout Promise" framed by Baden-Powell became both the central methodological element for young people's self-education, and the framework to verify that all scout associations share the same values, making thus possible the ideological unity of the movement.[29] The scout associations could reframe the Promise and the Law in a modern wording, adapted to their own cultural and social realities, a reframe that then had to be ratified by the corresponding world organization.[30]

Moreover, in the 1970s both world organizations carried out a process of clarification to identify and define the principles in place of hinting at them through the texts of the Scout Law and Promise. The result was a newly framed text that embodied the three principles, synthesized as *duty to God, duty to others,* and *duty to yourself.*[31]

However, the synthesized titles of the three principles do not give enough information on the principles' contents, and we should go deeper to fully understand them. For these principles constitute the rules and beliefs that have to be considered in order to accomplish the purpose of scouting, rules and believes that represent a social code for all the members of the movement.[32] Considering that the two world organizations' definitions of the principles are similar, and that the WOSM document *Fundamental Principles* makes them clearer, we will follow its reasoning.

The first principle, which addresses the spiritual dimension, is referred to by WOSM as Duty to God: adherence to spiritual principles, loyalty to the religion that expresses them, and acceptance of the duties resulting therefrom; or even more plainly, as "a person's relationship with the spiritual values of life, the fundamental belief in a force above mankind."[33] The wording of WAGGGS defines it as "Acknowledgement and search for spirituality." This definition means that the educational approach of the scout movement wants to help young people to transcend the material world by searching for spiritual values in life.[34] Despite WOSM having a more explicit reference to religion, there are several *laïque*[35] (secular) scout associations around the world that have existed since the beginning of the movement. All are active on the education of the spiritual dimension, which shows that educationally the search and development of the spiritual dimension in scouting does not necessarily have to focus on a specific religion. It is when these spiritual principles are linked with a particular religion that they should be consistent with the corresponding beliefs.

The definition of this principle—unlike its synthesized title—leaves interpretation open to non-monotheist or non-deist religions also present in scouting, like Buddhism, and it certainly includes the spiritual approach of existing *laïque* and open scout associations, like the French Éclaireuses Éclaireurs de France, founder of world scouting in 1920. In this sense, Laszlo Nagy, in his extensive Report on World Scouting, notices that

> even secular morals are not free from any spirituality. In fact, such morals rest on a very wide and non-codified moral conception, that of 'honest people' and, in as far as it is not tied up with atheist militantism, it in no way threatens the spirituality of associations which consciously purvey the ideology of a revealed religion. Collaboration is thus possible.[36]

The scout life experience, which can be seen in any summer camp, shows many of the nonmaterial goods that cannot be bought: to learn the value of friendship, to realize the wonder of nature, to value the achievements of your own effort, to enjoy the emotions coming from service, from solidarity, and from love... These all provide a sense of hope and purpose, and in highly consumer societies also show that when one has a rich spiritual and moral life, the need for consumption becomes less important.

The second principle, which addresses the social dimension, is defined as Duty to Others: loyalty to one's country in harmony with the promotion of local, national, and international peace, understanding, and cooperation and participation in the development of society with recognition and respect for the dignity of one's fellowman and for the integrity of the natural world. These two aspects of "duty to others" encapsulate the idea of citizenship education of scouting.

The cornerstone of community is that the idea of loyalty to one's country must be on a par with the promotion of peace, understanding, and cooperation at any level—local, national, or international.[37] The cornerstone of participation is clarified as the duty to serve others through the development of society, recognizing both the dignity of others and the integrity of the environment.

Scouting teaches that serving others provides a twofold satisfaction: it makes one less focused on their own problems and meets the needs of others. But the sense of belonging that conforming to community ideals brings—including national and religious—can be derived in the denial of the other: it is for this reason that the scout experience emphasizes that the sense of community is not more important than a sense of fellowship, and that the value of every individual—and every potential friend—is incalculable, just as the beauty and diversity of the environment where scouts have innumerable experiences.

The third and final principle addresses the personal dimension of scouting, and is defined as Duty to Self: responsibility for the development of oneself. This is perhaps the least controversial principle of the three and emphasizes the importance of the individual in scouting. It stresses the idea that the individual must take on responsibility for the development of his/her own skills. This is what the scout method achieves through intentional education, meaning through the process in which every boy and girl is in charge of their own achievements, growth, and enrichment as individuals.

Whereas these three principles express the values for the movement as a whole, for young people, scouting's values are expressed in the wording of the Promise and the Law, which brings together the principles to which all young scouts adhere. As the progressive educationalist James E. Russell pointed out, the Scout Law "stresses duties instead of magnifying rights," and it is "stated in positive terms, rather than in the form of the Mosaic decalogue: 'Thou shalt not.' "[38] What follows is the original text of the Scout Promise and the Scout Law, reproduced by the Constitutions of WOSM and WAGGGS (calling it scout/guide respectively) as a historical document *"intended to serve as a source of inspiration"*[39] from which each association adapts its own version.

Scout Promise (Original)

On my honor, I promise that I will do my best—
To do my duty to God and the King
(*or:* to God and my country);
To help other people at all times;
To obey the Scout Law.

Scout Law (Original)

1. A Scout's honor is to be trusted.
2. A Scout is loyal.
3. A Scout's duty is to be useful and to help others
4. A Scout is a friend to all and a brother/sister to every other Scout.
5. A Scout is courteous.
6. A Scout is a friend to animals.
7. A Scout obeys orders of his parents, Patrol leader or Scoutmaster without question.
8. A Scout smiles and whistles/sings under all difficulties.
9. A Scout is thrifty.
10. A Scout is clean/pure in thought, in word and in deed.[40]

As an example of how different associations adapt the Scout Promise and the Scout Law, below is the version created by the Mouvement Scout de la Suisse (Swiss Guide and Scout Movement):[41]

Scout Promise

With your help and happily I Promise to do my best:
(*or*: With the help of God, with your help and happily I promise to do my best:)
To study in detail the values of our Scout Law
To search for the meaning of my life
To be involved in each community where I live

Scout Law

We, the Scouts, wish:

— To be honest and sincere
— To rejoice in all that is beautiful and give joy to others
— To be thoughtful and helpful
— To choose to the best of our abilities and to commit ourselves
— To listen to and respect others
— To share
— To protect nature and to respect life
— To face difficulties with confidence

1.3. EDUCATIONAL METHOD

If a method expresses the means used to achieve its ends, the *scout method* represents the sum of interdependent educational elements that creates a unified and integrated whole to achieve the purpose of the movement. Every one of these elements has an educational purpose that complements the others, and for that reason, although not all the elements will be apparent in the forefront at any particular moment, over a period of time all elements will have been used actively.[42]

The scout method is defined as a system of progressive self-education through (i) shared principles and commitment to them (*Law and Promise*); (ii) learning by doing; (iii) teamwork in groups; (iv) active cooperation between young people and adults; (v) progressive self-development; (vi) nature and outdoor activities; and (vii) symbolic framework.[43] The method requires a certain level of maturity among the group members, which means that the method is unsuitable for too small children or for grownup youth–in their 20s.[44]

It is important to keep in mind that the scouting method is both intuitive and intentional. It is not necessary to study the components to be able to carry them out, because the dynamics of the movement integrate and reproduce them: this allows youth leaders to enter scouting with no prior experience and, in a short time, work with the method without even realizing it. At the same time, it is clearly intentional: each member of the scout movement is considered a unique individual who, from the start, has the potential to develop and can assume responsibility for their own growth.

The intuitive aspect of the scout method conceals the complex combination of elements that makes scouting a unique educational movement. These nuances make it more difficult for a scout leader to describe the scout method than to implement it in their group. Similarly, though a scout leader would probably be able to state the three fundamental principles, it is unlikely that he or she would be able to provide the detailed explanation you could find on the constitutional documents, and the same would probably happen with the seven elements of the method.

In the scout method, the youth is the protagonist of his/her own educational process, with the help and encouragement of his/her peers, of the scout leader (educator), and the experiences shared with fellow scouts. Scouting's self-education is also done progressively, which means that it tries to help every young person to develop his/her own skills and interests during the educational process and through life experiences. Scouting thus aims to stimulate youths to find constructive ways to meet their needs and open doors to future choices they want to make.[45]

A fundamental element of the scout method is the visualization of the leader as an older brother, and "not as a teacher, nor as an official, nor as a priest, nor as an instructor,"[46] as Baden-Powell wrote in 1919. This close relationship with the leader allows education through interaction, far from removed instruction, and in particular the possibility to educate the individual rather than indoctrinate the masses.

The practice of the movement can best be seen through its educational method more than through analysis of the definition, purpose, and principles of scouting. In some countries, the contrasting visions of scouting expressed in the ongoing evolution of the movement have led to erroneous claims that elements like discipline or use of uniforms define the movement. That is why to accurately explain the components of the scout method is important: because the constitutional definitions made by both organizations (WOSM and WAGGGS) clearly explain the elements that characterize the educational action of scouting around the world. The following diagram (figure 2.1) summarizes the interdependence of its elements:[47]

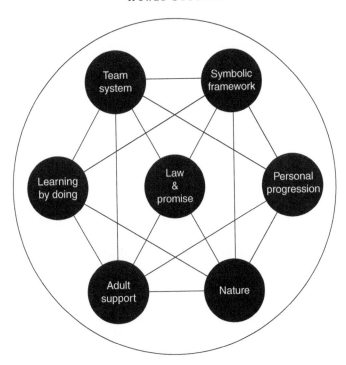

Figure 2.1   Elements of the scout method
Source: The essential characteristics of scouting (WOSM, 1998).

Taking a moment to focus on each of the seven elements provides a better understanding of this system of progressive self-education:

- The *shared principles and commitment to them* is the main methodological tool to involve youth in their own educational process: they are a statement of shared values (the *law*), accepted by the group, and the explicit, individual commitment of each member to the shared code of values (the *promise*), represented by the voluntary adherence to a lifestyle. It is what many boys and girls realize when they meet any other person who belongs to scouting, sharing the same values although coming from different backgrounds. The principles include the concept of service to the community.
- *Learning by doing* means that learning is not based on the transfer of theoretical knowledge, but on firsthand life experience. This practice is carried out through progressive and stimulating programs based on the interests of the participants, children and youth. In addition to including several elements from abilities and community service

to international exchanges, these programs use tools suited to each age: games for children, adventure for adolescents, and enterprise for young people. It is thus a way of helping young people to develop in all dimensions of the personality through extracting what is personally significant from everything that they experience.

— *Teamwork in small groups*, namely the patrol system, enables socialization and gives opportunities for boys and girls to discover and progressively assume autonomy, participation, responsibility, and leadership. It is in the teamwork in small groups where the peer education is more intense, allowing for character development and the acquisition of aptitudes and self-confidence, with trust and the ability to both cooperate and lead. The educational scout model promotes and assures the gradual participation of youth in the decision-making process through life experience.

— *Active cooperation between young people and adults* is the complement to peer education. Whereas scouting is based on the progressive assumptions of responsibility by young people, the interaction of them with adult leaders is fundamental to create an atmosphere of respect and autonomy in which the self-education of scouting can take place. In this environment, the scout leader helps the boys and girls discover their own potential, with a connection based on shared values and recognition of the personalities of each individual.

— *Progressive self-development* emphasizes that each individual is responsible for his or her own development, and that it will be the product of his or her own efforts. This commitment to self-improvement is a fundamental value that all scouts must share. But group and its programs also play a central role, since group activities are both the motor and means of individual progress.

— *Nature and outdoor activities* are the ideal backdrop for educational action. They offer abundant advantages: environmental awareness, physical well-being, sharpening of intellectual and spiritual curiosity, and the stimulating challenge of having to function with minimum comforts, work together to confront group challenges, and the appraisal of the richness of group life, and life in society.

— The last of the elements, the *symbolic framework,* is a set of shared symbols–both aesthetic and terminological–that creates a sense of belonging to a world brotherhood and reinforces the shared values. Starting with the emblem (a fleur-de-lis, or a trefoil for female scouting), the use of these symbols varies across different scout traditions: while the uniform and salute play an important role in some countries, the left handshake and the scarf (neckerchief) and its colors are enough in others.

In short, the scout method–a single method comprising the mentioned elements–is the main instrument of scouting for the education of young people. As it happens with part of the scout elements of identification (like the scarf), many other educational agents have adopted some of the elements of the scout method both in formal education and nonformal. While this is testimony to the harmony of the elements and their effectiveness in achieving the purposes of scouting, it can also sometimes call into question the originality of the movement in the mind of the public. However, it is only when the scout method is used entirely and in the leisure time, with an intense role of the peers in partnership with adults, that it has its full educational impact to self-develop autonomous, supportive, responsible, and committed persons.

2. A Highly Intuitive Educational Movement

Most of the times, scouting is better explained by how the eyes sparkle when someone tries to explain its wonders than by the words he or she uses. And this is so because scouting is much more about *life experiences* than about explanations, and because of its profoundly *intuitive nature*. Before analyzing the organizational structure of scouting, it could be useful to spend a bit of time analyzing how the scout movement actually operates, and also how we could extract from its intuitive educational action some information on what impact this educational action has.

2.1. More a Network Movement Than an Organization

Scouting is an educational movement based on voluntary commitment of individuals that operates as a network, carrying out their activities at local level through a global network of scout groups belonging to national associations organized worldwide. In this way, scouting is a movement that operates as a network and at the same time it has a membership-based associational organization.

In the words of Jacques Moreillon, former Secretary General of WOSM,

> it is true that when we become too much of an organization we run the risk of killing the *spirit* of Scouting. But if we are too much of a Movement, we go in all directions and *lose the coherence* and unity of purpose and principles that allow us to call ourselves Scouts. For this is the primary objective of 'organizing' World Scouting: to give worldwide *coherence* to our Movement, to ensure that all those who are officially recognized as 'Scouts' have the same *purpose*, base themselves on the same fundamental *principles* and use the same Scout *method*.[48]

There are three main levels of the organizational structure of scouting: the scout groups (local level),[49] which are the *nodes* of the network; the associations (national level); and the world organization (global level). On the roots, we could also add the patrols, which within the group is where the real citizenship education among peers happens.

The scout movement has then at its disposal decision-making bodies at the world level that establish its principles, characteristics, and main courses of action, with the direct participation of the national associations. It is democratic as long as the decision-making process is based on democratic procedures, on debate and equal votes. It takes shape through national associations that are at the same time subject of the rights within the world organization. And it has the local level as its main level of action not only that is where the educational action takes place, but also because that is where the grassroots democracy of the movement, with its million voluntary members, takes place as well.

Action at the local level in order to achieve goals at the global level has been a distinctive characteristic of scouting as a world movement since its beginning. As a recent WOSM document on Governance states, "the education to a 'global citizenship' starts from the promotion of full social, economic and political participation at the local community level."[50]

This action works worldwide, coordinated in a very loose and intuitive way as a huge network. The operations network of the scout movement fits the definition by the sociologist Manuel Castells: the components are both autonomous and dependent on the scout network and often share membership and goals with other networks.[51] It is true that the organizational structure of scouting does look to be the opposite of the network idea: world organization and defined decision-making processes, national associations, people in charge at different points, right up to local level. Nonetheless, the existence of an organizational structure does not mean that what is planned on a general scale is automatically applied to other levels; quite the contrary.

The role of the organization is to give coherence and historical continuity to the movement, which operates as a network. In this way, the World Conference, the World Committee/Board, and the World Bureau, as well as the national associations and their own scout groups, "are in fact living within this network, facilitating the quality of communications within the network, sharing knowledge throughout the network, but not controlling with hierarchical powers."[52]

In Malek Gabr's words, the scout movement is much more "like a loose network of colleagues, like a family, or a market place, united by history, by a belief in its fundamental principles sharing a unique indefinable 'spirit' and a common purpose."[53] The following diagrams show the

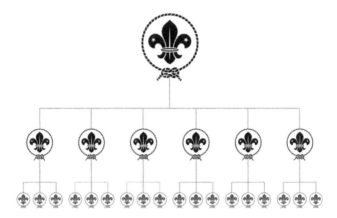

Figure 2.2   Apparent operation of world scouting
Source: World Scout Foundation, 2002.

difference between the apparent operation and the actual operation of scouting.

The first illustration (figure 2.2) reproduces how scouting appears to operate because of its structure: a world organization, below which there are national associations, below which are local scout groups. And though this seems to describe the organizational structure, the actual structure is quite different, much closer to the second illustration (figure 2.3), in

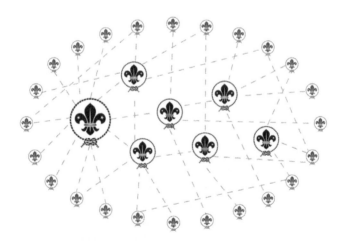

Figure 2.3   Actual operation of world scouting
Source: World Scout Foundation, 2002.

which the diverse actors interact in ways that cannot be hierarchically controlled. For instance, many changes made to the methodology or operation of national associations have been the result of contact with other associations (sometimes through the groups), which have given them ideas that they have then implemented themselves. The same has happened at local level with the scout groups, which have impelled changes coming from the interaction with other groups. The emergence of coeducation and mixed scout groups—and even the merging of associations belonging separately to WAGGGS and to WOSM—has been, in part, consequence of that effect.

The voluntary involvement of scout educators and leaders, the actual leading roles of the movement, is essential to understanding how the network operates around the world. Because these roles are neither obligatory nor paid, it is only strength of purpose and shared values that produce participation: there are no imposed directive hierarchies. A world organization of the size and scope of scouting, that has citizenship education as an objective, has often drawn the interest of authoritarian regimes that have wanted to use it as a tool for ideological manipulation, without success: the *movement* condition of scouting, besides the shared purpose, principles, and method, makes impossible any imposed ideological control.

A nonobligatory educational movement, in which the educators and leaders do not receive any form of monetary compensation for their tasks, needs a framework in line with the deep complicity between the ideals of individuals and the ideals of the movement. This complicity should guarantee that in the future there will continue to be people willing to take charge of the education of younger scouts. The adoption of joint strategies and lines of work, therefore, takes the movement as a whole in the same general direction, not through imposition, but generating shared projects. In this sense, the world democratic decision-making system is essential for giving legitimacy to the adopted decisions.

2.2. The Educational Impact and the "Magic" of Scouting

One of the greatest strengths of the scout movement is also one of its worst weaknesses: the deeply intuitive nature of its educational action. The greatness comes from the fact that, for young people, scouting is mainly about *enjoying*, not about *learning*. And that is why they become scouts, since early twentieth century, without thinking how the activities they take part in contribute to their full development as autonomous, supportive, responsible, and committed individuals. The weakness comes when many people interested in education only see the recreational appearance of scouting, unable to perceive the strong educational impact of this movement.

From an anthropological perspective, Edward Hall states that the assumption youngsters should be "motivated" to learn is wrong: "while it is not uncommon to find children who do not always like school, children as a whole love to learn, young people love to learn, and when the drive to learn ceases, that is a message that one should take seriously, because it signifies that there is little left in life to hold one on this earth."[54] Here lies one of the key elements of scouting's success: its capacity to arouse the interest of adolescents and young people to "paddle their own canoe," in Baden-Powell's words, and in doing so, giving them a purpose and making them part of their process of education.

The educationalist Joseph Farrell, following David Olson's thoughts on the big contrast between what cognitive science says and what schooling does, has summarized them in this outline:[55]

What Cognitive Science Says	*What Schooling Does*
What people learn depends on what they already know.	What they learn depends on what the school mandates.
People learn because they are intrinsically interested or because they love learning.	They pursue knowledge because they "need the credit."
Learning is inspired by the search for meaning and growth and understanding.	What they learn depends upon what books, chapters or pages they are responsible for.
The growth of mind is spontaneous and continuous.	It is a matter of obligation and duty.

When analyzing these comparisons, we could see that scouting was conceived under the elements of what cognitive science says today. Particularly, it has the clear intention to create a desire for learning in the adolescent, as Robert Baden-Powell explained in 1922 in his keynote speech at the 3rd International Congress of Moral Education:

> The craft and ceremonial and paraphernalia of the Red Indian or the Zulu has its appeal for every lad; the adventure of actual boat management, or exploration of a strange country, the clambering over wild mountains, naturalist research in woodland and forest, the camping and the woodcraft lore, the pioneering skill, all have their fascinations for him. *It is by using these attractions as the gilt that the pill of education can be administered.* Education as I read it means not so much putting knowledge into the boy as *giving him the desire and the method for acquiring knowledge.*[56]

We could find that idea to create desire for education while developing citizenship skills in John Dewey's essay "My Pedagogical Creed," when he states: "I believe that the only true education comes through the stimulation of the child's powers by the demands of the social situations in which he finds himself. Through these demands he is stimulated to act as a member of a unity, to emerge from his original narrowness of action and feeling and to conceive of himself from the standpoint of the welfare of the group to which he belongs."[57]

Indeed, the educational action of scouting cannot be seen in a picture, but rather in a film: it is the set of apparently modest elements that make scout activities be experienced as a parallel universe, and that little by little shape children's personality—humble rules from tying and wearing the scarf/neckerchief to wait to eat before everybody is ready, the feeling that effort has a reward on its own, persistence to achieve the goals, cheerfulness toward adversity, sense of belonging, friendship, cooperation, confidence when dealing with problems, spiritual discovering, self-government... "The scout curriculum may appear superficial to the pedagogue," Columbia Teachers College Dean James E. Russell said, "and doubtless much that is taught in neither systematic nor comprehensive. But scoutcraft is not intended to be a substitute for schooling. It is a device for supplementing the formal instruction of the schools, by leading the boy into new fields and giving him a chance to make practical use of all his powers, intellectual, moral and physical."[58]

Analyzing the educational impact of scouting as a whole differs from analyzing the educational effect of scouting in a particular society. As it is highlighted in *Comparative Education,* most macro-studies of education accepted the nation-state as the basic unit of analysis.[59] This holds true for scouting as well: there are plenty of studies on American scouting, British scouting, French scouting, Japanese scouting..., or even at a regional level, like African scouting, and each one assumes that it is talking *about scouting* as a such. But they are not: they only analyze one part of the whole movement. That is why, as comparative education has traditionally been a search for similarities and differences in education systems or activities, ideas and ideologies,[60] then the scout world movement should be a very attractive object of study for that discipline.

In an attempt to reveal in a comparative view what the actual educational impact of scouting is besides its intuitive running, the Jacobs Foundation (devoted to "foster child and youth development") sponsored a deep qualitative research in the mid-1990s, commissioned by the World Scout Bureau and entrusted to three independent researchers. They looked at three different cases of scout adolescent sections (13-18 years), in Scotland, France, and Belgium, using as a method a series of in-depth interviews held over a year with the scout groups, their leaders, and the youngsters' parents, and creating an in-depth analysis of how scouting affects adolescents. The result was the extensive sociological study *The Educational Impact of Scouting*.[61] Although the study has the obvious limitation of dealing only with European associations, there is no other study with the same characteristics, academic rigor, and analytical depth on the educational implications of the scout movement, so its results are very important.

One element to highlight is something that makes look "different" the diverse scout realities in the world even for many scouts: in the groups analyzed, the scout leaders have different approaches and stress different methods to contribute to the development of young people. Whereas in one group the emphasis is on the opportunity to strengthen relationships (focus on the group cohesion as a means for interpersonal relations), another's accent is on exercising responsibility (focus on sense of solidarity), and yet another put a wide variety of skills into practice (to exercise the capacity to lead).[62] Actually, as Nagy noticed, part of scouting potential as a world movement lies in its diversity and ability to adapt to different realities:[63] in a deeply local rooted movement, unity doesn't mean homogeneity.

If this diversity happens within three European countries, it may be even more intense among countries of the five continents. On this, in the 1960s Laszlo Nagy found the reason of the continental European scouting's incomprehension of the North American way of understanding scouting and vice versa. This misunderstood tension can be summarized by saying that the American approach is more pragmatic and skill based while European scouting is more intellectual and puts more emphasis on education than on training. It was a difference not picked up on until then and that had caused disagreements about the "true" way of understanding scouting. For Nagy, neither of the extremes is better; instead, a balance should be struck between the two.[64]

The research on *The Educational Impact of Scouting* has many other interesting conclusions, which could be compared with similar data on groups from other countries and cultural backgrounds. First, the adolescents believe that the scout leader is not a role model but rather a companion in the process of personal development in which personal experience and the exchange of different opinions is what counts. The fact that the leader is an unpaid companion in their adventures reinforces the idea of camaraderie between the leader and the adolescents, thus generating a strong intergenerational link between them. Non-remuneration is then relevant. Furthermore, in terms of the leader's contribution to the construction of a system of values for the adolescent, the study shows that the values are not internalized by inculcation or direct transmission, but by personal experience, and meaning is given to group experiences.

The work also points out that when the adolescent scouts become aware of a value that has a personal meaning for them, they try to change certain aspects of their behavior to match it to their beliefs, although they need the boost of the experience they gain as a group. Moreover, the structural impossibility of direct transmission of values or indoctrination in scouting can be seen in the way that the studied adolescent scouts critically extract the coherence of the suggested values with the practices: if the proposed value is internalized, they become critical with incoherent practices, even if they come from the leader. The coexistence in the patrol or section, which is a much more intense experience at summer camps, becomes the most important educational tool, by which they internalize their opening up, sense of responsibility to others and oneself and confidence in their abilities and capacities.[65]

This extreme appeal of scouting as an educational agent for adolescents was also emphasized in 1920s by the progressive educationalist Edmond Holmes. When analyzing what general principles continuation schools should be conducted on, he states: "The Boy Scout Movement is by far the most successful attempt which has yet been made to provide for the education of adolescents. And it owes its success to the fact that it makes due provision for the satisfaction of two imperious needs of man's nature,—the need to realize one's own self, and the need to work with and for others."[66] This double focus (the "duty to self" and the "duty to others" of the three scout principles) has the cleverness to achieve a great educational aim driven by his/her own interest: "The Scout is encouraged to develop himself in many directions to make the most of his natural capacities, aptitudes, and tastes. He is encouraged to do this, partly in order that he may realize his own self, partly in order that he may become a helpful member of society. For he is also encouraged to play his part as a member of a community, to indentify its interests with his own, to be loyal to it, to work for it, to serve it."[67]

There is a dynamic interaction between the group and the individual in scouting, particularly due to the voluntary nature of the participation, where the group doesn't impose on the individual but rather allows the individual to grow his autonomous moral and his confidence. This is also shown by Tra Bach, Huberman, and Sulser's research, which explains that the quality of the relationship and the constructive atmosphere of the scout experience seem to be a relevant factor in helping the adolescents to develop themselves and to the development of a sense of belonging: "The feeling of security, self-esteem, and motivation are enhanced through the relationships developed, which encourage the young people to progress in their skills and undertake more ambitious projects, responsibilities, etc., which also contribute to their self-esteem and confidence. Through the meaningful experiences undertaken together, the relationships are reinforced; the young people can explore with others the meaning and value of those experiences and relationships, and so on."[68] Probably that capacity to empower young people is what made Maria Montessori say that the scout movement freed children "from the narrow limits to which they have been confined."[69]

Scouting educational action is able to combine in balance the two continually opposing processes in character development, according to Russell: the one ("accepting guidance") that tends to restrict the subject's initiative, and the one ("guiding oneself") reinforcing his/her personal will. The combination of discipline and initiative.[70] "One force makes for identity of kind, conservatism and efficiency; the other, for individuality, initiative and progress," he writes. Thus, scouting combines the learning of habits and assumption of responsibilities through an educational program that "works adroitly, by a thousand specific habits, to anchor a boy to be modes of right living as securely as if held by chains of steel; but best of all, it exhibits positive genius in devising situations that test a boy's self-reliance and give full scope to his talent for originality and leadership."[71] Certainly, leadership is one of the main outcomes scouting gets from its educational action. Leadership means capacity and will to influence; more specifically, scouting generates what Burns called *transformational leadership,* namely a leadership that causes change in individuals and social systems, by creating valuable and positive changes in followers that make them develop into leaders themselves.[72] This explains not just the role of the scout movement in training autonomous individuals who become responsible citizens, but also how the movement perpetuates itself by having new generations of individuals who share values, principles, purpose, and desire to devote part of their free time to the education of young people.

The UNESCO Delors' Report[73] established the four pillars of education: *Learning to know, learning to do, learning to live together, and learning to be.* Scouting's educational action contributes particularly well to *learning to live together,* that is, "developing an understanding of other people, appreciation of interdependence, skills in team work and conflict resolution, and deep respect for the values of pluralism, mutual understanding, peace and justice."[74] As Miquel Essomba notes, scouting has four elements that make that possible: the projects young people implement based on freedom of choice, the group as unit of reference, the life experience that provides meaning, and the educational interconnection with the social environment. And all of this from three conditions: the unpaid character, which avoids the customer-product relationship; the diversity, which creates heterogeneous groups; and the commitment, based on freedom and also on responsibility.[75]

To sum up, despite the intuitive nature of scouting, there is some literature showing how this educational movement has been built upon quite solid foundations as understood by major pedagogical theorists, cognitive scientists, and anthropologists studying human learning.[76] But as Farrell points out, the question remains: Why do young boys and girls from so many countries of the world join the scout movement and stay? Why does the pedagogical method of scouting work so well that millions of young people, and volunteer adult leaders, around the world, across almost all the cultures, civilizations, and religions known to humankind, volunteer to participate it?

There is something both universal and eternal in an adolescent, Jacques Moreillon says: whatever the country or the culture, she will get a kick out of the same games, be challenged by the same situations, have the same doubts and the same fears. And the scout method has the ability to answer all these. It is this universality and timeliness that also explains not only why scouting spread so naturally and easily into so many countries, but also adapted so well to so many cultures. As Moreillon explained "I have always marveled, in my almost 500 missions to 105 countries for WOSM, at how much each Scout association, indeed each Scout group, perceived Scouting as something *local*, born in *their* country, in *their* city and in no way 'imported' from abroad. This, in my view, is due to the adaptability of the Scout method to what is both *universal* and *eternal* in every young boy or girl."[77]

Joseph Farrell adds that if one asks a scout, "as I have done in many cultures around our world," why they are in scouting, the most common response is: "It's fun. We get to do neat stuff that other kids can't, or won't!" For girls and for boys, therefore, scouting is freedom, friends, emotions, fun, adventure, and a sense of happiness, and there is always a strong sense of personal pride and accomplishment. But from a pedagogical point of view, Farrell underlines that the *genius* of the scout educational approach is that it does not try directly to "teach"; rather, it is designed to "enable learning," "which as I already argued"[78]—says Farrell—"is the way all of educational planning must go if it imagines itself ever to be successful. And Scouting does this by subterfuge in a way. Fun, adventure, and challenge is the attraction; learning is the outcome."[79]

In the ceremony commemorating the seventy-fifth anniversary of Catalan scouting, the then President of Catalonia, Jordi Pujol, who was one of the leaders of the resistance against Franco's dictatorship and who interacted with scouting in those years, added another element to this magic seen from the outside:

> When I saw you in the 1950s and the 1960s, and when I see you today, I have the feeling you have joyful spirits. There is a sense of joy in Scouting. And that is logical because serving produces joy, being useful to others produces joy.... And Scouting does so in a very personalized way, along the lines of a personal achievement: realizing one's potential doing positive things produces great joy. You all know that because you realize your potential by doing positive things that go beyond yourselves, which is why you have the right to feel joy and that also gives you a sense of wholeness.[80]

3. HOW THE ORGANIZATION WORKS: TOWN, COUNTRY, AND WORLD

After reflecting on the intuitive education and operations network of the scout movement, it is time to see its structure. Scouting is a democratically organized world movement, which means that its decision-making processes are based on deliberation, consensus building, and equal votes. This also means that the governing bodies of the national associations and world organization, through debate and votes, make decisions and can modify the procedures, operation, and even update the principles of the world organization.

Democracy is, in fact, a necessary precondition for the development of the scout movement and for its unity, as stressed in a recent document on the organization's system of governance, stating that "if active adult leaders are not involved in decision-making, they will not have the perception to share a common purpose and they will be tempted to quit the movement or to create dissident organizations."[81] Democracy at all organizational levels of scouting should merely be a continuation and application of the scout method—that is, the patrol system, the nuclear unit of democracy in the movement—by appropriately trained unit leaders. A scout association led autocratically, adds the document, would be incapable of applying the scout method, and could not involve the youth in the decision-making process. Likewise, it would not teach youth about citizenship nor shape them into adult men and women capable of fully participating in democratic environments.

The two world organizations (WOSM and WAGGGS) adopted a democratic decision-making model from their inception. As will be explained later, the Conference is the plenary body of the organization, composed of delegates from all the national member organizations, which all have the same vote. Only the Conference can accept new

organizations or expel members, in accordance with the regulated procedures approved by the Conference itself. It is also the Conference that
selects a committee made up of elected members with a limited mandate. This committee makes the decisions when the Conference is not
meeting.

The establishment of this system is not as obvious as it seems. When it
was created, the main founding countries of that moment—Great Britain,
United States, France...—could have been given a predominant role,
as they have on the United Nations Security Council. Or the founder,
Robert Baden-Powell, or the British association, as "proprietor of the
idea," could have been given the right to veto the decisions of the committee or Conference. But this was not the case. It was established right
from the start that all member organizations would have equal votes. And,
although fees are paid based on the census (and the payment of fees is
a constitutional obligation), each national member organization has the
same vote, regardless of its census.

It should be said that the Constitutions of WOSM and WAGGGS
do not specify that scout associations have to operate democratically in
order to be recognized as members: they only stress that they must be
"self-governed" and "independent," with the ability to form and implement their own program. In fact, it is important to keep in mind that
in many of the societies in which scouting operates democratic practices are not yet accepted, and even less so for women, although this
reality is evolving.[82] In many western countries, much before their society gave them the right to vote, women were the only decision makers
in female scouting. Despite the lack of explicit mention of democracy in the Constitutions, the requirement that member associations
be self-governing is now generally interpreted as requiring them to be
democratic.[83]

The progressive public commitment with democracy can be seen
clearly in the joint stance taken by WOSM and WAGGGS and the
Alliance of executives of youth organizations, described in the document "Children and Young People: Participating in Decision-Making":
"A child, whose active engagement with the world has been encouraged
from the outset, will be an adolescent with the confidence and capacity
to contribute to democratic dialogue and practices at all levels, whether
at a local or an international level."[84] And certainly, the three levels—
local, national, global—are equally important for the scout purpose of
citizenship building: the local level provides the roots to each social
reality; the national level provides a collective identity from which to
participate globally; and the world level provides the very real arena where
the brotherhood/sisterhood of scouting takes place.

3.1. THE LOCAL GROUP AND THE NATIONAL ASSOCIATION

Local Level: The Scout Group

The *scout group* is the basic unit in the structure of the scout movement and the only level where we can see the general scout educational program being implemented directly.[85] Within the scout group, the patrol system enables peer education and promotes citizenship building. Scouting was initially devised as an idea for educating adolescents from a single age range that was methodologically divided into small groups called "troops" or "patrols." After it was formalized as an educational organization, the age range was extended to include older and younger boys and girls in the form of *sections* or *units*. Therefore, the scout group is where the entire education process for children, adolescents, and young adults takes place, through its different sections and methodological subgroups.

The people who run the scout groups carry out their tasks (both educational activities and organizational ones) voluntarily, without remuneration and in their free time. It is there were internal democracy in the movement starts, with adult unit leaders being members of a "Group leaders team" and in this way be involved in the decision-making processes and be represented in the decision-making bodies of the national association.

The creation and maintenance of scout groups in most countries is done through *local sponsors,* such as civic associations, hiking groups, parents' associations, schools, youth clubs, churches, et cetera, which promote scouting because of its benefits for the community, though they also respect the autonomy of the scout group. This interaction between scouting and the local area's social network is its greatest asset: its establishment in local communities. "Scouting is growing from the local reality, self-sustained and supported by a variety of compatible local organizations that provide moral and financial support, meeting places, equipment, access to volunteers, etc."[86]

The National Scout Association

Whereas local groups are the basic unit in the structure of the movement, national scout associations are the central governing unit of scouting at world level, since they legally compose the world organization and have the right to vote at world conferences. It is in the framework of the scout association of each country—which must be self-governed, independent, and nonpartisan—that the scout movement's principles and method are guaranteed and where they are adapted to the host country's social reality.

At the same time, national associations are usually the collective basic reference of belonging from where to feel part of a world community, as it could be seen in international gatherings.

Only one scout organization is recognized per "country" and, in exceptional cases where a country has more than one scout association—because of religious plurality or, less often, cultural plurality—a singular federation must be set up to represent that country's scouting in the world organization.[87] We use the expression "national association" to encompass both single national associations (most of the cases) and federation of associations (around 12% of the total).

The role of the association is very important. In particular, the association of each country is responsible for adapting the language and essential characteristics of scouting to the social reality of the host country. The right management of this adaptation makes it perfectly fitted to the society where it is found, as can be seen in many countries, from Catalonia or France to Korea or Haiti, and from Egypt or Senegal to the United States or Indonesia.

Similarly, the associations are responsible for training the scout leaders, watching over the quality of scout activities, coordinating groups and the geographic areas of groups, representing the movement in front of public institutions, weaving cooperative networks with other collectives, maintaining links with old members, and creating links between the members of the association and the world movement.

To accomplish all of the previous tasks, the world organizations have stated from the start that national associations should have an "international commissioner." These figures gradually became responsible for the "diplomatic" relations between scouts in each country, and were put in charge of contact with other member associations and with the world organization itself. This also ensured that the relationships were made with recognized scout associations, and not involving "fake scout" organizations.

The emergence of the Internet, however, has transformed these practices. Many local scout groups and even individuals can now keep in touch with groups and people in other counties through their websites, making possible interactions, which, 15 years ago, were only possible by letter correspondence and with the help of the international commissioners, who had the information to set up such exchanges. This may foretell the development of the role of these international commissioners to become one of guiding and supporting local groups that are directly in contact through the Internet in the wider framework of relationships among organizations.[88]

3.2. WHEN A COUNTRY HAS MORE THAN ONE ASSOCIATION

As we now know, the Constitutions of both world organizations establish that only one member association may be recognized per country. In the majority of countries, like it was in the United Kingdom since early scouting, this association has been open to all, non-denominational, and allowed both religious and cultural diversity. Even though the French case at the beginning of the twentieth century—which it will be discussed later—opened the door to exceptions due to religion, which joins the cultural factor, exceptions of this sort have always been in the minority. Of the 170 plus national organizations that are members of WOSM and/or WAGGGS, only 20 have a federative structure due to religious or cultural factors, or both. Keep in mind that only "religious" or "cultural" factors can be accepted as justification for a country having more than one association within a national organization.[89]

The trend, in particular in WOSM, is to reduce even further the exceptions to having a single national association, for how that contributes each society to indentify scouting with one subject instead of several ones. Excluding new independent countries since the fall of the USSR, practically none of the newly recognized countries have a federation (except Bosnia Herzegovina, which also is a federated country). The possibility of creating new Catholic associations has also been rejected—as in Guinea and Benin. Moreover, WOSM has successfully encouraged some countries (Argentina in 1996, Ireland in 2004, and currently Flanders in Belgium) to merge their open and Catholic scout associations into a single scout association.

Countries with Federations on Religious Grounds
Without a doubt, religion is the main reason for there being more than one scout association in a single country. Of the 20 federations, 18 have one or more associations linked to a church or denominational organization; of these, 14 federations were created on religious grounds: Burkina Faso, Chad, France, Gabon, Germany, Ireland,[90] Italy, Ivory Coast, Luxemburg, Madagascar, Norway, Portugal, Senegal, and Sweden.

For the most part, these uni-denominational associations are linked to the Catholic Church, while open associations are largely pastoral commissions that have ties to their respective denominational institution. In every case, however, scouting has had to remain open to both and girls without regard to religious beliefs.

France was the first country to be recognized as a federation in 1922, when the membership of the world organization was formalized: their then three preexistent associations (one *laïque,* one Evangelical, one Catholic) were incorporated in WOSM as a federation called French Scouting. On the grounds that in France the existence of uni-denominational associations was justified because a *laïque* one existed, the Catholic Church promoted the creation of Catholic scout associations in countries and territories where open scouting existed: Belgium, French Canada, Catalonia, Germany, Ireland, Italy, Luxemburg, Spain . . . , in addition to the several former French colonies in Africa.

The models of these federations are different. Today, the French federation contains five associations: *laïque, Catholic, Evangelical, Jewish,* and *Muslim,* an unusual case; whereas the Portuguese, the Italian, and the Spanish contain only two: Open and Catholic, as it is in several African French-speaking countries—although there the open association is mainly Muslim, as society is. The case of Norway and Sweden is different, as a result of the link between scouting and some youth Christian organizations.

Countries with Federations on Cultural or on Religious and Cultural Grounds

Although most federations are founded on religious grounds, the "cultural" factor touches the cases of national or cultural communities that do not have their own independent State but hold certain recognition, including the case of displaced people. The world organizations handle these cases with extreme care to make sure that scouting is not instrumentalized by exclusionary nationalist movements that along the history have tried to use the movement on their favor.

The use of the cultural ground is rooted in WOSM's 1929 recognition of associations of exiled Armenian and Russian scouts in France. Though the Russian exile association lasted only a few years, the Armenian association continued to be recognized until the 1990s, when WOSM once again recognized Armenia as a member country with full rights. After World War II, scouting was forced to change its policy of recognizing exiled groups, given the huge numbers of refugees and displaced persons.

Today, there are only seven independent countries where recognized scout organizations with different associations for "cultural" reasons exist: Belgium (Flemish and French-speaking communities); Bosnia-Herzegovina (copying the federal structure of the country); Canada (French-speaking communities); Denmark (Faeroe Islands and Greenland); Israel (besides the case of Palestine); Lebanon; and Spain (Catalonia). Except for Bosnia-Herzegovina, the other six scout organizations also have associations linked to certain religions.

Interestingly, there are five exceptions in scouting that also exist due to cultural factors: *Boy Scouts of China,* which is only active in Taiwan, is a member of WOSM but began as an exiled scout association (China banned scouting in 1949). *Scouts du Canada* is a Francophone Catholic association present in the French territories of Canada that is associated with (not federated with) the open Anglophone association *Scouts of Canada,* which has membership with WOSM. In *Hong Kong* there is one WOSM and one WAGGGS association, which have remained in existence even though Hong Kong became part of China. Moreover, the case of *Scouts of Palestine* is unique: it is an association acting in the Palestinian National Authority territory and which WOSM recognized (without conferring the right to vote) in 1996, proposed by the Israeli federation. Finally, the Catalan federation (WOSM and WAGGGS member) has a differential status within WOSM similar to that of *Scouts du Canada,* but with a certain capacity for international decision making (one third of Spain's votes), and it is also one of the two components of the WAGGGS federation in Spain.

Interaction between Associations of WOSM and WAGGGS

We have already explained that in a country can exist more than one scout association due to religious or cultural factors; nevertheless, an important detail has not been mentioned: the existence of different scout associations in one country is many times due to the separation by gender (boys or girls) or due to the separated belonging to one of the two world organizations—WOSM and WAGGGS.

Though the British model of two scout associations separated by gender was initially generalized around the world, by the 1960s associations in many countries, principally European, had begun to see the advantages to educating boys and girls together in mixed groups. The evolution of this approach has had several consequences for the scout realities in many countries. In a good number of cases, the boys and girls associations—members of WOSM and WAGGGS, respectively—began to work together, to the extent of turning into one single association belonging to both world associations. The associations that belong both to WOSM and to WAGGGS have been called "Scout and Guide National Organizations" (SAGNOs).

This is now the case within most European countries, including Austria, Belgium, Catalonia, France, Italy, the Netherlands, Poland, Switzerland, and the Scandinavian countries. In 2010, of the 161 member organizations of WOSM, 34 were also members of WAGGGS. In some cases, the result of the merging kept the double reference both in the name of the association ("Scouts y Guías de Chile," "Scouts et Guides de France") as well as in the age groups ("pionniers/caravelles"). When the name used does not differentiate between masculine and feminine, the naming is easier: "éclaireuses et éclaireurs" (French) or "esploratori ed esploratrici" (Italian), for example. The double nomenclature keeps the idea of separation by gender, and possibly for that reason, many of the associations belonging to both WOSM and WAGGGS—such as the Swiss, Swedish, Dutch, or *laïque* Catalan—have opted to use an entirely new name: "Mouvement Scout de Suisse" ("l'Organisation faîtière nationale des scouts et scoutes de la Suisse"), "Svenska Scoutförbundet," "Scouting Nederland" ("all members of Scouting Nederland are called *scouts*"), "Escoltes Catalans."

But the trend toward coeducation involved more than simply a fusion of the male and female associations in some countries: in the cases in which this was not possible, many organizations, mainly masculine, opened to both genders, to the point that modifications to the Constitution of WOSM in the 1970s allowed both boys and girls to join. As a result, only 20 of the 161 WOSM associations are today exclusively masculine: the others have both male and female members. These statistics are much different for the 145 associations that belong to WAGGGS, however: of this number, very few are open to both boys and girls. If the 34 associations that belong to both world organizations are not counted, practically most the remaining WAGGGS member associations are exclusively feminine. Even so, there are a good number of countries in which WOSM and WAGGGS, though not organized together, enjoy a stable and ongoing cooperation.

3.3. World Organization(s) and Global Belonging

The scout movement has been formalized since the 1920s into two international organizations, the World Organization of the Scout Movement (WOSM) and the World Association of Girl Guides and Girl Scouts (WAGGGS), which have 161 and 145 national associations, respectively, of which 34 belong to both organizations.

Both world organizations are similarly organized around three bodies: the Conference, the Committee/Board, and the Bureau—an structure reproduced at continental level, with the called "regions," levels of decentralization of the world organization. English and French are official working languages of both world organizations, and WAGGGS also has Spanish.[91]

The *World Conference* is the governing body of the organization. Is composed by all national member organizations and each has the same number of votes.[92] It meets every three years, and its tasks include determining the policy and standards of the world organization and its rules of operation, electing the members of the World Committee, and approving the recognition or exclusion of member organizations. The venue of the World Conference is chosen by the conference itself from the applications submitted.

It must be noted that in WAGGGS only female delegates have the right to be elected in the committees—both world and regional. This means that a male member of an association of WAGGGS cannot be chosen at a regional (for example, European) or world level. The opposite happens in WOSM with former merged associations paying the female fees only to WAGGGS: in these cases, female members cannot be elected for the World Scout Committees.

The *World Committee*[93] (called *World Board* in WAGGGS) is the executive body of the organization and acts on behalf of the World Conference when it is not held. It is composed of twelve people elected[94] by the World Conference (non-remunerated), the Secretary General (WOSM) or Chief Executive (WAGGGS), the treasurer, and the chairmen of the Regional Committees (non-remunerated). Whereas in WAGGGS regional chairmen have the right to vote, together with the 12 elected members, in WOSM regional chairmen have no vote. In the two cases, the top executive doesn't have the right to vote.

One chairperson and up to two vice-chairpersons of the Committee are chosen from among those elected. Besides implementing the policies approved by the World Conference, the World Committee can recommend or suspend the recognition of a national association and approve the Constitutions of associations—including the Scout Law and Promise—and their amendments. A Constitutions Committee appointed by the World Committee assists with scout legal issues.

Constitutionally, once they have been elected, these individuals cease to represent whoever put them forward and represent only the world organization from thereon. There is no quota of any kind: either territorial or, in the case of WOSM, for gender.

The *World Bureau* is the permanent secretariat of the organization, headed by the Secretary General (WOSM) or Chief Executive (WAGGGS), who report from the respective bureau to the Committee and are appointed by the Committee itself. The professional structure of the two world organizations has evolved over the years from a rather amateur model—until 1946, the position of director of the World Scout Bureau was unpaid[95]—to a model comparable to that of any other large international NGO.[96]

In fact, WAGGGS' annual budget for 2006 totaled 5 million pounds sterling, 33 percent of which came from member fees and 23 percent from the services of world centers. In 2004, WOSM's budget was 11.5 million Swiss francs (approximately 4.8 million pounds sterling), 50 percent of which came from member fees. The member fees that each associ-ation pays on behalf of its members is adjusted according to the per capita income of the host country. The remaining income of the two organizations comes from donations and financial aid (27% and 21%, respectively) and aid from their respective external financial support struc-tures: the World Scout Foundation (15%) in WOSM's case and the Olave Baden-Powell Society (5%) for WAGGGS.

WOSM introduced the Secretary General position in 1968, which had more political content—right to vote on the World Committee—than the old position of Bureau director. WAGGGS changed the name of the *Bureau Director* to *Chief Executive* in 2005, to give the latter more say in strategic management while denying it any formal powers in World Committee decision-making processes. In 2008 a WOSM constitutional amendment established that the Secretary General has no vote. The role of the Bureau is important as a promoter of the unity in diversity and of the consistency of the movement. An excessively strong World Bureau could have the temptation to impose its vision on how scouting should be; but on the other hand, a too weak World Bureau would jeopardize the unity of the movement.

The world organization is decentralized into continental *regions*[97] that depend on the structure of the world, rather than being autonomous and constitutive bodies.[98] So although the regions adapt the world struc-ture to a smaller scale—with a conference, elected committee[99] and bureau—their legislative capacity is constitutionally subject to world regulations,[100] and their bureau is a decentralized part of the World Bureau.[101] The WOSM World Bureau has its headquarters in Geneva and regional offices in each region. However, due to financial constraints, WAGGGS regional executives work at the World Bureau headquarters in London, with the exception of the European region, which has had its headquarters in Brussels since the failed attempt to create a joint WAGGGS and WOSM region in the mid-1990s.

The regions issue brings us to the greatest concern of the world orga-nization: the fear of shattering the unity of the movement. In reality, a world organization with such internal diversity will always have a ten-dency to fragment, particularly because of the two factors that justify the existence of scout federations in a single country: culture and religion. If the world organization gave greater powers to the regions, this would give more legitimacy to the imposition of their own cultural vision of what scouting should be and how it should be organized, which could cre-ate a situation whereby the geographically decentralized world movement becomes a federation of regional movements that zealously protect their own identity and put their own unique features above those of a common world membership. Therefore, as in other issues, a balance should be attained.

Many international organizations are, in practice, a federation of national associations. However, in scouting this is not the case. A differential characteristic of the scout movement is that not only do the national associations belong to it, but also the individual members. The constitutional belonging to the *world organization* is conferred on the *national associations,* not on the individual members of the associations, but the belonging to the scout movement is denoted on an individual basis through personal commitment to the scout values system (the Law and the Promise).

This personal commitment can only be made within a national association, which has the power to formulate the text of the Promise and the Law with the approval of the world organization. This is the meaning of its actual *dual membership*: legally, the national organizations are the subjects, but the conscious membership of *individuals* in scouting as a world movement, meaning, the condition of *being a scout,* is conferred through the personal commitment to the principles of scouting that his or her national association adopted according to the world-established criterion.

This very sense of dual belonging is what makes it possible for scouting to be a true world movement rather than a federation of countries. A scout knows that he or she has a special link—a common belonging—shared with scouts all over the world. It is this experiential link, evident in the many activities, meetings, and jamborees, that becomes more salient than a scout's nationality or religion, without overshadowing or minimizing these aspects of identity, that fosters a true sense of global citizenship in scouts.

3.4. THE GENDER APPROACH: WOSM AND WAGGGS SEPARATED... FOREVER?

As Tammy Proctor has noticed, whereas differences based on race, ethnicity, language, or religion are always thorny problems for a youth organization, "the most significant factor in Scout and Guide past and future policy comes with its treatment and understanding of gender."[102] And certainly, though the purpose of the scout movement is the same when referring to youth in general, there is one important difference forming the basis for the separation of the two organizations: their asymmetrical approach to gender.

This difference is particularly obvious in the *mission* statement, a simplification of the purpose that the two organizations formulated between 1996 and 1999. WAGGGS says that "The Mission of the World

Association of Girl Guides and Girl Scouts is to enable girls and young women to develop their fullest potential as responsible citizens of the world,"[103] while for WOSM, "The mission of Scouting is to contribute to the education of young people, through a value system based on the Scout Promise and Law, to help build a better world where people are self-fulfilled as individuals and play a constructive role in society."[104]

Just as it does in its purpose, the mission of WAGGGS clearly refers to its contribution to the development of *girls* and *young women* in achieving their full potential; while the mission of WOSM refers to its role in the education of *young people* in general, without reference to gender. However, this difference complements rather than cancelling out the common main purpose, which is to contribute to the development of young people as responsible citizens.

As a document comparing the respective missions by two members of the WAGGGS/WOSM Consultative Committee[105] points out, the missions of the two world organizations are compatible since they both speak of the achievement of the full potential of every scout, whether boy or girl, and the specific reference to girls is an understandable recognition of the reality that the needs of girls and young women—to varying degrees around the world—are often subordinated to the needs of boys and young men.[106]

Precisely, the clear option of WOSM to actually move from a male-oriented organization to a fully coeducational one, has as one of its tools the research "One of the Boys? Doing Gender in Scouting," published in 2003 as part of the implementation of WOSM's gender policy adopted in 1999. The research, directed by Oslo-based Prof. Harriet B. Nielsen, studied coeducational groups from Russia, Slovakia, Portugal, and Denmark, focusing on WOSM's ability to switch from a boy-based model to one in which boys and girls come together. The approach was designed to highlight contradictions in assumptions and provided some tools needed to progress toward the coeducational model.

As Nielsen points out, girls in scouting look for the same as boys: "freedom, friends, fund, and adventure."[107] However, and besides the coeducational experience of several merged WOSM-WAGGGS associations, scouting has had a highly masculinized image since its early years, which means that whereas the main concept of activities does not need to be changed, "what *should* be worked on, however, is the symbolic gender and the gender culture surrounding these basic activities."[108] Therefore, it should change the perceived dichotomy or separation between activities and relationships, the hierarchy between the interests and relationships of girls and boys, and do away with the tendency to underrate girls' competence in scout activities. The study points out that girls in scouting should not aspire to become "one of the boys," because girls will never be boys. The conclusion, then, is to redistribute and recognize: redistribution means that all tasks and activities must be experienced generally in the same way by girls and boys; and recognition means that all gender cultures must be able to be experienced within the group so long as they do not limit the rights of others to express themselves, they are not put forward as universal, and, as a result, they are not established as the norm.

The growth of mixed coeducational scout associations within each world organization, particularly in WOSM—which has adopted coeducation, has made the complementarily of the diverse approaches even more evident: coeducation in mixed associations in societies with a greater extent of equality between men and women, and associations just for girls in societies where gender inequality is more prevalent. Even so, the largest associations of WAGGGS are in western countries and exclusively for girls and young women: the US association (Girl Scouts of the USA, 4 million members) and the British association (Girl Guiding UK, 550,000 members).

The will to move toward a single world organization, where boys, girls, and mixed associations can exist together, has been a constant demand of some associations, especially those that belong to both world organizations. In fact, as a consequence of this tradition, in 1995 the European conference of WOSM and the European conference of WAGGGS agreed to create a joint European region, with one singular committee and bureau. But the fragility of the foundation and the impulsive attempt at unification and the reluctance of the world officials, blocked the progress three years into the initiative, reducing it to a minimal partnership between the two regional organizations and establishing paths of collaboration—although they gradually have found new forms of cooperation.

The idea of creating a single world organization was still too immature, and the European attempt backfired: in 1997 the World Scout Committee (WOSM) decided not to recognize any new association in which girls paid membership fees to WAGGGS and boys to WOSM—which until then was characteristic of the dual belonging—and, following this, in 1998 the World Board of WAGGGS decided not to recognize any new association open also to boys. The purpose of these moves was to differentiate the profiles of each world organization and thereby avoid any sense of aggressive competition. But as any country where more than one scout association exists know, a systematic action of an organization to differentiate from another could end modifying the perception of the movement, confusing elements of organizational culture with the main values of the movement. In this author's personal opinion, having been

International Commissioner for both WOSM and WAGGGS, and having attended regional and world conferences of both world organizations, both organizations, and also the movement, have much more to gain than to loose working together. It is not simply a question of having boys and girls together in a group or in an association—different traditions and approaches could have reasons for each choice; it is more to be able to put together the diverse rich traditions of different approaches to the individual, to gender, to what is fundamental and what is secondary, and to be better prepared to face the future.[109] I would say, though, that the long path of antagonism and disputes of the WOSM and the WAGGGS associations of the United States has an enormous influence on the current relations of both world organizations and on potential future ironing out of the difficulties.[110]

Be that as it may, these strategic positions culminated with the World Board of WAGGGS explicitly stating in 1999 the possibility of merging with WOSM, which was rejected by WAGGGS' World Conference in 2002, and also deciding to end the admission of boys in associations that did not have any male members by that time. This position reinforced WAGGGS' identity as an organization essentially for girls and young women, but put in an uncomfortable situation its mixed gender member associations, whereas WOSM could state that it is the only world organization of the scout movement accepting both boys and girls. Since then, a consultative committee linked to the two world committees and the world organizations is devoted to exploring possible avenues of collaboration.

4. Recognition and Belonging

Scouting is a global movement that, besides shared purpose, principles and method, has a series of self-established regulations and decision-making systems. Nonetheless, with its international scope and great cultural diversity, it is difficult to differentiate scouting from the many existing attempts to imitate it, ever since it was established, which have adopted its appearance or some of its practices in order to take advantage of its public image. Beyond merely profiting from the prestige of scouting, these attempts at imitation can also have a destructive effect on it when they are of dubious quality or when their ideological profile is discriminatory or goes against the principles of the movement. It is by the procedures to mark out who does and does not belong to scouting that we can consider it as a defined subject. In both world organizations of scouting, WOSM and WAGGGS, this practice is known as the "recognition policy."

4.1. RELEVANCE OF THE RECOGNITION POLICY

In 1923, the League of Nations unanimously passed a resolution put forward by the Chilean delegate urging governments to set up special mechanisms for when recognized scout associations visited the countries of other associations. When the Austrian scout association asked its government, "the Austrian Government had replied that they did not know what constituted a 'recognized Association' within the meaning of the resolution."[111] It was then suggested that the governments of the *League* be sent a list of scout associations recognized by the Boy Scouts International Bureau (BSIB, which was at that time WOSM's name).

Sixty-five years later, on July 22, 1998, four adolescents and a boatman died in an accident on what was, as far as French public opinion was concerned, a scout activity: four scouts had died in a scout activity led by a "fundamentalist priest" and the cause of the accident was "undue care and deliberate failure to meet the safety obligations."[112] However, the group was not actually a scout group: it consisted of members of the self-styled *Association Française des Scouts et Guides Catholiques,* an association that doesn't belong either to WOSM or to WAGGGS, made up of few fundamentalist Catholic groups that had broken ties with the Vatican.[113]

In October of the same year, a child living in the French town of Fréjus who belonged to the self-styled *Guides et Scouts d'Europe* (an ultraconservative association not member of WOSM nor of WAGGGS) was sent a mail-order catalogue by a company with connections to the extreme-right-wing Front National party that sold books and CDs with Nazi SS songs and the thoughts of the excommunicated right-wing Archbishop Lefebvre and Jean-Marie Le Pen. When the boy's father realized that the layout of the details on the label was identical to the one of the supposed "scout" association, he demanded explanations and he was told by telephone that a member of the association had processed the details "by mistake."[114]

This two cases of fake scout associations made the Scoutisme Français federation, which is the member of WOSM and WAGGGS, subsequently drew up a "Charte de Qualité du Scoutisme" *(Quality Chart of Scouting)* to assure the general public that "recognized" scouts had no problems with safety or extremist ideology. But more crucial than their fight for quality was the battle for the "brand," which they eventually lost: after ten years of legal trials for misappropriation of the term "scout" and for "educational practices dangerous for young people," the extreme-right association won the court case and was able to be registered as the "Association Française des Scouts et Guides Catholiques."[115] The term "scout" therefore was legally allowed to be used by fake scouting against the principles of openness, tolerance and dialog of the scout movement.

These examples demonstrate the importance of the "recognition policy" of scouting. At the beginning of the movement, nobody viewed the rapid spread of associations self-considered "scouts" in countries outside British influence as a threat, nor was any type of worldwide structure anticipated. Nonetheless, the traumatic experience of World War I, the ideal of the League of Nations, and the ideological commitment that Baden-Powell undertook with the idea of promoting peace showed the opportunity but also the necessity to organize scouting all over the world under the same shared principles. That was the birth of what now is WOSM in 1920. Until then, *scouting* had legally been a British organization, the practices, image, and name of which had been adopted in diverse countries from different standpoints. After 1920 though, under the enthusiastic leadership of Baden-Powell followed by British scouting, a world organization was set up as the single world authority on the bases of scouting, which were no longer a matter for the opinion or interpretation of the different countries by themselves.

From this point on, all founder associations of the world organization, including the British association and its founder, agreed to submit to a single authority on scouting, that is, international laws that they themselves legislated. Through collective deliberation and a guarantee system, the new world organization will, for instance, establish that scouting is not militaristic, agree that no scout association could place national loyalty over international fraternity. It will also impose ideological and organizational limits that could not be overstepped either by new candidate associations or existing members. Likewise, it will "recognize" as new associations any that met the established common conditions, which would then become members, and it could withdraw recognition from associations that breached these conditions. Since 1920, then, scouting has become an integral world movement, which means that local groups, national associations, and the world organization at global level form a whole.

The politics of recognition in scouting was primarily concerned with ensuring that the term "scouting" (and translations) was not used to refer to practices that went against the principles of scouting: exclusionary nationalism as opposed to national commitment with a cosmopolitan vision; paramilitarism as opposed to educating the character of the individual; partisanship as opposed to freedom of opinion; discrimination as opposed to openness; instrumentation as opposed to independence; compulsory as opposed to voluntary. In fact, in the first quarter of the century many fascist and communist youth movements—such as the

Nazi German *Hitler Jugend*—took advantage of scouting's popularity by adopting many of its aesthetic elements.

Additionally, it is important to keep in mind that many countries replaced the original English term *scout*, with terms or adapted synonyms more deeply rooted in their own tradition, such as *escolta* in Catalan, *éclaireur* in French, or *pfadfinder* in German, showing that there is no single term that encompasses the entire movement throughout the languages. The recognition system through the belonging to the world organization, then, enable to organize a worldwide movement based on the same principles but with a wide diversity of image and terminology from country to country, and prevent its image from being used for ends other than its own.

Membership and international recognition are intrinsic to the scout identity. Scouting is more than the straightforward conformity with its principles and following of its method; precisely because of its combination of citizenship education, loyalty to one's country, and global commitment, it must be integrated in the world organization that gives meaning to the movement's triple axis of local, national, and global action. Without being part of the world organization, the ability to think, prepare, and have an impact from supranational to local level, is merely discursive, and thus cannot adequately contribute to the purpose of the scout movement.

Scouting is not a federation of national associations that have come together to share experiences; it is a structured movement that clearly sets out the ideological and organizational limits of those who form a part of it. In a statement by Robert Baden-Powell at the 1928 constitutive WAGGGS International Conference, he stresses that "We must from the outset avoid making our International Conference a 'Parliament'—that is, a meeting of *representatives* of different countries. . . . The work of delegates [at the International Conference] is to bring their experiences from all parts of the world to bear upon and help the better training of *the girl*. Unless and until we are not assured of the right spirit it would be better that we should not attempt to start an International organization."[116]

The inseparable dual national and global dimension of scouting, which respects the diversity of national frameworks while maintaining a set of common minimums established democratically for everybody, is one of the least studied and yet most relevant issues of the scout movement. It bases its model of a movement that educates citizens combining the classic republican idea of loyalty to one's country and the cosmopolitan idea of the sense of belonging and commitment to the community formed by all human beings. This combination is not only a constitutional condition that scouting has established for all its members worldwide: the personal experience that its vast network provides—pen pals, exchanges, international development projects, international camps, jamborees—is also part of the educational action carried out by scout associations in order to achieve it.

This brings us to analyze international recognition from a different point of view. If scouting's citizenship education combines national loyalty with the sense of global belonging, through both the establishment of a legitimate world organization and the experiences made possible by the organization itself, then the "recognition" of an association involves much more than the straightforward authorization to use the name. For an association that considers itself scout, being "recognized" involves being subject to the world organization rights and duties, accepting shared authority, being subject to the established rules of the game and participating in their renewal, and taking part in the international experiences that stimulate the sense of global belonging, instead of limiting itself to formulating these as an abstract idea.

4.2. Differentiating between What Is and Is Not Scouting

The historical narrative in each country has contributed to confusion between scouting and movements that call themselves this without actually being scouts. When a country talks about the "start of scouting," it does not differentiate between the time the association was created and the time it was recognized. This confusion makes total sense because, in several cases, the world organizations were set up after the national associations, which actually founded their organizations. As a result, the world organizations tend to indicate the year in which the national associations were founded, along with the year that scouting was recognized in the country, which suggests that a scout association existed before it was recognized, thus giving rise to confusion.

Germany is an example of this: before 1945, we know that there were a number of associations in Germany that called themselves "scouts"; these were outlawed by the Nazi regime in 1933[117] with the requirement that they join the *Hitler Youth*. However, neither WOSM nor WAGGGS recognized any of these organizations until after World War II because of their fragmentation and exclusionary (even expansionist) nationalism. The case of Germany illustrates the confusion that often arises when discussing the ideological profile of scouting. First, if we do not know that since 1920 the world organization(s) of scouting has had the exclusive authority to determine which associations meet the common requirements allowing them to be called scouts, we cannot differentiate between recognized scout associations—those that constitutionally form part of scouting as a world movement—and associations that adopt the name of *scouting* without being part of it. Second, if we fail to make this differentiation, we could fall into the trap of analyzing scouting on the basis of associations that are not part of scouting, even though they call themselves "scouts."

To continue with the example of Germany, if somebody were to analyze scouting in Germany and say that "before 1945 scouting had an exclusionary nationalist discourse," we would have to answer that there was no association in Germany before 1945 that could be considered a "scout" association based on world criteria. The threat of imitation has been a constant in the history of scouting ever since it was founded in England. In the British Empire, the monarchy's rapid institutional recognition dispelled any doubts about the exclusivity of the representativeness of *scouting*. However, the international spread of associations calling themselves "scout" associations from 1909 to 1920 looked set to downgrade the quality standard that Baden-Powell sought. To cite an example, the first documented activity of sort of "scouting" in Catalonia dates back to 1911, when an excursionist called Ramon Soler organized a series of activities for boys in Barcelona . . . simply by imitating a set of postcards from the Boy Scouts Association UK with pictures of *scouts* on them!

From the outset, the aesthetic aspect played an extremely important role. With the creation of the BSIB in 1920 (which later became WOSM), followed by that of WAGGGS in 1928, scouting was worldwide institutionalized into two organizations (male and female) and three main axes were established to mark the difference between what scouting was and was not: the essential characteristics (definition, purpose, principles, and method); the promotion of its unity; and the defense of the brand and intellectual property.[118]

As has been explained in detail, the essential characteristics of scouting—the first axis for determining what scouting is and is not—has served as the ideological and organizational basis of the movement, and has established the limits that cannot be crossed in order to be part of the it. The second axis, the promotion of unity, has been a practice geared toward avoiding breaking up and weakening, trying to slow the atomizing tendency in a movement that brings together enormous cultural, territorial, and religious diversity, and to maintain the policy of a single organization per "country." And finally, the defense of the brand and intellectual property has been the legal side of scouting actions designed to prevent any fraudulent use of the scout identity—name, emblems, uniforms, et cetera. For example, the prestige of the scout uniforms in Britain's African colonies caused them to be trafficked in various countries.[119] The policy of the world organization has been to encourage each recognized association to register the copyright of the world emblem in their respective country. The relevance of this axis lies in the need to avoid public confusion between recognized scouting and organizations that use the scout name when they are not members and, particularly, do not share its defining principles and elements.

The ability to grant or withdraw the recognition of a scout association is probably the most significant power of the two world organizations of scouting, WOSM and WAGGGS, since it is this practice that allows them to ensure the unity and uniformity of the movement in the midst of such diversity. When the world organizations were set up, they established the capacity for recognition by combining the application of intellectual property rights with a democratic decision-making system. First, because Robert Baden-Powell, the man who invented and defined *scouting*, establishing its purpose and principles and institutionalizing it as an association in Great Britain, was also the man who spearheaded the creation and development of the two world organizations of scouting, male and female, which always recognized his moral authority.[120] And second, because these world organizations immediately established a democratic decision-making system to guarantee that what was and was not scouting were defined through the collective debate of all member associations of the world organization and not, as could have been the case, the result of arbitrary and unclear decisions made by a self-invested elite.

Since their establishment then, the two world organizations have been the legitimate subject both for setting the standards that scout organizations must meet and for recognizing what scouting is and is not. This system differs from that of other civil society organizations around the world. In some cases, such as many federations of youth associations, the international organization is a federation of organizations that carry out the same type of action (educational, cultural, student, etc.) and perhaps have a set of very general principles. In others, such as Amnesty International or Greenpeace, the national groups operate like franchises that follow guidelines set down on a worldwide basis. Even the international organizations of political parties only ask their formations to assume a foundational manifesto, that is, to indicate their agreement with the general principles.

Scouting asks for more. The Constitutions of the two world organizations, WOSM and WAGGGS, establish that only one association can be recognized per country and that this association must adhere to the purpose and principles of the scout movement, that it must wholly adopt the method, that it has a Promise and Law text approved by the world organization, and that it is open, without discrimination, to all those who wish to adhere to the principles of the movement. Furthermore, the national association must be independent, nonpartisan, self-governed, and voluntary. The competent body for accepting new national associations as members is the World Conference, at which all member national associations have the right to vote.

4.3. RELIGION, CULTURE, TRADITION: MOTIVES FOR SPLIT IN SCOUTING

Despite the established procedures, the recognition policy of scouting, beginning with its very name, is still the Achilles' heel of the movement. Neither of the world organizations has developed a clear line of argument on the link between democratic membership, recognition, and the possibility of generating change from within, which has led to the creation of associations, particularly in the last 15 years, calling themselves "scouts" but which don't belong to any of the scout movement world organizations. Without making a rigid classification as such, we will highlight the three main elements found at the heart of many splits and which, paradoxically, have been crucial to the growth of scouting: the religious factor, the cultural factor, and the factor of organizational tradition.

The first factor of disunity, the *religious* factor, comes from the decision of many religious denominations to create their own scout associations, rather than participating in open associations, which is the model adopted by most of current WOSM and WAGGGS member associations. Given that the development of the spiritual dimension of the individual is a fundamental part of the educational aspect of scouting, its interaction with religious organizations has been important since the beginning, especially with the major religions, both sponsoring groups at local level or taking part in the spiritual education process. The ability of scouting to be seen as "own" by different cultures and religions is, certainly, one of the reasons for its success, and its explicit commitment to religious tolerance in the face of fanaticism takes on special relevance when taking into account the strong presence of the scout movement in countries with a fundamentalist religious grounding. But as a recent WOSM statement clearly says, "Scouting cooperates with the family, the school, the State, the churches and the spiritual community, but it is not subordinate to any of them."[121] For this reason, the existence of confessional networks in scouting worldwide is a way of avoiding denominational splits and maintaining different spiritual and religious life experiences within the same movement.

For the most part, the few uni-denominational scout associations are linked to the Catholic Church, while in many countries it is the pastoral commissions that have links to their respective denominations.

In all cases, however, scouting has had to be open without regard to religion. Even though since 1948 the Catholic scout associations and commissions have been officially organized with the recognition of the Vatican and WOSM, at the end of the 50s an unrecognized ultraconservative association—the self-styled "Scouts d'Europe" was created in Germany and then in France, split from the recognized Catholic scouting. This association does not belong to WOSM or WAGGGS, and has been structured at supranational level, although it has a modest international dimension, with only 55,000 members in several countries, mainly in France and Italy (in most associations membership is between 500 and 2,000), while the recognized Italian and French Catholic scout associations alone have more than 240,000 members.

In spite of the strength of Catholic scout associations in Europe and of the discriminatory nature of the self-styled "Scouts d'Europe," in 2003 the Vatican officially approved the bylaws of this association under Canon law,[122] causing a crisis within recognized Catholic scout associations that saw how the Catholic Church gave support to a movement that used the name "scout" contravening the requirements and fundamental principles of scouting. The Statutes of the self-styled "Scouts d'Europe" make it clear that, in contrast to scouting, they are not an independent association, nor open to everyone, but an instrument of the Catholic Church only open to young Catholic Christians. For example, its bylaws also establish that "chiefs" (leaders) must belong to the church, an obligation that does not exist in Catholic scout associations. Furthermore, in that unrecognized association the premise that scouting should be open to all is ignored, even though the term "scout" is used, since the Statutes establish that non-Christian children and young people can only be members in exceptional cases, and that any individual who has not been baptized cannot make the "Scouts d'Europe" version of the Promise.[123] As we will see later, regrettably this practice—which is clearly against the fundamentals of scouting, could also exist in particular religious-sponsored scout units in the United States. If so, the world organization should supervise those practices to guarantee the fundamentals are fulfilled by all member associations.

The second source of split within the scout movement, the *cultural* factor, stems from two different typologies: associations with exclusionary nationalist visions and against any supranational legitimacy, and the cases of national or cultural communities without official recognition or its own independent State. The first form has appeared along the history in countries like Great Britain, France, and the United States, where appeared associations that have tried to use the "scout" name while advocating against any international legitimacy or any influence from other countries, which contradicts the fundamentals of scouting. The first cases were the already quoted British Boy Scouts[124] in England, and the "Fédération Nationale des Éclaireurs Français" in France, which in 1913 declared that "they were resolutely French and hostile to the supremacy of any English-speaking culture and any international organization in which this influence prevails."[125] In the United States, legal action by the BSA in 1918 prevented the equivalent of the British Boy Scouts splinter group, originally called the "United States Boy Scouts" or "American Boy Scouts," from keeping the scout name and they were forced to be renamed the "American Cadets."[126]

As it has been explained, the second form of the "cultural factor," the one of unrecognized cultural or national communities, started in the 1920s to justify the existence of different recognized scout associations originally from the groups of refugees from Armenia and Russia. After World War II, with the large number of displaced peoples and many countries under the new Soviet regime, this policy changed and no further scout groups of exiles were recognized. Even so, we have seen that there have been several exceptions: associations that represent territories or collective cultures, for example the Flemish and Walloon communities of Belgium; the French-speaking community of Canada; the Faeroe Islands, Greenland, or Catalonia. There are also three territorial exceptions: Taiwan, Hong Kong, and Palestine, of which only the latter is a clear case of the "exceptional" recognition of a non-independent-state national community.

Although scouting has had to adapt to the independence processes that have taken place over the last century—particularly as a result of decolonization and the collapse of the USSR—scout jurisprudence has been very careful not to use culture as a way of encouraging the creation of separate associations in areas seeking independence. In his report quoted earlier, former Chairman of the World Scout Committee John Beresford points out that, "there is today increasing pressure from ethnic and other minorities in some countries to seek independence for their region. Scouts and Guides in these regions may feel loyalty toward the aspirations of their regional and local communities and press to become separate Associations."[127] Even so, both world organizations have adopted policies based on similar criterion used by the United Nations for recognizing a sovereign state, and do not allow more than one scout organization in the same independent country. The current strategy is to prevent scouting from becoming involved in the conflict that generally precedes independence; however, as soon as a country obtains internationally recognized independence, the organization quickly sets about creating an independent scout organization. The WAGGGS bylaws have a specific point that deals with these cases, entitled "National Organizations in countries attaining political independence."[128]

The third cause of disunity in scouting, the conflict of interpretation over the "organization tradition," lies in some recurrent claims that traditional elements of the movement (both aesthetic ones and practices) cannot be changed. The intuitive nature of scouting could create insecurity on what makes scouting *Scouting*, which brings about people to cling to traditions and symbols for fear to lose authenticity. It is also a discrepancy between the argument that associative cultures change, sometimes for the better, and the argument that denies an organization legitimacy to change any of what it considers its founding elements.[129] While the founder of scouting lived, he had both the legal and moral authority recognized by everybody as the man in charge, first of UK scouting and after 1920 of world scouting; it was he who dispelled doubts about what scouting was. On Robert Baden-Powell's death in 1941, a debate emerged on how to interpret his thinking, particularly regarding changes in the defining elements of the different associations. Because the organizational system of scouting does not impose a single model of associative culture (in terms of how to implement the worldwide minimum standards), the changes in the various associations over the years have had supporters and detractors who have not always reached an agreement. As a result, the evolution of the methodology and image of scouting in many countries has transformed or replaced formal and practical elements that were originally part of the associative culture, which has led to splintering.

In general, associations that have been created by splitting have tended to be from the groups that were most resistant to change. The first case dates back to 1964, when the Boy Scouts Association UK set in motion a process to study all aspects of scouting and to update them. The implementation of these updates included changing elements such as the uniform, the name of the association (removing the word "Boy"), methodological elements and characteristics of the sections, and also organizational changes. Some people in the United Kingdom strongly disagreed with the proposed changes, because they saw them as abandoning the traditions and intentions of Robert Baden-Powell. In 1970, after the changes had already started to be implemented, some detractors formed a new British association self-styled the "Baden-Powell Scouts." Interestingly, the group split from the scouting established by Baden-Powell because it refused to accept the changes agreed in a democratic decision-making process, but it adopted the name Baden-Powell as a source of legitimacy for its new project. There were similar splits in a number of countries,[130] mainly in Europe, and although they were numerically irrelevant and never became WOSM members (they were splits), they did enable the general public to question the unity of scouting and its contemporary, relevant image. Therefore, while many WOSM member associations tried to dispel the stereotyped image of military-like uniforms or formal stagings that were at odds with central western values, the splinter associations based their existence on "loyalty" to these elements, which were—to them—what "Baden-Powell's Scouting" was all about.

In 1996, a number of these associations set up the self-styled "World Federation of Independent Scouts" (WFIS) to give associations that called themselves "scouts" but were not members of world scouting an international federation through which they could organize camps, rallies, and collective training together. The only requirement for becoming a member of this international federation is not belonging "to another world organization" and "to follow, and use, Baden-Powell's original program, traditions, uniforms, morals, ethics, and structure as laid out in Baden-Powell's *Scouting for Boys.*"[131] According to their data, WFIS has 30,000 individual members around the world, mainly in the United Kingdom. To make a comparison, the Scout Association UK, member of WOSM, has half a million members.

The "international" membership of the associations belonging to WFIS is, to all effects, rather unrealistic. Its website indicates that WFIS "acts as an umbrella association for regional scout organizations."[132] As an organization, it does not have a shared set of ideas or bases other than that of not belonging to any other world organization, and its international structure is also rather dubious: the website states that members of its World Council are voted over the Internet.[133] A very different case can be found in the United States, where groups of scouts in opposition to the discriminatory policy of the BSA opted to use advocacy or pressure groups, like "Inclusive Scouting" or "Scouting for All," rather than creating a splinter "scout" association.

If we analyze the Report on World Scouting that Nagy made in 1967, we find three important conclusions about the recognition policy of scouting. First, that some large, nonrecognized associations are growing and will continue to grow, regardless of whether they are recognized. Second, that when dealing with nonrecognized or splinter associations, the children and young people who need scouting should be put before the adults in charge, which would allow a more open approach to finding solutions.[134] And third, that the principles of recognition must focus first and foremost on educational conditions rather than ideologico-political matters.[135] Toward the end of the 1960s, this latter element in particular heralded a turning point in the recognition policy that world scout organizations—mainly WOSM—had adopted since the end of World War II, in a context of changing frontiers, displaced persons, refugees, and exiles, and communist regimes in Eastern Europe where scouting was banned. The new constitutional reform, which was brought in by Nagy and adopted during the 1970s, ensured that the definition of the principles was incorporated into the educational elements and that these were evaluated during recognition.

Religion, culture, and organization tradition are then the three main elements threatening the unity of the scout movement. But it is important to differentiate when unity is threatened because the intolerance of those who do not allow consensual changes and updates and choose to leave, and when unity is at risk because the associations' culture prevents any debate or dissent.

"Glocal" Citizenship Education

> Girl scouting: Small steps. Huge Impact. Lifetime legacy.
> **Leymah Gbowee**, Liberian activist, Nobel Peace laureate
> Address to the Young Women's World Forum, 2010

National identities are the result of historical processes in which several different "opportunities" or paths were possible. They are not, therefore, a given and permanent fact. Moreover, whereas national identities are a good source of cohesion and solidarity, they could also be a source of exclusion and xenophobia. Liberal nationalism and cosmopolitanism have been debating about these two faces of identity for years. Is it possible to combine national identity and global commitment? Many scholars, opinion makers, and politicians believe that strengthening the sense of global belonging weakens national identity, and vice versa. While that is certainly rooted in the nationalistic perspective, many promoters of the cosmopolitan vision also assume that to educate in national loyalty inextricably leads to values that contradict the idea of global citizenship, and that only through some sort of national disaffection can we create a true sense of global belonging.

I am contrarily convinced that a citizenship education based on civic and inclusive values, promoting commitment and loyalty to one's own national community, can also reinforce rather than debilitate the sense of global belonging and the commitment to the world community. And furthermore, I am certain scouting shows that national identity and sense of global belonging could be synergic.

A deep and multidisciplinary analysis of scouting shows how a nongovernmental, voluntary worldwide educational movement with a local-rooted activity and commitment to the respective national community has continuously promoted the sense of global belonging as global citizens among its members ever since its early days, using a model of citizenship that combines both the republican civic values of liberal-democratic nationalism and the values of cosmopolitanism. This chapter attempts to present so.

1. CITIZENSHIP EDUCATION AND SCOUTING

1.1. WHAT DOES TO EDUCATE CITIZENS MEAN?

After the totalitarian experience, Hanna Arendt explained that the government must not be seen as a group of people ruling over their subjects and introducing laws that the latter must obey; instead, governments must be made up of individuals whom the citizens have empowered to legitimately exercise authority in their name. Thus, although the government has the ultimate authority to adopt binding decisions in the community's name, its decisions must represent the public consensus.[1] The dual meaning of citizenship (active/passive) takes on a special relevance in this context. While the *passive* side of the legal status identifies the member of the political community and subject of rights, the *active* side emphasizes the fact that citizens are not only governed by a system of rules and governing practices, but that they also have a fundamental role in the definition and development of the latter. In this view, if the rules to which citizens are subject are imposed by tyranny, a foreign power or illegitimate political institutions, individuals then become passive subjects instead of active citizens. The political capacity of citizens lies in their self-government, their popular sovereignty, and their self-determination.

According to Bernard Crick, who in 1998 coordinated the Advisory Group on Citizenship fostered by the British Government, "the very project of a free citizenship education, as distinct from a would-be indoctrinating one, whether ideological or simply patriotic, must be based on a limited number of presuppositions," which he calls procedural values: freedom; toleration; fairness; respect for truth; and respect for reasoning.[2] We cannot talk of citizenship education then without taking into account the tension between education and indoctrination or between the chosen reproduction of the model of society and imposed maintenance of the majority vision, and the conflict with religious or cultural values that are at odds with constitutional values. However, the legitimacy of the values that must foster citizenship education lies in their contribution to living in harmony in a democracy and the development of individual ideas of common good, since they allow for public debate and are based on respect for the diversity of those involved in the debate.

Nonetheless, diverse points of view have argued that schools should not necessarily be responsible for this education in civic virtues.[3] The family, for example, has traditionally been the transmitter of civic virtues, although mainly within a moral framework established by religion and, in all events, with no guarantee that the transmitted values would be shared. Religion itself transmits civic values, though these may conflict with the principles governing common life in pluralist societies, as is the case of the Catholic Church and divorce, abortion or the recognition of homosexuality. It has also been argued that market expansion would teach civic virtues such as initiative and self-sufficiency. However, the regulatory mechanisms of the market are not sufficient to ensure that equally negative values do not prevail.

Moreover, many thinkers have focused on democratic participation as a tool for transmitting civic virtues that allow for democratic common life, even though the emphasis on participation does not guarantee that citizens will participate responsibly. Whereas some argue that the transmission of civic virtues takes place in voluntary organizations of civil society[4] some others answer that only organizations aiming to have an impact on the political agenda can encourage participation.[5] Nevertheless, the main aim of most of these associations is not the transmission of civic values, as Kymlicka notes, and hence, the transmission of civic values may be implicit but not guaranteed. "Some associations, like the Boy Scouts, are designed to promote citizenship," he adds; "but they are the exception not the rule."[6] In a similar vein—though 80 years earlier— the Columbia educationalist James Russell concurred with the analysis of scouting's potential role, stating that the education given at school has in scouting an excellent partner for citizenship education in the sense that the scout program "is essentially moral training for the sake of efficient democratic citizenship."[7]

As we have seen in previous pages, the purpose of scouting is the *education of individual persons* and not the direct transformation of society. This is so because the scout movement does not attempt to establish a particular vision for how society should be. Rather, it wants to shape responsible citizens, with moral autonomy and critical thinking, as well as with leadership skills, so that it is they who, grounded in their shared inclusive principles, participate in the definition of their model society and contribute to making it a reality.[8]

Nevertheless, this characteristic is not obvious, even to scout leaders themselves. Scouting has never escaped the debate, either internally or externally, between those who believe that its social agenda is too timid and those who think that its will for social change is excessively bold. For that reason, it is appropriate to clarify that scouting is not a recreational movement that avoids facing the problems that affect people, nor a disruptive movement that promotes social confrontation. Its educational activities do not seek to force rapid social change, but rather to facilitate a progressive yet intense transformation, led by people who have critical thinking and moral autonomy and who play an active and responsible role in their own societies.

Furthermore, western-centered perspectives make people forget that scouting takes a clear and explicit decision to educate for global citizenship being rooted in a broad range of societies and cultures. And this diversity, based on millions of volunteers, makes it inevitable that scouting experiences different behaviors according on the predominant social values within each country, which also vary through cultural changes. The modest, but powerful aim of the scout movement is to contribute that in every community citizens share civic virtues that allow strengthening inclusive societies, committed to liberty and to peace. Nevertheless, the promotion of these civic virtues does not have the same priority in democratic societies as it does in those that are not democratic. In her study *Critical Citizens,* Pippa Norris shows that while in liberal democracies citizens' demands for accountability are essential to democratic governance, in countries in transition toward democracy demands for accountability have a more basic role in guaranteeing respect for human rights.[9] An active and critical citizenship, then, has a very different role if a liberal-democratic system is already established than if authoritarianism and a lack of guarantees rule the political game.

Yet we can ask ourselves if this model of citizenship of scouting, the one that counts on the deep involvement of public institutions in many countries, has as its goal to perpetuate the status quo or to transform it: What meaning do we want to give to the scout motto "leave the world a little better than you found it"? In order to better understand how scouting, rooted at the local level, can build loyalty to one's own country from the perspective of a global citizenship committed to the betterment of society, we will explore those topics.

1.2. THE ASSUMPTIONS OF "CITIZENSHIP" IN SCOUTING

Scouting is an educational movement, the aim of which is to contribute to the development of young people in achieving their full potential as individuals, as responsible citizens, and as members of their local, national, and international communities. The movement is grounded in the voluntary action of its members, leaders, and educators: from the local scout group to the national association and the world organization. Citizenship education has continuously been an aim of scouting from its early steps in the United Kingdom. In fact, the foundational book of the movement, *Scouting for Boys,* already contained the concept of citizenship education in its subtitle: *A Handbook for Instruction in Good Citizenship.* But in order to understand all of the controversies that the western ideas of "citizenship" and "education" have generated within a global movement, it is necessary to begin by understanding the baseline assumptions of the concept of citizenship in the context of England in the early twentieth century.

We cannot forget that scouting appeared in a moment when nationalism was beginning to flourish in the European culture. At the end of the nineteenth century, with the emergence of new nationalisms, the concepts of "state," "nation," and "society" converged, and the elite that promoted this convergence created new rituals, traditions, and cults through which it could be communicated to the public.[10] In the British Empire, the early scout movement was clearly an instrument of this convergence, as it also was for most of the countries that reproduced and adapted the movement to their societies before 1920. There are though other sociological factors that fostered the birth of scouting and made it more appealing, like the emergence of "youth" as a separate life stage, the extension of the concept of *leisure* or free time, and a greater appreciation of nature and the countryside as opposed to life in the industrial city. On the ideological grounds, three factors from Victorian society conditioned the scout movement in the United Kingdom at the beginning of the century: the theory of progress of civilizations, the secularized religious moralism, and the liberal-democratic tradition. Let's take a quick look to them.

In turn-of-the-century England, there was widespread acceptance of the theory of progress,[11] according to which some communities are more advanced than others—both comparing different countries and civilizations as within single countries (in reference to social class)—and that progress could be achieved between one stage and another. This theory was an ideological basis of British imperialism, conferring on it the mission of helping to civilize the world, and it can be felt in very early writings of Baden-Powell and of scouting in England. In addition, the strong religious moralism existent in the United Kingdom also influenced early scouting; but unlike in other countries, that moralism was not dictated by any external religious power, such as the Vatican for Catholic ones, since in England the monarch is the head of the Anglican Church. And third, the long liberal tradition of British democratic parliamentarianism is also the basis of early scouting's citizenship model: in that tradition, the monarch's legitimacy is derived from loyalty to the institutions and good governance, the democratic practice precedes the partisan system, and the government is required to account for its actions to the citizens.

All these elements can be found at the base of Baden-Powell's methodological proposal in *Scouting for Boys* in 1908 and in his idea of "good citizenship"; and more specifically, they could be found in the values of the Scout "Law" and "Promise," which became the point of reference for the principles of the scout movement, as a shared code of behavior. The early twentieth-century British context is then essential for understanding the scout references to loyalty to the King and to God, as this was a society that, despite the moralizing influence of the Edwardian-Victorian, had strong liberal foundations. Thus, the creation of the Boy Scouts Association in 1909 Britain became a reference for the immediate imitation of the model in many counties around the world (although few had the British liberal culture): a nonformal educational association for teenagers under the protection of the king as patron, and which had the cooperation of the Church and public institutions, including schools and the army.

Nevertheless, Baden-Powell's ideology and aims evolved substantially between 1907, when he wrote *Scouting for Boys,* and 1920, when the Boy Scouts International Bureau (BSIB, later on "WOSM," or the World Organization of the Scout Movement) was founded. In fact, this evolution wholly conditioned the idea of citizenship in world scouting when it was formalized in 1920, giving it a civic republican slant with a strong liberal component, and combining patriotism based on cosmopolitan convictions with a commitment to world peace. We can divide this ideological evolution into four axes: an interaction with the progressive educational movements that promoted active learning; an emphasis on openness and critical thinking; an internationalist approach; and a commitment to peace.

Regarding the first, the interaction with educational movements promoting active learning, it is important to highlight the considerable similarities that rapidly show up between Baden-Powell's scout method and Maria Montessori's active learning pedagogy: the importance of the role of the educator, the building of the individual's character through self-education, the child's taking on of responsibilities as an educational tool, respect for nature linked to the idea of transcendental creation, social involvement, tolerance, understanding, willingness to help, et cetera. The cross-references between Baden-Powell and Montessori demonstrate the complementarity and complicity between the two initiatives: while the former brought the practice of scouting closer to the concept of active learning proposed by Montessori, the latter explicitly recognized the similarity between her approach in school and the scout's educational practices outside the school.

The second axis, the emphasis on openness and critical thinking, in contrast to the blind obedience of military instruction or even of the schooling of the era, was closely related to the grafting of active learning groundswells. Explicitly, scouting stressed that its role was not to instruct the masses, like the army did, but rather to train the individual's character.[12] Thus, the apolitical nature of scouting's proposal meant independence from, rather than absence of, criteria on public life.

Third, scouting's internationalism emerges in parallel to its geographical expansion across the British Empire. The patriotic discourse that led to the creation of scout delegations in British dominions also existed in many other countries, when even before 1912 many self-considered *scout associations* were created: from Chile to Denmark, from the United States to Malaysia.[13] It was this international hatching of the scout project, along with the impact of World War I, which led to the "international conversion" of Baden-Powell. The result was the disappearance of the idea of cultural or national superiority and the explicit statement that loyalty to one's own country was inseparable from brotherhood between countries and that, as a result, there could be no discrimination not only on the grounds of class (as established in 1908), but not either on the grounds of origin.

The commitment to peace is the fourth and last axis that explains the ideological transformation of the scout movement in its early stage. Neither a single document nor reference in world scouting, since its formalization in 1920, casts the slightest shadow of a doubt over the devoted commitment of the scout movement to peace, through the joint education of young people from different countries: the idea of a universal fellowship, strongly present in scouting. The impact of World War I proved decisive for the adoption of this stance, but so did the informal international dimension that scouting had taken on before 1920.

However, we must take into account that the international spread of the model of scouting born in England occurred in parallel with these four axes of ideological transformation of the movement. Actually, the cultural nationalism of early UK scouting was already on the scout proposal in many of the countries where the movement was appearing before the world organization was established. So, the fact that quite before 1920 scout associations were created on the five continents adopting the original British model generated a paradox: over the years, both visions—the early one with cultural nationalism bases, and the constitutionally established at the world level in 1920 with an indubitable international commitment—have had Baden-Powell's texts as a foundation. That is why, in looking for references, it is necessary to look for the positions and practices of the world organizations and its member associations since 1920, which do not contain the contradictions that one can find in the early steps of scouting in the British Empire and in some other countries.

A very good example of this tension is the shock that occurred around 1919 between Robert Baden-Powell and the distinguished men who promoted the Boy Scouts Association in the United Kingdom. Baden-Powell had adopted an explicit, active, and enthusiastic commitment to the project of the League of Nations (a precursor of what is today the United Nations), up to the point to make explicit that scouting was in the service of its internationalist ideals. As Mario Sica explains, certain conservative members of the Committee of the Council of the Boy Scouts Association (UK) criticized for its alleged "political" character the link between Baden-Powell and the internationalist League of Nations Union, created in England to promote the international institution. They even questioned Baden-Powell's idea of a great international meeting that gather young people of the associations from around the world that shared scouting ideals. But despite that opposition, Robert Baden-Powell maintained his vision, and the international meeting finally occurred in 1920: it was the First World Scout Jamboree.[14] That same year, in an article in the magazine of the UK scout association, Baden-Powell explicitly encouraged scouts to collaborate to promote the League of Nations Union: "Probably a local branch [of the *League of Nations Union*] exists in your town; if so, you should ask the secretary if you can help him in any way, such as distributing handbills for meetings."[15]

The episode with Baden-Powell and the League of Nations Union demonstrates that, possibly, those who today believe that the inclusive, shared values of scouting are too weak, undervalue the transformative power of the principles that have grounded the great internationalist initiatives of this century: the League of Nations, the United Nations, the Universal Declaration on Human Rights, the UN Convention on the Rights of the Child, the International Criminal Court, the UNESCO, the UNICEF, and the other agencies within the United Nations system, as well as the international conferences that they have driven. Opponents of Baden-Powell's internationalist enthusiasm saw it very well.

1.3. VALUES TO PERPETUATE SOCIETY VERSUS VALUES TO
TRANSFORM SOCIETY

The early British scouting adopted the values of citizenship education already present in the first editions of the book *Scouting for Boys*, expressed for the kids under the idea of "good citizenship." That idea essentially meant active and socially acceptable behavior, based on daily *good turns*: "a Scout is active in doing good, not passive in being good,"[16] Baden-Powell wrote. However, this model of active citizenship was cautious about a trend of order destruction that appeared by the time around ideas of class struggle. For example, in the same book, while Baden-Powell shows his proximity to the socialist ideal of eliminating social extremes—neither millionaires nor people living in poverty—he also offsets this view with the liberal distrust, saying that this should not come at the cost of a loss of liberty,[17] and warns that "it is easy to pull down; the difficulty is to do so without damage to the country. We ought to begin by building up on a sounder foundation before destroying the old."[18]

The idea of daily good turns explained in *Scouting for Boys* evolved as it happened with the mentioned four axes of the ideological change of scouting's founder discourse: educational emphasis on active learning, openness and individual critical thinking, internationalism, and commitment to peace; and so, in fact scouting discourse became rooted on the idea to build a better society based on the values of an inclusive, just, and peaceful coexistence. The idea that no country, culture or religion is superior to another, together with the adherence to the ideals of the League of Nations, left no room for neutrality on expansionist nationalism nor for religious fanaticism, when in 1920 the world organization was established. In this sense, since then the role of the two international organizations (for boys and for girls) became crucial here in preventing these trends, present in many countries at various points in their contemporary history, from being incorporated into any recognized scout association.

Many of the 30 countries that met in London in 1920 to agree on the creation of the BSIB had, emulating the British association, been given the explicit support of their highest national institutions, thus combining apoliticism with institutional loyalty. Just as King Edward VII of England was *Patron* of the Boy Scouts Association, in many countries a similar position was held by the corresponding head of state: the monarch in Scandinavian countries, the Netherlands and Spain; the president of the Republic in Italy; the president of the United States; or the governors of the Empire in the British colonies. As we have previously seen, the support of public institutions came principally from a confidence generated by the discourse of service to one's country, loyalty and order that emanated from the scout movement. In a historical setting in which government institutions might have been reluctant to participation—given the potential for generating social conflict—the scout movement would hardly have found this support if it had explained its goal of training young people to have moral autonomy and critical thinking and to act accordingly.

However, over the years, the growing emphasis that in many countries scouting has placed on character education has not caused it to lose institutional support. This is still the model in place today, as explained in a recent WOSM document on Governance: "notwithstanding the independence of the National Scout Organisations, in many cases national authorities play a relevant role in Scouting, and the Head of State is often recognized as the Patron of local Scouting in a country."[19] Even in modern South Africa, where scouting was introduced as a colonial instrument and existed during the apartheid, President Nelson Mandela became patron of South African scouting in 1994.[20]

The official protection that scout associations enjoyed and continue to enjoy in many countries lends an interesting aspect of its role on building global citizenship. Like the League of Nations, scouting as a world movement was consolidated by an enduring combination of national loyalty and a clear sense of global belonging. Nonetheless, the protection of state institutions did not change the idea shared by Baden-Powell and by scout leaders all over the world that scouting should be independent, self-regulated and voluntary. Thus, there were rejected both the compulsory characteristic that the schooling system has and the aspiration to enjoy the massive public resources that indoctrinating (and compulsory) official youth movements were receiving in totalitarian regimes—like Germany, Italy, Spain, and the USSR.[21]

The successful spread of early scouting around the world was not only due because the great reception of boys all around the world. As the historian Timothy Parsons states, it was also because the adaptability of its values for sociopolitical stability. Those values were flexible enough to uphold the established political order in each country where new associations were created, through alliances with the legitimate institutions of authority, making social values and norms prevail without overstepping the limits.[22] This goal of stability is explicit in the resolution of the International Scout Conference on the Scout Promise, approved in 1931, in which "[t]he Conference desires to make it clear that in the Scout's Promise, the promise of duty 'to my country' means duty to the constituted authority of the country concerned."[23]

This very solemn statement should, however, be qualified: What would have been the position of Baden-Powell and the distinguished men promoting British scouting if Germany had occupied the United Kingdom at the end of World War I? Would they have accepted this newly constituted authority? Most certainly not. But that shows one of the most problematic aspects of citizenship education in scouting: it is ambiguous on how far it has to promote submission to the authority of existing institutions and political structures or, on the contrary, at what point this authority should be questioned. Actually, for instance, the reaction of scouts in different European countries under the Nazi invasion or Mussolini and Franco's fascist regimes was clearly against the new "constituted authority," help-ing the resistance and fighting for freedom.[24] But world social realities are very diverse, and to fight for a democracy that had been defeated is not the same than to fight against an authoritarian regime in a society that had have few or no democratic past. Therefore, it would probably be useless to try to establish a casuistic on that topic within an educa-tional voluntary movement existing in many different societies, only a part of which were democracies. A certain ambiguity about it was there-fore needed, within the limits of the shared values, later on specified on the Human Rights.

That ambiguity not only applies in the example of an invasion. In early twentieth century England, the accountability that characterized its polit-ical life took it for granted that democracy did not mean giving a *carte blanche* to the government to do as it pleased: it had to account for its actions. In that sense, a first interpretation of the principles behind the scout "law" and "promise" from 1908 *Scouting for Boys,* which explicitly require loyalty "to the King, and to his officers, and to his country, and to his employers,"[25] would appear to defend the established order and status quo. However, the same text also states on its point 4 that a scout is a "brother to every other Scout, no matter to what country, class or creed the other may belong," which has egalitarian consequences as strong or even stronger than the previous reference to loyalty.

Parsons' analysis of the case of scouting in British African colonies shows how the movement was "both an instrument of colonial author-ity and a subversive challenge to the legitimacy of the Empire."[26] Parsons explains that colonial officials introduced scouting in the belief that the point of loyalty to the King in the "scout law" would encourage the loy-alty of African young members of the movement. But on the contrary, the fourth point of the "Scout Law" that says that *a Scout is a brother to every other Scout* became the key element for natives to reject the social discrimi-nation they were suffering under colonialism. One might assume that one of these points would have more weight than the other. It seems that the colonial officials thought so, as well as the distinguished men in England and in many other countries who gave their support to scouting. But to what extent could it be said that those who saw scouting as a movement of order were underestimating the consequences of the deeply egalitar-ian content of its principles? In that same way, Laszlo Nagy explains in his Report on World Scouting that in many African countries, includ-ing Senegal, Guinea, or Algeria, scouts became, "the first leaders of the movement for national independence, although its activity, in accordance with existing laws, were regarded by colonial authorities as illegal and subversive."[27]

Indeed, although in the original Scout Law there is an explicit reference to obedience,[28] the interpretation that has been made does not entail obeying beyond one's own conscience, which is in line with the writings of Baden-Powell on the matter, when he said that "a Scout thinks a thing out for himself, sees both sides, and has the pluck to stick up for what he knows to be the right."[29] In fact, the liberal-democratic background to the concept of citizenship in scouting actually ended up sparking the contradictions that appeared when facing discriminations or authoritarianisms, both in the British colonies and in other countries. The scout references to obedience, then, should be understood under the first of what Russell called the two educational processes in the development of character: "One way consist in yielding to guidance; the other, in guiding one's self."[30]

In a 1936 article by Robert Baden-Powell on scouting in South Africa, for instance, he explained that, in a society totally segregated into black, Hindi, and white races, "our policy of Scouting being open to all 'regardless of class, creed, or colour' was found to be impossible in practice," because of the legal constraints; but he added that, nevertheless, the attempt of one sector to make scouting for whites only was "impeded," and a federation was set up with three branches, one for each ethnic group, with a view to contribute to socially blur that separation in the future.[31] Like in that case, in many others the values of scouting have become values of social transformation when they have been adapted to societies other than the British context, and particularly when they have been adopted by sectors of resistance to the established order, even against the official position of the organization: whether on issues such as national identity or anticolonialism, opposition to dictatorships, assertion of the civil rights of ethnic groups, assertion of gender equality, or the opposition to the discrimination for sexual orientation in the United States.[32]

The values that shape societies are not static, but dynamic. And we should see them as part of the changes that the various societies of the planet experience differently. If we take a historical look at the last one hundred years, we will see an extraordinary transformation of values and a great acquisition of social rights in many countries. Those issues that some decades ago were considered revolutionary have come to be seen as normal: female suffrage, labor rights, the abolition of racial segregation, social protection, or the rights of self-determination of former colonies.

If we focus on social and human rights, in the western countries this change occurred in several stages until it arrived at political reforms, with which the modern political parties institutionalized social rights and, primarily in Europe, gave birth to the welfare state. But scouting was created at a time of heightened tensions, during a period of social mobilizations and workers' claims that, in Russia, were culminating with a revolution and the establishment of the USSR. Perhaps this is why scouting was very cautious about anything that could generate social conflict—"it is easier to pull down things than to build": a scout had to be above class divisions and, in consequence, above the confrontational discourse of class struggle.

Hence, there were many interpretations of the concept of "active citizenship," particularly in non-democratic societies, and even a potential for manipulation. What was the role of scouting in Austria when it was annexed to Nazi Germany, or in the fascist regimes of Mussolini in Italy or Franco in Spain? What were the Catalan scouts, outlawed by Franco's regime, to do when the Catalan institutions of self-government were abolished, the President of Catalonia executed, and their language banned? What was the role of scouts in countries where racial discrimination was legally established? What happened in the processes of decolonization, where scout leaders led the independence processes? What was the right option for an "active citizen" in Colombia in 1980s: to side with the guerrillas as a way to fight inequality or to side with the army and defend the established authority? What did the Argentinean scouts have to do when active citizens disappeared killed by the dictatorial repression?

The answers to these questions are as diverse as the situations they are asked about. Regarding regimes changes, the position of the world organizations, after the exceptions of recognizing Russia and Armenia in exile during the 20s, was to not recognize scout associations as members in countries where the movement was not allowed, though contact was maintained if they existed illegally. Individually, each scout acted on the basis of his/her own understanding of "active citizenship." Associations did not have a homogeneous behavior either. In Fascist Spain in the 1940s, for example, while Spanish scouting at that time sought to connive with the regime (seeking its recognition), the illegalized Catalan scouting organized itself to resist it.[33] Another example is the recent statement of the Board of Scouts de Argentina, harshly condemning the dictatorship of the 1970s and inviting its members to organize activities to recover the collective historical memory and celebrate the democratic system.[34] In decolonization, on the other hand, scouting played a key role as an instrument of social construction for the new independent countries: infrastructures, collective identity, nation building, et cetera. And more recently, in 2011 I noticed how individual young scouts in Arab countries were very active around the so-called Arab Spring in Tunisia or Egypt, claiming their role as real *citizens*, despite the institutional relations their scout associations enjoy with the status quo. This is something that should be studied in the future.

The already quoted constitutional amendment approved by WOSM in 1977 added the concept of "responsible citizen" to the purpose of the scout movement, a step beyond that of "active citizen," in assuming that responsible citizens have the ability to analyze, apply their own critical thinking and distinguish what is positive from what is negative. It also explicitly stated that the reference communities of this responsible citizenship were local, national and international. These two concepts—responsible citizenship referred to local, national and international communities—are now set down in the constitutional aim of the scout movement in both WOSM and WAGGGS (the World Association of Girl Guides and Girl Scouts). Carefulness on this issue is necessary, providing the "inherent power" that Warren notices the scout movement has: "otherwise, why should totalitarian regimes ban them, and why should they reappear so quickly once such regimes fall?."[35]

To play with the fires of the several concepts of citizenship without burning oneself with political discourse is nearly impossible. And scouting, little by little, has realized it. The distinguished British men behind the Boy Scouts Association who, at the end of World War I, told Baden-Powell that promoting the League of Nations would have political connotations, were not wrong. They were not, certainly, connotations of a partisan character; but the implication of scouting in society, from broadly shared principles, grew and grew. Its beginning was the timid "good turns" and the aforementioned idea that the scout is "active in *doing* good, not passive in *being* good." Thus, in little time the concept of "service to the community" was introduced, locally promoted in scout sections and groups. With time, and in particular in those societies with extreme inequities, the nearest service to the community opened up the concept of "community development." It meant a process that seeks to create the necessary conditions for the social and economic progress of a community, favoring that members of society actively participate and take initiative, so that they become more autonomous to be able to determine their own future stages.[36]

Community development can be given within one society, as in England at the beginning of the century or today in many African societies, where scouting plays a central role. It can also be given from one society to another, and in that case it is called "cooperation for development." This last axis, which combines with the sensibilization role of the development education, was introduced as part of the strategic action of scouting in the 1970s, in the light of the new world stage resulting from decolonization (with many new countries joining world scouting) and the progressive "globalization" of the scout movement: that is, raising consciousness of global action through local action.

In this way, we can say that the concept of social involvement in scouting came to consist of four progressive lines that mark out a logic of service to the community with actions from local to global level: Community service; community development; development education; and cooperation for development.[37] These four axes must be understood as educational tools that provide meaning to the logic of the active social implication of the scout movement, bringing actions and programs that are carried out by groups at the local level, associations at the national level, and groups of associations, continental regions, and the world organization at the international level.

However, its educational character has not meant world scouting is exempt from the increased involvement of international NGOs and associations in the global agenda. During the 1990s, many international NGOs that had traditionally adopted a cautious stance of apoliticism began to play a more active public role, particularly because of the impetus of diverse UN summits held in this decade, including those on the environment (Rio, 1992), Human Rights (Vienna, 1993), population (Cairo, 1994), social development (Copenhagen, 1995), women (Beijing, 1995), and the respective "parallel summits" organized by international movements of civil society.

The position of both WAGGGS and WOSM on the issue has changed substantially over the last 15 years. It started in the mid-1990s, with the initiatives by Lesley Bulman and Jacques Moreillon, the then top executives of WAGGGS and WOSM,[38] to create an alliance with other youth organizations' top executives, to adopt a public stance in favor of nonformal education for young people. The result was the document "The Education of Young People: A Statement at the Dawn of the 21st Century" (1997), which was followed by documents on national youth policies (1999), on the social role of girls and young females (2001), about the situation in Africa (2003), and on the participation of young people (2005).[39] Technically speaking, these documents were not adopted by the organizations; they were statements made by their CEOs, making the decision-making processes to define the position easier. Moreover, the model of an alliance with diverse organizations not only reinforced the public image of scouting, it also reduced possible apprehension at a statement coming exclusively from the scout movement.

As was mentioned in the historical section, the two world organizations have traditionally acted with prudence in regard to their international public positioning, to avoid invading elements of individual choice: scouting should not impose its vision on how society should be. However, the UN summits of the 1990s made the lack of global political governance evident—a wide-ranging issue that the international NGO community could seek to mitigate and that went beyond individual choice. This encouraged many international NGOs, including the scout world organizations, to take a more active position with the aim of having an influence. Thus, at the end of the 1990s, WAGGGS and later WOSM began to also slightly play the role of an advocacy institutions.

Advocacy means to promote and defend an idea with the purpose of influencing its achievement. But when one refers to citizen organizations, *advocacy* designates the pressure that is applied to institutions, governments, and corporations so that they change their behavior, with regard to causes of public interest and not in defense of the particular interests of the members of the organization.[40] This last item constitutes the principle difference between *lobbying* and *advocacy*: whereas the former is for the benefit whomever is promoting; the later is to benefit a broad community. WAGGGS understand advocacy as a democratic process to "influence people to take decisions that will improve our lives and the lives of others," where "to influence" always includes *Speaking Out, Doing,* and *Educating.*[41]

The evolution from a prudent distance to the advocacy in the international public positioning came, above all, from the hand of WAGGGS, who thought that the situation of the girls and young women was too tough around the world to let the world organization not to claim rights on their behalf. In the year 2006, the then Chief Executive of WAGGGS, Lesley Bulman, said that in the past the world organization was much more timid on its public positioning because it feared being seen as a "political" if these positions were uncomfortable from the point of view of some cultures or traditions, even if the practices of these traditions were harmful to girls and young women. Nevertheless, some member associations started to ask the world organization to take a more active role in front of the situations of injustice at global level.

Thus, many associations that in the past had been uncomfortable in the face of reporting controversial topics now wanted WAGGGS to be more of a spokesperson, on many issues. They were associations that, for example, were fighting against the expansion of AIDS, and had to learn how to deal with sexual and reproductive health issues that had been taboo or that would have made them uncomfortable. That is why, Bulman said, girl scout/guide associations were now addressing those and many other subjects that generate strong cultural controversy in many societies, like female genital mutilation.[42]

WAGGGS commitment to advocacy has led it define that term in an internal document, as "taking a stand and putting pressure on those who can bring about change and help build a better world." It also illustrates how female scouting carries out advocacy in three ways: "Speaking up on issues that affect girls and young women and influencing opinion formers; doing projects that address root causes of issues affecting girls and young women; and educating girls, young women and society at large in areas such as leadership, nutrition, peace, and world citizenship."[43]

That stance has been boosted by a thus far unheard of initiative: a direct global survey on adolescence health to over 6,000 girls and young women that belong to WAGGGS associations in one hundred different countries. The results led to an overt advocacy campaign launched in 2005 under the slogan "Girls Worldwide Say,". The answers on the extensive survey were aimed mostly at subject matters related to health and, from these, they selected seven messages as axes of the campaign: "Fight AIDS"; "Make healthy food choices"; "Prevent adolescent pregnancy"; "It is important to talk about sex"; "Let's talk about the danger of drugs"; "Ban smoking in public places"; and "Discover your potential" (the later related to image and self-esteem). An example from this advocacy campaign is the public positioning of WAGGGS in support of the agreements that several governments have taken to forbid tobacco in public places, pointing out that 83 percent of the 6,000 polled girls agreed with it and asking for the fulfillment of the Convention on the Control of Tobacco, from the World Health Organization. More recently, in 2011 WAGGGS launched a world campaign in partnership with UN Women to stop violence against girls, creating a nonformal education curriculum to empower girls and young women and being part of the UN Women initiative "Say NO—UNiTE to End Violence against Women," a global online platform that records advocacy efforts from around the world and collects actions to end violence against women and girls.

WOSM's attitude toward advocacy has also been changing, though not as overtly as WAGGGS. In 2004, WOSM launched an educational project called *Scouts of the World*,[44] to encourage young people all over the world to get involved in achieving the Millennium Goals adopted in 2000 by the United Nations. In early 2005, strict criteria were established for working with corporate partners, and WOSM explained that it would not allow partnerships with organizations whose actions conflicted with the principles of WOSM.[45] Moreover, a 2006 press document issued by the World Scout Bureau explains how the social impact of scouting is twofold, with "global advocacy" and "local action."[46] Likewise, WAGGGS launched in its 2008 World Conference the Global Action Theme "Together we can change our world," "encouraging girls, young women and members of all ages to make a personal commitment to change the world around them" through being involved with the UN Millenium Development Goals.[47]

There is a very fine line between the impartiality necessary in a movement that aims to be open to everyone to give each one the opportunity to picture his/her model of society, and the neutrality that, based on apoliticism, turns a blind eye to anything which detracts from the tolerant, inclusive, and peaceful environment that scouting aims to foster. In fact, the main purpose of scouting is to train individuals for them to develop moral autonomy, critical thinking, and social commitment; and the advocacy initiatives and the actions of commitment with the principles of the United Nations, as the many local community involvement initiatives, should also be educational means toward that purpose, and not aims on itself. In any case, these initiatives follow in the line of reinforcing the idea that the citizenship education that scouting promotes has duties that go beyond national limits and bonds, and that reach the human community: it is an education for global citizenship.

2. Consistency and Incoherencies in a Global Movement

In contrast to other international citizenship movements, scouting is based on strong local roots, with all the diversity that this entails. In fact, the changes brought about by globalization do not necessarily lead to the homogenization of the planet or the disappearance of cultures. On the contrary, as Roland Robertson argues, globalization cannot be separated from localization—"global" is increasingly taking on the meaning of "translocal." This is why he suggests the use of the neologisms "glocal" and "glocalization," to complement the use of "global" and "globalization," given that "globalization has involved and increasingly involves the creation and the incorporation of locality, processes which themselves largely shape, in turn, the compression of the world as a whole."[48]

Scouting is then clearly a *glocal* movement, based on local rooting and a large voluntary and unpaid individual membership, grown in national loyalties, and committed to global challenges. In effect, scouting is characterized by its combination of education of individuals as citizens without discrimination, national loyalty with an international vocation, spiritual development, commitment to improving the living conditions of individuals and dedication to peace. Moreover, in most countries Scouting has been supported by State institutions and religious denominations since its initial foundation. And additionally, in the past—and this is still the case in many countries—boys and girls have been separated within the scout movement. Taken as a whole, this means that scouting simultaneously coexists, promotes, and conflicts with national identity (and loyalty) and state interest, with religious identity and beliefs, with gender identity, with civil rights, and with the idea of social progress.

All those elements have been on the base of the principal axes of conflict in the twentieth century: imperialism, self-determination, xenophobia and racism, the separation of church and state, religious conflict, the founding of pluralist societies with no single definition of *good* and *evil,* mass migration, discrimination on grounds of gender or sexual orientation, and the struggle against social inequalities. In many places, scouting looks like supporting the status quo in the main spheres of society, upholding the legitimacy of the state, national commitment and religious loyalty. But this reality, most likely base of the social support scouting receives, has also another side in the inevitable conflict that occurs when the ethical principles of its members contradict the official view in cases that surpass acceptable limits of dissonance, like when the legitimate State power discriminates, or when national identity is used to attack others, or when religious denominations act in a sectarian or fundamentalist way.

On these cases, the standing and claims of individuals have been the driving force for social change. The United States of America, a highly diverse society able to produce both a long-lasting legal racial segregation and an internationally leading civil rights movement, holds similar controversies on its scouting experience. It might be useful to get to know better this case before going on.

2.1. SCOUTING IN THE UNITED STATES: CONTROVERSIES AND CULTURE WAR

The adoption of scouting by other organizations, including religious ones, is mentioned in the very first edition of *Scouting for Boys* in 1908. The introduction, addressed to "instructors," says: "the [scout] system is applicable to existing organisations such as schools, boy's brigades, cadet corps, etc., or can supply a simple organisation of its own where these do not exist."[49] The founding of the Boy Scouts Association UK, however, meant that the alternative ("to supply a simple organisation of its own") was put into practice and organizations wanting to apply the scout method were then subject to decisions made by the scout association. This difference is very important. If the model had been maintained whereby a book inspired a method called scouting in which each group or organization had absolute freedom as to how to apply it, we could not discuss scouting as a defined organizational subject; we would have to refer to it as a more or less defined educational system. However, the creation of a legitimate organization to set the standards, first in Britain (1909) and then throughout the world (1920), forced associations who wanted to employ the scout method to do so in accordance with the methodological and ideological guidelines of the scout movement.

There is one exception to this: Boy Scouts of America (BSA), founded in 1910 and that in 1920 became founder of WOSM. This is the only association that has always had a system in which sponsors ("chartered organizations") are responsible for much of the program's implementation, in some cases even down to the selection of Scoutmasters. Kunz defined this model of scouting sponsorship as a special case of interorganizational relations where the sponsored organization uses other organizations to implement its program at a basic level.[50] The big advantage of this model lies on its fast spread and strong roots; the disadvantage lies when the weight of the sponsor organizations' ideological vision conditions the one of the scout association. The parallel history of development of the two US associations of scouting, Boy Scouts of America (BSA) and Girl Scouts of the USA (GSUSA), as well as their problematic interaction, is much more than a simple domestic issue for world scouting.

In the conflict between the values and practices of the scout movement worldwide, three reasons suggest to analyze the particular case of the United States of America. First, because of the large amount of influence that the two US associations (BSA and GSUSA) have in WOSM and WAGGGS, including in the international debate on gender education and on a potential common future for the two world organizations. Second, for the social implications of BSA's explicit discriminatory policy on grounds of sexual orientation and religious belief, in a society where an extremely active culture war is going on. And finally, and as a result of the previous reason, for the influence that US scouting has, through global mass media, on the image of scouting worldwide.

Just as the network operation of the scout movement is complex to grasp when analyzing it as an organization, the same difficulty occurs on a national scale: all too often the dynamics of national scout associations are confused with the practices carried out by their scout groups. The historian Ben Jordan, for example, has shown how the BSA tended to educate children separately on the basis of age, gender, race, or social class during its first 20 years (1910–1930)—despite claiming to be "open to all boys"—although it was pushed toward more inclusive policies after pressure from its own scout units.[51]

Because of this, rather than analyzing the broad spectrum of individual units in US scouting, we will try to examine the official policies of the two national associations to see their impact on scouting globally. It is important to keep in mind that the United States is the country with the third highest population in the world, though it is still a long way behind the two leaders: China and India. As such, the two US associations (BSA and GSUSA) exert a considerable influence on the two world organizations (WOSM and WAGGGS), both in censuses—total numbers—and fees—which are weighted according to GDP—as well as for their impact on ideology and world strategy, as aforesaid.

According to the World Scout Bureau (2011), the BSA has almost 6 million members, representing 22 percent of the world census of WOSM, and its fees make up 39 percent of WOSM's total income from this budget heading worldwide. Additionally, a large proportion of the funds of the World Scout Foundation come from donors linked to the BSA. Also of weighty importance, GSUSA contributes 3.2 million members to the WAGGGS census, representing 31 percent of the total, and this figure increases when it comes to finances: 50 percent of WAGGGS' world income from fees comes from the US association.[52] The weight of US associations in the budgets of WOSM and WAGGGS gives them an important influence on the respective world organizations, even higher to that of the United States of America in the United Nations, where its financial contribution accounts for 22 percent of the total budget, the highest one.[53]

Before delving in more deeply, a bit of history: the BSA was founded in 1910 by the Chicago multimillionaire publisher and philanthropist William D. Boyce, with Ernest T. Seton as first Chief Scout, and run after 1911 and for three decades by James E. West as Chief Scout Executive. West was a former executive of the Young Men's Christian Association (YMCA)[54] the main office of which became BSA's first national headquarters. In that same year, the YMCA organized 400 summer camps, which were attended by 15,000 boys. In 1911, one year after its creation, the BSA had printed 300,000 copies of its *Handbook for Boys*. The following year, it was present in every state of America.[55] Based on the already mentioned sponsorship system, the *Church of Jesus Christ of Latter-day Saints* (the Mormons) was the first religious "chartered organization" to adopt scouting as its official youth program in the United States (1913), as part of the church Mutual Improvement Association program for young men.

Since its beginning the BSA embodied a typically American patriotism, with the president of the United States serving as the association's honorary president. In June 1916, the US Congress approved a *Federal Charter* for BSA, recognizing its important contributions to the country and giving exclusivity to the name "boy-scout."[56] It also had the support of distinguished scholars. To James West, the bureaucratization of the BSA was a way to provide efficiency and standardization, that is, good administration.[57]

The girls' association, GSUSA, was founded in 1912 by Juliette G. Low, an American woman from Georgia who embraced the outdoors, the arts, and was known for standing on her head. After meeting Baden-Powell she devoted all her energies to developing the idea of scouting for girls. The model for girls encouraged them prepare not only for traditional homemaking, but also for possible future roles as professionals and for active citizenship outside the home. Additionally, girl scouting welcomed girls with disabilities—an idea that seemed quite natural to Low, who had remained active in life despite grappling with deafness, back problems and cancer. As with the BSA—albeit 34 years later, in 1950—Congress approved a Federal Charter for the Girl Scouts.[58] Since the beginning, though, relations between the two associations were not easy: although James West tried actively to avoid GSUSA to use the term "scout,"[59] the girl scouts insisted on their right to use it[60]—and they won.[61]

Both associations, from their different origins, succeeded in making American scouting a popular and widely practiced pastime, and garnered plenty of societal support. The tradition of male and female scouting in the United States has made this movement an all-American product that society considers to be homegrown. As a result, the two associations have received much private funding. An example of this is the 50–50 transfer of rights to BSA and GSUSA of "God Bless America," a peace song by the exiled Jewish composer Irving Berlin popularized in the US in 1938 during Hitler's rise to power in Europe.

Yet, while both associations are regarded as "all-American," their practices over the last 40 years have placed them at quite divergent places on the spectrum of social values. Both BSA and GSUSA went through an important decline of membership in the 1970s, and according to Barbara Arneil, the reason for that decline lies in the rejection by the civil rights generation of many of the traditionalist norms on which American scouting was based. Nevertheless, that decline was reversed in GSUSA in the 1980s, whereas BSA continued decreasing. It seems to Arneil that this is consequence of the different responses the two associations gave to the critical juncture of the civil rights generation: the willingness and effort of GSUSA to adapt to the challenges posed by this new generation, in contrast with the reaction of BSA, which rejected change in favour of keeping faith with its traditional views.[62]

It seems that GSUSA has been more sensitive on discrimination. From the 1970s onward, when the women's rights movement was starting to take off, the association began to adopt approaches favoring the movement, including the incorporation of the intellectual and feminist leader Betty Friedan on its National Board. And when GSUSA was sued in 1992 because the duty to serve God in the Promise breached the freedoms established in the US Constitution, it reacted by setting in motion a process of change that was completed a year later and subsequently allowed girls to change the term "God" for another that fitted better with their individual beliefs, a formula adopted by other countries.[63] Additionally, unlike BSA, GSUSA upholds the view that issues surrounding sexuality are a matter for girls and their parents. They therefore adopt no official stance on homosexuality, although they do not accept the discrimination of individuals because of their sexual orientation.[64]

Furthermore, nowadays, despite a long history of close contact with American society and the citizenship education of countless generations, the BSA has been surrounded by the controversy over its official discriminatory policy against homosexuals—as well as against atheists—in a country with a huge social disparity of opinions on those topics. In actual fact, as Jay Mechling notes, the BSA said nothing about sexual orientation until early 1980s.[65] The controversial manner in which BSA executives have dealt with issues concerning homosexuality and atheism is not dissociated from its very unique model of operation.

As it has been mentioned, the BSA is the only scout case in which the association does not carry out activities directly; instead, "chartered organizations" do it. They include schools, religious congregations, parent's associations, groups of citizens, Rotary or Lion clubs, and even fire stations, and they are chartered to provide the scout program for the neighborhood, are responsible for the meeting place, and in some cases have oversight of the volunteer leaders. Although the BSA provides the general program, inter-unit activities, professional support and information, trains leaders, and teaches the volunteers in charge, the chartered organization[66] is similar to a franchise, and in cases like the Mormons it might even select the leaders. As Nagy explains, this relationship means that the chartered partner is responsible for the effective implementation of the programs and activities, although the values and method references, quality control, and adherence to standards are overseen by the BSA.[67] This manner of operation can, of course, create a conflict of interest between the principles of scouting and those of the chartered partner, and vice versa. But at the same time, for BSA the chartered partners have always been an essential priority.

The Mormon (LDS) and Catholic Churches as chartered organizations together represent one fifth of all BSA members.[68] In fact, BSA's relationship with Christian religious institutions is at the same time one of dependence and a strategic bid, since it sees in these religious institutions the biggest "market" for its growth.[69] To illustrate this point, since 1913 the Mormon Church has posited its *own* youth organization in the BSA;[70] in other words, as a chartered partner of the BSA, the church's youth activities are carried out through BSA units sponsored by the church. As a result, the Mormons, a church representing less than 2 percent of America's total population—and which has practiced racial discrimination and rejects homosexuality as immoral—now makes up more than 13 percent of BSA's membership. In 1974, for example, the discriminatory doctrine of the Mormon Church against African Americans led to a dispute of the National Association for the Advancement of Colored People (NAACP) against BSA and the LSD, because although the scout association did not have an official policy on racial discrimination, the groups sponsored by the Mormon Church did.[71] The case was settled and the BSA was under a court order to not discriminate on the basis of race.

A deeper analysis of the case of the Mormon Church within BSA could lead to the conclusion that it has similar incompatibilities than the ones we saw in the case of the discriminatory self-styled *Scouts d'Europe*. Like it happens with the ultraconservatives fake scouts in Europe, the Mormon Church has a very instrumental view of scouting, stating: "Scouting is about learning and living the gospel. Scouting prepares boys to become righteous men who hold and honor the priesthood of God. Scout leaders have the responsibility to help each boy connect what he is learning in Scouting to his priesthood preparation and his future as a covenant keeping missionary, husband, and father."[72] Furthermore, the Mormon Church also sees scouting as a way of educating future priests, instead of a way to train autonomous individuals: "Scouting is part of the Aaronic Priesthood activity program. The Duty to God Award is a priesthood award, having requirements that will help young men develop spiritually and fulfill their priesthood duties."[73]

The fact that the BSA was complicit in allowing the LDS and others to practice racial discrimination, even after 1968, when all forms of segregation had already been declared unconstitutional by the Supreme Court, and despite the association's stated openness to all, highlights that it is not always the scouting principles that prevail in this complex relationship.[74] Actually, many of the chartered partners of the BSA have traditionally been denominational institutions—churches and groups with religious affiliations. As revealed in a 1969 article by the sociologist Phillip Kunz, and, though he considers it an efficient model—"large-scale organizations could avoid many organizational costs by using the device of sponsorship"—, he also warns that a weakness of the *sponsorship* model "seems to be its inability to accommodate a beneficiary organization to a very pluralistic society."[75]

The inflexible stance of the BSA Board is further strengthened by the values expressed by some of the chartered partners that support units.

One example of this is the expulsion of children who confessed to be nonbelievers in Virginia in April 1985, for saying that they did not believe in God. This was followed by similar events in Chicago and California in 1991, with the expulsion of children aged 8 and 9 years for the same reason.[76]

More famously, the policy of BSA to exclude members for their sexual orientation has resulted in a number of legal cases since 1980, the largest and most notorious one being the expulsion of a young New Jersey Assistant Scoutmaster, James Dale, from the BSA in 1993 for being identified as a homosexual through his membership of a Gay association at his university. Merely belonging to this association was seen as grounds to exclude him from the BSA, using the argument that homosexual conduct is inconsistent with the "traditional" values espoused in the Scout Promise and Law and that an avowed homosexual cannot serve as a role model for those values.

Dale, an Eagle Scout, filed suit against the BSA for violating New Jersey's antidiscrimination laws. Eventually, the New Jersey Supreme Court ruled in Dale's favor. And he won the case. Nevertheless, BSA appealed again in 2000 to the Supreme Court of the United States and won by a very narrow 5 votes to 4 in the much-publicized *Boy Scouts of America v. Dale* case.[77] While the Mormon and Catholic Churches supported the discriminatory stance of BSA, other sponsors such as one arm of the Methodist Church or the Unitarian Universalist Church came out in defense of the antidiscrimination law.[78]

In April 2001, the Presidents of nine big BSA councils (New York, Los Angeles, West Los Angeles, Chicago, San Francisco, Philadelphia, Minneapolis, Boston and Orange County CA), also members of the BSA National Council, presented a resolution on matters of sexuality for consideration at the Annual Meeting of Boy Scouts of America on June 1, 2001, asking it to change its member-admission policy not to exclude anyone on the grounds of sexual orientation. Particularly, the resolution included the statement "Membership and adult leadership positions in the Boy Scouts of America are open to persons regardless of their sexual orientation, subject to compliance with Scouting's standards of conduct. The Boy Scouts of America does not inquire about the sexual orientation of its members and adult leaders, nor does it inquire about the sexual orientation of prospective members and adult leaders in the course of recruitment and registration."[79]

For those council presidents, the US Supreme Court's decision to allow the BSA to determine its own fate on the issue of membership and leadership standards did not validate the BSA position of prohibition of homosexuals from membership and adult leadership roles: however it did validate the BSA's legal right to take that position if it chooses to do so. "Now that the legal right to determine our own membership and leadership standards has been confirmed"—the background document supporting the resolution stated—"we should broaden the discussion among our constituency and our professional and volunteer leadership as to what the best standards and policies are for the future. Many of us believe we should adopt a policy that preserves the right to self-determination on these issues at the sponsoring Chartered Organization and Unit Committee level." And goes on: "Prohibitions against sexual misconduct, advocating a homosexual lifestyle, or condemning a homosexual lifestyle should be maintained just as we maintain a prohibition against advocating a particular religious faith or political position. We should not allow the BSA to be polarized by these issues."

The international repercussions of this BSA policy, particularly on the image of scouting in Europe, led most European associations of WOSM and WAGGGS, meeting at the European Scout and Guide Conferences in July 2001, to adopt the following resolution:

The Conference

- considering that society is evolving;
- recognising that Scouting has always followed the evolution of society in so far as it remains compatible with its fundamental principles;
- noting that homosexuality is generally recognised and admitted in European society;

recommends that National Scout Organizations not consider homosexuality a reason for any kind of discrimination within or outside Scouting/Guiding.[80]

By 2002, 25 BSA councils were asking BSA to allow *local councils* to formulate their own policies on membership regarding individual's sexual orientation.[81] Despite the social pressure that these public entreaties created[82] the BSA National Executive Board reiterated its defense of its current policy of excluding homosexuals and atheists in a resolution of February 2002.[83]

However, it is worth noting that, beyond any moral considerations, the beginnings of the whole controversy over the discrimination for sexual orientation probably has more than a little to do with the identifications some of the public make between homosexuality and the abuse of minors and pederasty. In fact, and similarly to what happened to the Catholic Church, BSA faced in 1980s some reports for child abuse committed in the 1960s and 1970s—and it still does. In 1991 the *Washington Times* did probably the most thorough study on abuse committed within BSA, that culminated in 1994 with a book authored by the main journalist involved, Patrick Boyle. The vast sums of money paid out by BSA during the 1980s to avoid abuse scandals discovered from the 60s and 70s suggests concern about the possibility of abuse and the implications this would have for the organization.[84] Boyle's data make it clear that there is no connection whatsoever between child abuse and homosexuality—in fact, what the study shows is that abusers were often abused themselves as children; however, Mechling suggests that, by barring entry to homosexuals, the BSA wrongly also thought that it was excluding the majority of pedophiles from among its leaders.[85]

The controversy generated by the decision in the Dale case in 2000 surpassed the radicalizing limits of the public stance of the BSA defending their right to refuse membership to homosexuals and atheists, to the point that various public and private institutions withdrew their financial support and tried to take away their public protection.[86] As Mechling explains, the BSA's inability to react and adapt to social changes in the same way as GSUSA did is due to the historical connection between Christianity and an aggressive view of masculinity, reinforced by the BSA's ties with the strong religious culture that gripped the United States in the 1950s: "the religious conservatives who control the national office of the BSA see themselves as important troops in the culture wars" for religion and masculinity, whereas "the Girl Scouts, quite simply, have no stake in the masculinity part of the tangle."[87]

Thus, in the "culture war," a battle over moral authority and values, Mechling believes that BSA clearly took sides. Citing sociologist J.D. Hunter, he explains how we are seeing polarizing forces coming from two sides. On one side, the "orthodox" Americans—mostly conservatives and moral traditionalists—maintain that moral authority lies in an external, definable, and transcendent authority. On the other side of the spectrum, "progressive" Americans—mostly liberals and cultural progressives—believe that moral authority is not set in stone and that this area tends to re-embody historic faiths according to the prevailing assumptions of contemporary life. For Hunter and other culture-war theorists, these categories, which extend beyond religious traditions, deal with a new element of identity on which personal political positions are based, one that does not end with gender, race, social class or religious tradition. The abandonment by BSA executives of the project of maintaining a nonpartisan balance between reverence and tolerance, Mechling states, even made BSA to actively punish religious members whose opinions on homosexuality and atheism departed from the more conservative views.[88]

To Mechling, "the Boy Scouts [of America] was 'nondenominational', to be sure, and there were religious badges representing each major religious group. But 'nondenominational' could not include agnosticism or atheism in 1950s America, for 'nondenominational' meant only that no one religious denomination could impose its theology and practices upon the organization. Boys from all faiths were free to join the organization, but 'faith' was the key. A boy had to have a faith, for atheism—and probably agnosticism—was the characteristic of Communists, our sworn enemies."[89]

Supporting the idea of a "culture war," though glossing over the considerations, legal scholar Madhavi Sunder puts forth a carefully thought out perspective on the BSA v. Dale polemic in her extensive article *Cultural Dissent*. On it, she states that the view of culture as static, imposed, homogeneous and unitary is anthropologically incorrect. And she precisely argues that the battle over the interpretation of the texts during the trial was between those trying to prove that the BSA was genuinely an institution against homosexuality and those attempting to show that traditionally it did not have a clear stance on the issue.

Sunder believes that, regardless of the BSA's true position on homosexuality, what matters most is not what it could be understood from historical documents, but rather what the present-day members of the BSA—and not merely its executives—decide, as the nine members of the BSA National Council claimed in their 2001 resolution proposal. If society has changed, and the members of the association have changed along with it, therefore, the association's stance should be able to change as well. Otherwise, the members must only choose between "loyalty" or "exit." When, in the context of a debate over cultural views in an association, the Supreme Court, rather than the association's members, decides which view must prevail, the law is effectively acting as a defender of cultural groups against the dynamics of modernization and change.

In trying to discern the BSA's view on its members' sexual orientation, Sunder states, the Supreme Court could make the association impenetrable to the organic transformation that may have been happening within. Thus, she states, "legally enforced cultural boundaries could, conceivably, accord powerful members of cultural groups the ability to suppress *any rumblings* for change in a culture, particularly by censoring or excluding those members who challenge power relationships within a culture and threaten the status quo."[90] The debate on whether the courts could impose a vision to the internal debate of an association has several consequences. On the exclusion of atheists, for instance, Weinberg states that a court has no right to impose a different belief system on the BSA, although he also points out that "the question of whether the BSA has the right to exclude nonbelievers from their membership is an incredibly complex issue that implicates almost every First Amendment question possible."[91]

In the polemic around BSA we see again the tension between the "movement" and the organization," because the discriminatory stance of the BSA's National Executive Board does not make its local realities a discriminatory movement. As Mechling explains, the BSA as a legal corporation is not necessarily the "real" scouting of the very diverse scout units. Along the same line as the observations of Parsons and as the cited study *The Educational Impact of Scouting*, Mechling points out that many groups "define themselves proudly as different from (and superior to) the national or council office, especially when they think the national office has strayed from the basic message of the Boy Scouts."[92] Exactly alike that the study shows it happens with the European adolescent scouts, that extracted the coherence of the suggested values with the practices: critical thinking, or in Baden-Powell's words, "individual power of judgement." For example, the main network for the abolition of discrimination in the BSA, *Scouting for All*, was launched by individual members of the BSA. The network encourages resistance with a badge that all scouts can sew on to their uniform to show their rejection of the official discriminatory policy. "Eagle scouts and other who have been critical of the BSA's exclusionary policies say that the BSA they value is the one that teaches tolerance and inclusion; they accuse the present BSA leadership of departing from these fundamental principles of Scouting."[93]

Many contributions note the huge potential of the scout movement in the US in contrast with the organization's resistance to change, like a book by the *New York Times* journalist Peter Applebome. After spending time on camps with his son's group, Applebome highlighted and applauded the positive impact of scouting's educational undertakings but made it clear that the BSA has to change if it does not want to find itself caught up in a downward spiral. On that, he suggests to face key measures such as ending discrimination, finding dynamic leaders, getting rid of the traditional uniforms, embracing diversity, and increasing commitment to community services.[94]

The foundation for a scout association equipped to face the challenges of today's American society does exist. And very important inclusionary work is implemented every day in its thousands of scout units. While it does certainly have strength in numbers, its members come from an increasingly diverse variety of backgrounds—75 percent of the 80,000 scouts in Los Angeles were from minority groups, mainly African American, Latino, and Asian communities, and 92 percent of these came from single-parent families.[95] The BSA has had a successful African

American President, as GSUSA had, and today has as one of its driving forces the reaching of the Hispanic youth population and a considerable effort is being embedded on it. However, it is unclear whether this necessary evolution, which is already happening organically within the movement, will spread to an increasing acceptance of plurality and of social values evolution. Bureaucracy is resistant to change, and especially it seems so that of the BSA, reinforced both by the powerful influence of two churches that control many BSA units, and by the legal blockade produced by the inflexible position of the Supreme Court, which has been used by BSA national executives to oppose the members who legitimately wants a more open association according to its society.

2.2. SPIRITUAL DIMENSION AND DEPENDENCE FROM DENOMINATIONS

Whereas scouting worldwide opted for the model of forming its own associations instead of chartering others, it always sought the cooperation of civic institutions, associations, parishes, and schools to promote the movement, and it is this model that has made it so strong. The model is based on a symbiosis, in the sense that some of the principles of the collaborating institution are implemented through the principles of the scout movement. The prevalence of the principles and characteristics of scouting over those of the institutions that collaborate with it has been—and is still—a very contentious subject. Although there have been instances where a public institution has tried to use scouting as a way to transmit the ideology of the regime in question, this problem has occurred and still occurs today mainly with religious institutions. According to Allan Warren, "in almost every national association there had been a tension between those who saw Scouting and Guiding as an attractive, informal educational youth program supporting evangelism and church survival, and those for whom the less dogmatic concept of 'spiritual' growth was only one of the critical elements within a comprehensive program of personal development, that would ultimately enable the young adult to make an individual decision about faith and worship."[96]

"Duty to God" is certainly one of the three main principles of world scouting, and as we have seen, it could be defined as "Adherence to spiritual principles, loyalty to the religion that expresses them and acceptance of the duties resulting therefrom,"[97] or even more plainly, as "a person's relationship with the spiritual values of life, the fundamental belief in a force above mankind,"[98] in WOSM wording; or as WAGGGS states, it could be understood as "Acknowledgement and search for spirituality."[99] Therefore, it is a role of scouting to contribute to the individual's spiritual development. Moreover, according to Nagy, a main role of spirituality in scouting is to encourage solidarity on a world scale, so the future of the movement does not lie in the debate between religious or nonreligious morals, but in finding the path to encourage "truly universal solidarity and brotherhood."[100]

Robert Baden-Powell, in his address to the 1926 Joint Conference of Scout and Guide Commissioners, stated that "Our object in the Scout movement is to give such help as we can in bringing about God's Kingdom on earth by inculcating among youth the spirit and the daily practice in their lives of unselfish goodwill and co-operation"; and he added that "By the term 'God's Kingdom' I mean *the prevalence of love in the world in the place of dominance of selfish interest and rivalry such as at present exists.*"[101]

Spiritual dimension and religion are not the same. As Raül Adroher explains, human beings need to find a rational explanation for what they do, beyond just *magic*. This search for meaning—not simply magic, not merely rational—is what shapes each person, what makes her unique and gives her personality. "Searching, thinking, living, doubting, deciding": this is the realm of the *spiritual dimension.*[102] At the same time, the logical result of the search for meaning is the creation of several deeply rooted ideologies and beliefs that have had a market effect on certain aspects of culture: *religions*, as complete ideological systems, offer a key to meaning. And churches are the organizations that believers create in order to develop those systems.

Certainly, the Boy Scouts Association founded by Baden-Powell in England took on the role of religion and churches on the spiritual development of youth, as later happened when the world organization was created. However, the interpretation on what the role of religion in scouting should be diverges when it is in hands of an open scout association or when an association that depends of a particular religious denomination does it.

The British model of scout association established in 1909 assumed that the full range of beliefs are covered by a single association and that no church or confession should be above any other in the association—besides the option of setting up internal committees for a given confession. When the movement expanded all over the world, this model was adopted by almost 90 percent of WOSM and WAGGGS member associations, and it is currently the organizational basis of world scouting. However, in the 1920s the Catholic church pushed to have its own Catholic scout associations, an inclination toward religious particularism which led to the creation of associations linked to a single religion. In Nagy's words, this was mainly caused "by the inflexibility of various religious leaders who found it hard to accept the universal and ecumenical character of Scouting, which regarded all religions as means of satisfying the spiritual needs of youth"[103]. The roots for this tension are found in early-century France, which, in December 1905, passed its Law on the Separation of Church and State.[104] In 1911, before the world organization of scouting was established, the association Éclaireurs de France was set up: it was specifically a *laïque*[105] (secular) association, and whereas its Promise made no mention of God, it was clear that it adopted the British *scout* method—*éclaireur* is regarded as a synonym for *scout* in French. That same year saw the creation of the Éclaireurs Unionistes de France, a Protestant association backed by a leader of the Unions Chrétiennes de Jeunes Gens, the equivalent of the YMCA.[106] This is how France came to have both a specifically *laïque* association—that is, one that did not carry out religious activities of any kind, unlike the British association—and a denominational association, i.e. explicitly linked to a church—also unlike the British case, which did not depend on any other institution.

The Catholic Church was initially cautious about scouting, mainly because it was a movement of English origins that also contained elements reminiscent of Freemasonry: just as the Freemasons establish that members must believe in a supreme being, obey the laws of God and men, and extend charity and brotherly love, the principles of scouting established that the scout had to believe in God, be loyal to the King, and always help others. Nonetheless, in the 1920s, the Catholics finally conceded although adopting as in the French Protestant case the single religion association model.[107] The Vatican therefore began to promote the creation of separate Catholic "scout" associations, under the direct responsibility of Catholic dioceses, in countries where open associations already existed. "Many considered this step as 'spiritual imperialism' contrary to the universal basis of Scouting as well as dissidence or even an attempt to attract potential priests," says Nagy.[108] The first case was the Associazione Scouts Cattolici Italiani in 1916; it was followed by the Scouts de France (1920, and by the Guides de France in 1923), the Portuguese Corpo Nacional de Escutas-Escutismo Católico Português (1923), and the Catholic Boy Scouts of Ireland (1927). Although the Vatican officially recognized the educational value of scouting in the 1930s, it did so referring to the model of separate Catholic scout associations, one that was maintained in many French-speaking countries after decolonization and adopted in a number of other cases after World War II, as Spain, Argentina, Chile, and Uruguay in the 1960s. In all of the above instances, Catholic groups split from the recognized scout organization and set up a separate one.[109] But in later more recent cases, as Benin and Guinea in the 1990s, the possibility to create new denominational (Catholic) associations was rejected by the world organization.[110] Notwithstanding, the future might bring other changes among the few existing denominational associations. In the last decade, for instance, in Belgium whereas the *laïque* French-speaking scout association became pluralist, the two WOSM Catholic ones have become open, as a response to the changes happened in their increasingly diverse societies and the need to be certainly open to everybody.

It was because of France's separation of *laïque* and denominational scouting, as opposed to the British model of one, non-denominational type of scouting with religious inspiration, that the Boy Scouts International Bureau (WOSM) accepted federations when it was formalized in 1920. At the Second International Scout Conference, held in Paris in 1922, one of the hot topics of the new constitutional framework, which was to transform the Constitution into a tool to prevent fragmentation and dissidence, was whether international recognition could only be granted to single associations, as in Britain, or to federations of associations, as in France. This was when "all national Associations were recognized without any preconditions, as had been promised two years earlier in London. This meant that in some of the founder countries, secular Associations without any explicit reference to service to God were accepted."[111] Nonetheless, the subsequent 1924 Conference passed the resolution quoted earlier on scouting principles, which included a comforting reference for those who saw both the acceptance of *laïque* and secular scouting and the existence of associations not linked to any religion as the start of an agnostic or atheistic departure, despite making it clear that there was no room for a clash between religions.[112]

This situation has generated tensions at different points in the past. In their book on *laïque* French scouting, Kergomard and François note that an attempt was made in 1949, at the twelfth International Scout Conference, to exclude from WOSM those associations with Promises that did not mention God or religion.[113] Although this is not recorded in the official Conference Report, it does appear in an internal report written by the British delegate to the conference, a copy of which is kept in the archives of the World Scout Bureau. In it, he explains that the Dutch association submitted a document on scouting and religion, which led as a negative reaction to a resolution proposal stating that: "Since the Scout promise is the basis of all our Scoutwork it is essential that all Associations registered as members of the Conference should accept the Scout Promise of Duty to God (or to my religion). Those Associations which do not accept this Scout principle cannot be regarded as members of our International Scout Movement."[114]

Although the British report does not say so, Kergomard and François note that the greatest pressure at the 1949 Conference to exclude associations was brought to bear by the US delegation. The French authors notices that the *laïque* and "open" associations with no-denominational links were mainly from European countries at the time: Belgium, France, Italy, Luxembourg, and Netherlands, and claimed that "they were subject to a three-day attack orchestrated by the American [BSA] delegation. In a private conversation, the leader of this delegation stated that the Éclaireurs de France were atheists and hence, communists."[115] Although the position taken by the French delegate, Pierre François, was that his association could not accept a mandate like the one being proposed, voting went ahead regardless with the result of 72 votes for and 72 against. The Canadian Chair of the meeting voted against and it was finally agreed to remove the resolution from the minutes and pretend that it had never existed. But it *did* exist: as Colquhoun, the UK scouting delegate, says in his report, "At any rate, there is no doubt that the International Committee will watch the position of future applicants for membership most carefully."[116] And this is just what happened: to date, there has been no backing down with regard to the official view that scouting and belief are inseparable, even though the existence of *laïque* scouting proves that the formula can be overlooked keeping the commitment to educate the spiritual dimension without scouting losing its identity.

On top of that, tensions toward a more clear "religious" scouting, consequence of the mentioned separation of Catholic associations in some countries, had jeopardized the world organization in 1948 when the International Catholic Scouters Conference (ICSC) was established for Catholic scout associations and the Catholic offices of open associations. To prevent the split that had occurred in some countries from spreading worldwide and thus preserve the unity of the movement, in 1962 (the same year that the Vatican approved the Statutes and Constitution of the ICSC), the World Scout Committee (WOSM) gave the ICSC *consultative status*, as it would later do with two other similar entities of Muslim and of Orthodox; Jewish, Buddhist, and Won-Buddhist platforms also exist. The World Committee must approve the consultative status of an entity, and they are a way of avoiding unidenominational splintering and maintaining different religious approaches in the same movement. On the basis of religious criteria, these platforms assist national scout associations (i.e., members of world scouting) linked to a single denomination, whether as an association or a religious secretariat in an open association. Its role is to provide a framework in which to share their common beliefs, although they might also alter the unity of the movement when trying to be representatives instead of supply of resources.

Besides, in 1983, seven French-speaking *laïque* scout associations (three European and five African) set up the Coopération Francophone du Scoutisme Laïque (French Cooperation of *Laïque* Scouting, COFRASL), to organize a formal network of development cooperation activities. Regardless of that aim, the experience began to stir the interest of other European scouts associations working on the spiritual dimension from a nonreligious perspective, which were considered *laïque, pluralist,*[117] or even *open,* depending on their language. Some of them promoted the creation of an international network of non-denominational scouting, set up in 1996: the Union Internationale des Associations Scoutes-Guides Pluralistes/Laïques, though the enterprise did not have continuity after few years.[118]

A number of initiatives have been developed to encourage interreligious dialogue within scouting. All the seven quoted denominational groups around WOSM work together since 1997 as a World Scout Interreligious Forum, to organize and run interreligious activities in world scout events, to promote understanding, tolerance and peace. Actually, all this shows how the spiritual dimension in scouting is not only a tool for the integral education of young people. It should also be a tool to avoid exclusion, sectarianism, and fanaticism. And the interreligious dialogue, as well as interaction from different believes, are tools for that purpose. Similarly of its interaction with national identity, scouting does not diminish religious beliefs, on the contrary: it promotes that people live their beliefs intensely; nonetheless, it limits the beliefs with the right of the others to have their own beliefs and their own vision on how society should be, according with these beliefs. That is why no moral authority outside scouting, no single vision on what is good and evil, should be over another within the movement. As the cited document says, "the spiritual dimension in Scouting unifies people and should not divide them. A *true* Scout activity (and the same applies to a *true* religious activity) should give birth to or reinforce a feeling of tolerance, respect and understanding of the faith of others."[119] Religion and spiritual dimension in scouting should, therefore, be compatible with the movement's independence, unity and inclusiveness.

An important example of that dialogue was an initiative promoted by the European joint conference of the WOSM and the WAGGGS regions in 1983, that created a six-year ad hoc Working Group on the Spiritual Dimension on Scouting and Guiding, with six members representing spiritual traditions of scouting: a British Catholic priest, a Greek Orthodox woman, a French Jew woman, a Turkish Muslim man, a German Lutheran woman, and a Catalan agnostic man belonging to a *laïque* association. They stated that "the development of spiritual awareness must consist of wondering 'why'; wondering 'why not'; seeking meanings; and discovering values". They also added that "there are three kinds of possible relationship between Scouting/Guiding and the religious and spiritual families: Open associations; denominational associations; and *laïque* associations."[120]

Dialogue on spiritual dimension in scouting also benefits from this diversity. As Laszlo Nagy wrote in his 1967 influential "Report on World Scouting," "even secular morals are not free from any spirituality. In fact, such morals rest on a very wide and non-codified moral conception, that of 'honest people' and, in as far as it is not tied up with atheist militantism, it in no way threatens the spirituality of associations which consciously purvey the ideology of a revealed religion."[121] In other words, as Mechling observes when analyzing scouting, "there are many ways to be a good person besides the religious way."[122]

The development of this *spiritual awareness,* which is the role of the scout education in the spiritual dimension, is not based in indoctrination. Baden-Powell's approach on spiritual development was that it has to be "caught," not "taught," and further more, to him the best environment for this development was in the outdoors: "Nature study gives the most understandable and eagerly grasped method...We try to teach them through precepts and elementary theology, within school walls, while outside the sun is shining and Nature is calling to show them through their eyes, ears, noses and sense of touch, the wonders and beauties of the Creator."[123]

Spiritual dimension is therefore an integral part of the educational program of scouting. But spiritual dimension does not mean religious education: this is why in 2001, WOSM's document "Scouting and Spiritual Dimension" stated that "Scouting has its own way of introducing and developing spirituality and the spiritual dimension in young people."[124] As Dominic Bénard wrote, "in the area of spiritual development, the role of the Scout leader is not to give religious instruction, nor to tack religious observances onto Scout activities. It is to use the kind of experiences offered by Scouting to help young people discover a spiritual reality and incorporate it into their own lives."[125]

The move toward an institutional secularization that does not neglect spirituality happening in many societies coincides with WOSM's efforts in recent years to return to the original model of a single open association per country, fostering that the Catholic and open associations in countries like Ireland, Uruguay and Argentina merge into one. WOSM is also going for a vision where spiritual development in scouting is not externalized, but internalized, as explained in the *World Scouting Report 2006*, which states that for many years, the Scout Movement used to delegate responsibility for spiritual education to the religious denominations it was associated with. The ministers of these associated denominations were responsible for educating the Scouts, each according to his or her own religion. The religious part of the program was provided as an addition to Scout activities. With the new Program approach, the Scout Movement wishes to return to its original role, which consists of showing how recreational and educational activities can, in themselves, guide young people in their spiritual development.[126]

2.3. Social Values, Cultural Change, and Critical Thinking

The relationship of scouting with identities—religious ones, national ones—is at the same time fruitful and problematic. The scout movement, being an accommodator of multiple identities, also mitigates their excesses. Under the guise of the principle of nondiscrimination, the scout values are attacking the very core of identity essentialism to insist on the notion that no one nation is better than another, that no religion is above another, and that no race is superior to any other. If we take up the analysis of scouting in colonial Africa, we could say that the seed of equality is intrinsic to scouting and that this gave rise to a contradiction between the apparent dominant logic of the scout movement as an upholder of the status quo and its underlying ethics that encourage decolonization as a process that breaks racial barriers, stands up to discrimination, opposes fundamentalism and, in short, fights for justice.[127]

The values of scouting, that is, the values formulated for all the world from 1920 onward, are inclusive in nature: citizenship, which means responsibility in common life; nondiscrimination, which involves empathy, taking into account and acknowledging others; living together in peace, which requires prioritizing the dignity of human life over any conflict; and improving the present to build a more inclusive future. Why, then, has scouting so often been accused of having exclusionary values? First, because it cannot be isolated from the social reality and the prevailing values in each society; but also because it unavoidably interacts with two elements that border on the limit between inclusion and exclusion: nation and religion. Baden-Powell was well aware of this. In the past, he himself had transgressed the limit, as we can see in some of his pre – World War I writings praising the British Empire and the central role of Christianity, though on the contrary later on he acknowledged that "as in nationalism, so it is in religion. Support of one's own form of belief is a right and proper thing, but it becomes narrow sectarianism when it does not recognize and appreciate the good points in other denominations."[128]

Indeed, nation and religion, as a source of identity, can be both inclusive and exclusionary: inclusive when used to unite people and create a sense of community, and exclusionary when used to delimit who belong "inside" and keep others "outside."[129] Nation and religion can be used to keep those who are of the same identity, blood, origin and color away from those who are not; to separate those who believe from those who do not. Even if the identity politics of discriminated and threatened groups can be good tools for fighting against inequality and injustice, as Amartya Sen explains, identity politics can also be used—and often are used—by privileged groups with seek to suppress and terrorize others.[130]

When scouting was formalized at the world level, with Baden-Powell's explicit commitment (as *Chief Scout of the World*) to the values of the *League of Nations*,[131] the role of these key concepts of nation and religion took a new importance, becoming a tool rather than an obstacle for promoting the values we now call of global citizenship: an awareness of belonging to the world community, acceptance and respect for diversity, citizens' involvement with a will to serve others, the commitment to trying to leave the world "a little better than you find it."[132] As Fernando Reimers notices on global citizenship education, a universal commitment to global values, including to universal human rights and tolerance, is essential to prevent civilizational conflicts.[133] These global values of world scouting were summarized in the resolution (official statement) on the "Principles of Scouting," adopted by the second meeting of the International Scout Conference (1924), establishing the national, international, and universal character of the scout movement:

> The Boy Scouts International Conference declares that the Boy Scout Movement is a movement of national, international and universal character, the object of which is to endow each separate nation and the whole world with a youth which is physically, morally and spiritually strong. It is *national*, in that it aims through national organizations, at endowing every nation with useful and healthy citizens. It is *international* in that it recognizes no national barrier in the comradeship of the Scouts. It is *universal* in that it insists upon universal fraternity between all Scouts of every nation, class or creed. The Scout Movement has no tendency to weaken but, on the contrary, to strengthen individual religious belief. The Scout Law requires that a Scout shall truly and sincerely practice his religion, and the policy of the Movement forbids any kind of sectarian propaganda at mixed gatherings.[134]

The controversial duty to one's country and its institutions as well as to the religion one professes is therefore found in the scout principles. Hence, the two major elements of social identity, nation and religion, are a constitutive part of the scouting model of citizenship. Nevertheless, as it is shown on this resolution, the limits to the national reference are clear from the very start, both in the statement that "there is no national barrier in the comradeship of the Scouts," and in the fact that it "insists upon universal fraternity between all Scouts of every nation." The religious reference is also tinged when the resolution states that the policy of the scout movement "prohibits any kind of sectarian propaganda" at gatherings and meetings. Global values and tolerance, therefore, are on the core ideological fundaments of scouting, and not one of the resolutions passed by the respective world conferences in the more than 90 years since the two organizations were created contradicts these principles.

Furthermore, the commitment of scouting to the Universal Declaration of Human Rights and the UN Convention on the Rights of the Child is explicitly clear. Up to the point that a recent Statement of the World Scout Committee clarifies that "if any Scout leader finds himself or herself in a position where their personal convictions on any matter affecting human rights are inconsistent with Scouting's purpose, principles or method, as defined in the WOSM Constitution, and in particular the requirements of the Scout Promise and Law, or Scouting's commitment to universal human rights, the World Scout Committee calls on them to withdraw from their position in the Scout Movement." In that sense the statement reminds that, if necessary, the Committee could promote "the suspension or expulsion from membership of WOSM of any National Scout Organization whose actions place the reputation of the Scout Movement in jeopardy."[135]

If the shared values of human rights and the rights of the child are therefore clear, one of the most difficult elements of scouting's citizenship education model is delineating to what extent it should foster submission to the authority of political structures and institutions, or, to put it another way, how to know when it is time to question authority. Because of the fine balance between fostering citizenship and encouraging morally autonomous critical thinking, in the 90 years of world scouting there have been cases of incoherencies between values and practices. However, the majority of cases have not been connected to the aforementioned contradiction between loyalty to one's country/religion and the principles of fraternity/nondiscrimination, so much as connected to clashes between the values of scouting and the predominant values of their respective societies that were slowly changing.

The potential danger of transgressing the reasonable limits of patriotism and religion is continually monitored by the two world organizations, which have paid close attention to the interpretations made by national associations and have even withdrawn memberships when the balance could no longer be guaranteed. There is though one issue difficult to resolve and clearly contradictory: which position scouting should adopt when the legitimate authorities of a country are overthrown. If England had been invaded by Germany in World War I, Baden-Powell would have probably called for scouting to become a resistance movement, and today its narrative would be quite different.

Thus, the possible "incoherencies" in scouting practices in the past 90 years have not been because its values contradicted the global values of tolerance and peace; despite, they have aroused mainly because of the clash between its inclusive and nondiscriminatory nature and the prevailing social values and norms in each country on issues such as racial segregation, religious authority, the role of women, and sexual orientation. The human trend toward discrimination of difference is a permanent threat. On that, it is interesting to stress that a recent research explains that discrimination and stereotyping is a reaction to cope with chaos, a mental cleaning device in the face of "disorder"[136]—and difference; therefore, a matter for education.

If we analyze legal discrimination by race, now thankfully erased from the laws of every country in the world, we should notice it was an important issue in the last century. Decolonization generally ended this practice, with the exception of South Africa, the last country that had legally established racial segregation. The consequences of that segregation can be still witnessed today in both South Africa and the United States—which ended legal racial segregation in 1964, 20 years after the fall of the Nazi regime in Germany. In the BSA, the last council to drop the ban against African Americans was in 1942, and the last council to end segregation was in 1974. Looking at the role of scouting in South Africa, we see that it maintained its ideal of openness to all, and that as a result the association was multiracial. Certainly, it cannot be said that this meant multiracial coexistence in the groups, given that the legal separation extended to the association itself; nevertheless, in 1977 the South African scout association unanimously decided to dissolve the four racial branches of the association and make it multiracial and open to all as a whole, 13 years before the end of apartheid announced by President De Klerk.[137]

Whereas legal racial discrimination was decreasing throughout the last century until its disappearance, the case of the role of women is quite different and more socially pervasive: it deals with an inequality situation that, in one way or another, affects the entire planet. As revealed by the UN Development Report, women around the world work significantly longer hours than men, including many hours spent on non-remunerated activities. Notwithstanding, even in the developed world, women generally earn less than their male counterparts and spend more time on unpaid work. Poverty is the cause and result of much of the inequality that affects women, who account for 70 percent of poor people on the planet and possess just 10 percent of the wealth. Furthermore, women are visibly underrepresented in governments around the world, holding a very low percentage of ministerial positions.[138]

As we have seen, the active debate over the best way of working toward a society in which the role of women is not subordinate to that of men is still on the fundaments of the separation of scouting in two world organizations. Moreover, cultural, and sometimes legal, elements encourage the continued existence of national associations separated by gender. In particular, in countries where inequality between men and women is higher than average, or even with legal discrimination, the existence of a single association for women guarantees that, at all levels, decisions are made by women, which contributes to the formation of new generations of female leaders. This is the core argument of many female leaders in Arab countries, for example. A comparative research on changes in gender roles worldwide published in 2003 by sociologists Inglehart and Norris,[139] reveals that opinions on gender equality and sexual freedom represent the biggest gap between western and Muslim countries. Moreover, whereas each new generation is becoming more equal in the western world, this evolution is not observed in a relevant degree even among women themselves in most Muslim countries, although some recent changes in Northern African societies like Tunisia bring some signs of change.

A recent sociological research based on the World Values Surveys (WVS), starting in 1981, provides very useful data on how these "prevailing values" behave in different societies and on their evolution. The WVS were designed to provide a comprehensive measurement of all major areas of human concern, from religion to politics to economic and social life and two dimensions dominate the picture: Traditional/Secular-rational, and Survival/Self-expression values.[140] The relevance of that research lies in that it shows one value across multiple societies at four different times over the course of 20 years, allowing us to see the evolution of that value in both the same generation was well as between different age ranges. Though an anthropological approach could raise doubts about these findings because the same question from the survey could have different meanings to those surveyed from very distant cultures, the sociological analysis shows consistency on the responses over the years and generations and give clues for a better comprehension of world society.

The research covering four periods between 1981 and 2001, made by Inglehart and Welzel and published in *Modernization, Cultural Change, and Democracy* (2005), shows that much of the world is undergoing cultural change that is shifting values, although there are some social values that are deeply ingrained and do not vary significantly. In particular, findings show that the socioeconomic development of most countries has gradually reduced—to differing degrees—the restrictions on human autonomy, creativity, and freedom of choice, and has generated a two-dimensional cultural change: the secularization of authority, stemming from the industrial era; and the emancipation from authority, stemming from the postindustrial era. The results of this are a change in both social values and intergenerational values in approximately 80 countries—which make up 85 percent of the world's population—in aspects such as the acceptance of women's equal role in society, relativization of the sense of national pride, substitution of obedience to religious or civil authorities for increasing self-expression values, human freedom and choice, and a discreet but growing acceptance of homosexuality in some countries.[141]

Following this study, it is interesting to revise the interaction of scouting with certain values founded in religious beliefs, and in particular with religious authorities themselves. It is already been mentioned that most scout associations do not depend on a religious denomination, and so this situation arises mainly in Catholic countries, former colonies of the latter, and in Muslim countries—besides the US case of chartered partners. Nonetheless, these cases, which have strengthened the social roots of scouting throughout the twentieth century, could become a source of conflict if the evolution of social values contradicts the values defended in religious institutions on issues such as the role of women, the use of contraception to protect against AIDS or the discrimination of people for their sexual orientation in countries where these values are increasingly accepted.

One example was the 2006 Roverway event, a European scout camp of WOSM and WAGGGS for 5,000 young boys and girls, held near Florence (Italy). The camp was an official activity of the European region of the two world organizations hosted by the Italian Scout Federation, which belongs to WOSM and WAGGGS and contains two associations—a catholic one and a *laïque* one. When the camp commenced, the representatives of the Catholic association vetoed the participation of a lesbian association in an activity of Roverway in which several institutions would organize workshops to discuss sensitive issues: in this case, the proposed workshop was about homophobia.[142] Despite the tension that this decision caused, the link with the Catholic Church probably weighed far more heavily in this case's controversial decision.[143]

Nonetheless, according to the mentioned study on the World Values Survey, the expansion of the knowledge society has led to a gradual reduction in the authority of religious institutions in postindustrial societies over the last 20 years, though this has not meant the disappearance of spirituality; in fact, quite the contrary: "there is a shift from institutionally fixed forms of dogmatic religion to individually flexible forms of spiritual religion," the study reports. Thus, it seems that, in parallel with socioeconomic development, the role of religion is changing from institutionalized forms of dogmatic religiousness to an individual search for spirituality. Something not far from the approach of *Millennial Generation* American teenagers to what they understand by "religion": something that "helps them in knowing right from wrong, making good decisions, providing a sense of hope and purpose in life, navigating them to be moral and altruistic, and helping them get through hard circumstance," a thing also that is not necessarily attached to a particular denomination, and that could even be part of a "new Civil Religion."[144] These social changes could have further implications when the independence from the religious authority is not clear. Inglehart and Welzel make the point that the stability of democratic institutions does not depend on the society's degree of religiousness only if the religious authorities do not try to control the political system;[145] something that could also be applied to scout institutions, as the Italian case demonstrates.

When talking about discrimination and prevailing social values, the issue of homosexuality is perhaps the most conflictive of all in the disparity of values among different world societies, something we cannot forget when analyzing how scouting deals with it. The key difference between sexual orientation and other traditionally discriminated features, like gender and race, is that homosexuality could be seen as a *behavior*, which many times is condemned by religion or by prevailing social values. The study based on the World Values Survey reports that in 2001, of the 77 countries on which data is available, only in ten countries do less than 49 percent of the population disapprove of homosexuality. In most countries, the vast majority of the population—75–99 percent—disapprove of homosexuality. Furthermore, more than 70 countries prosecute its citizens on ground of their sexual orientation (even some US states did so until 2003), and five of them even have death penalty for sexual orientation: Iran, Mauritania, Saudi Arabia, Sudan and Yemen—plus some parts of Nigeria and Somalia. Nonetheless, in postindustrial societies the socioeconomic evolution is also leading to a change in perception. While in 1981 40 percent of the Netherland's population disapproved of homosexuality, by 2000 this number had gone down to 22 percent. The move toward greater tolerance can be observed to varying degrees in all of the world's societies, an increase in tolerance parallel to the increase in socioeconomic level. Thus, we see a decline in rejection from 50 percent to 26 percent in the more developed countries between 1981 and 2001.[146] Likewise, legislations are also evolving toward an inclusive approach, and not only in postindustrial societies: whereas some countries and even US states legalized same-sex marriage in the recent years, just in 2009 homosexuality was decriminalized in India, the second most populated country of the world. Furthermore, in 2010 the US Government has made two important steps to end discrimination for sexual orientation: first, the US President signed into law a bill repealing the "don't ask don't tell" law and allowing homosexuals to serve openly in the US military; and later, the Secretary of State publicly declared in the United Nations that "gay rights are human rights", and that the US Government will fight discrimination against gays and lesbians abroad by using foreign aid and diplomacy to encourage reform.

In the last ten years, therefore, the public and legal acceptance of homosexuality has been evolving very fast. Precisely, the issues between scouting and sexual orientation, traditionally absent, had a public stand for the first time ten years ago, with the already discussed controversial decision of the National Council of Boy Scouts of America to exclude homosexuals as members, instead of the "don't ask, don't tell" policy existing until then. In fact, that decision and its relevant social and media repercussions—given the importance of scouting in the United States and the weight of US media around the world—garnered the already quoted unprecedented negative reaction from European scouting. This is a particularly explicit debate in Europe and in the United States because the evolution of the public perception on sexual orientation in these social realities, but also changing rapidly all over the world.

However, and especially when talking about twenty years ago, in many countries homosexuality was not even an issue up for debate, including the denial that something like "sexual orientation" could even exist besides moral deviation. Thus, when in 1992 the World Scout Committee was debating whether the first steps of BSA executives to discriminate against homosexuals went against the principles of scouting, members of the Committee from non-western countries simply refused to discuss the issue because homosexuality was taboo in their societies. Similarly, the authors of the aforementioned study on the World Values Survey (1981–2001) explain that they do not have time-series data on attitudes toward homosexuality from any Islamic country "because our Islamic colleagues were extremely reluctant to even ask about this topic."[147] And so, the research found that although "dramatic shifts toward increasing tolerance of gays and lesbians have taken place in postindustrial democracies," "these changes have had less impact in the ex-communist and developing countries, and almost none in the Islamic world, the region with the lowest civil rights scores."[148]

This means that, whereas European scouting has taken a clear position defending the rights of homosexuals, scouting, as a world movement, has not been able to make a statement on homosexuality to avoid creating a break-up because the important clash with the social and individual values of many of its members. In fact, as a movement based on volunteers from all over the world, scouting cannot escape the controversies brought by the debate between preservation or change of cultural values that each society experiences. And these changes imbue the movement composed by the individuals, and lead to the change on the organization level in each country. On this, scouting does not appear to be a vanguard movement. Besides, as it happens with all identities, in scouting there are also people trying to interpret them in a univocal way, forgetting that cultures and social values evolve through the freedom of individuals to maintain or change elements of their own culture;[149] but at the same time, the interaction with other cultures and beliefs, in a framework of tolerance, gives opportunities to understand the other's point of view.

As a matter of fact, the scout movement, with its strong local roots but also with its wide international dimension, is faced with a difficult conundrum: if the values of scouting cannot avoid the influence of potentially exclusionary predominant social values, beyond the trend toward change, how can it guarantee its role of responsible, inclusive citizenship education? The answer may lie in part in the already cited study on *The Educational Impact of Scouting*. One of the core findings of the research is the extraordinary importance of scouting's educational impact in helping young people integrate into their peer group in their unit and establish social relations. The study points out that, contrary to what was believed, the main importance of the scout leader is not to pass on values to the group as a role model, but to accompany each adolescent in his/her learning process, in which the most important factor is their personal experience and the exchange of different opinions.[150]

In scouting, therefore, values are not internalized through inculcation or direct transmission, but through personal experience as shown in the study: "*The most powerful element in the construction of the young people's values appears to be personal experience*, and the meaning that he or she makes of the experiences, much of which takes place within the peer group itself. The climate of mutual respect and trust promoted by the leaders facilitates dialogue and the young people's attitude to express their views."[151]

Given this, we can better understand why attempts at using a linear transmission of values, for example in colonial Africa, were doomed to fail, since young people learn through their critical thinking to extract the coherence of the values both from the example of the leader and the official formulation by the association. This can be seen even more clearly in the example on religious values presented by the cited sociological research. Although most of the adolescent scouts of the research "attach importance to seeking spiritual values, many of them strongly criticize formal religious practice as they experience it. In their view, *what they actually experience often seems incoherent with, or contradictory to, the values that they are expected to seek.*"[152]

These results thus imply that what Parsons perceived as a rejection of "official" scout values in the anticolonial African reaction was actually a triumph of scouting's own potential: the preeminence of inclusive values over particularist values, which occurs at association level and does not take into account the stance of the leaders of the national association. In fact, Parsons himself actually reaches the same conclusion by comparing his knowledge of scouting in British colonial Africa with the fact that his scout group, member of the BSA, had features that were far removed from the dominant view of the organization, saying: "As social historian, I now recognize that my old troop demonstrates that official Scouting as defined by national Scout associations is rarely representative of how Scouting is practiced at the local level."[153]

As we have seen previously, according to Russell, scouting's education combines positively the two opposing processes in character development: the one that consists of accepting guidance, and the other consisting in guiding oneself.[154] Critical thinking cannot be based on an empty box, and the inclusive values and models of behavior of scouting are the fundaments to turn young people into autonomous, supportive, responsible, and committed individuals. It is from this moral autonomy that a person could exercise his/her critical thinking.

From this ability of scouting to reinforce personal autonomy, it is interesting to highlight the idea of the cited study on the World Values Survey that, in the evolution toward societies where personal choice is increasingly central, the "rising emphasis on autonomous human choice is inherently conducive to anti-discriminatory conceptions of human well-being,"[155] in seeing the other as an equal. This view concurs with what Robert Baden-Powell stated on his 1912 article "The Other Fellow's Point of View." On it he explains an incident in Portland, Oregon, when a small political activist group tried to sabotage an event in which he was to expose what scouting was. The episode surprised him very much because the activists purported to defend freedom of expression but did not respect the principle when it came to others. And he complains: "Justice and fair play do not always form part of our school curriculum. If our lads were trained as a regular habit to see the other fellow's point of view before passing their own judgment on a dispute, what a difference it would at once make in their manliness of character!... Such lads would not be carried away, as is at present too commonly the case, by the first orator who catches their ear on any subject, but they would also go and hear what the other side has to say about it, and would then think out the question and make up their own minds as men for themselves."[156]

Baden-Powell therefore points out the importance of deliberation and critical thinking in character education: to see the other's point of view means to accept the other as a moral subject the discernment of whom could be relevant. And he concludes that "so it is in almost every problem of life; *individual power of judgement is essential, whether in choice of politics, religion, profession, or sport*, and half our failures and three-quarters of our only partial successes among our sons is due to the want of it. *We want our men to be men, not sheep.*"[157]

The resoluteness of Baden-Powell's emphasis to place autonomy in moral judgment above what is already established by politics or religion is particularly interesting. Much more considering that the struggle for national and religious identities is, in many cases, a struggle for the hegemony of those who *interpret* them. If we compare Baden-Powell's approach with the results, 90 years on, of the study on the educational impact of scouting, we see that character education, the primary objective of the Scout movement, prevails over the transmission of particular values. Thus the study points out that "many of the older adolescents' comments indicate that it is especially the values and attitudes to life (including openness to others, a sense of responsibility toward others developed through group life, etc.) and a feeling of confidence in their resourcefulness that they have had the opportunity to develop that will remain as major acquisitions in preparing for adult life."[158]

In a comparative post–World War II study on the educational action of US scouting and the Hitler Youth, the psychiatrist Herbert Lewin reached the same conclusion: in contrast to the indoctrination of the Hitler Youth, "the Boy Scout context emphasized strongly the importance of an end for the sake of the *individual's* perfection and satisfaction." Lewin also added that "for the Boy Scout, 'happiness' is an end which stems from, and is to be experienced in, his face-to-face group; for the Hitler Youth 'happiness' originates for a satisfactory status of his nation and is a feeling to be shared by *all* folk comrades, i.e. it should be experienced on the national community level."[159]

Besides the coherence between the inclusive and universalist values of scouting and its practices, it is unavoidable that the social values specific to each scout's respective society influences how his or her worldview is formed. This influence is relevant even though the values of societies continuously evolve, and despite the educational model of scouting has a greater impact on creating autonomous individuals with critical thinking than on the transmission of prevailing social values.

The World Value Survey study points out that there is a "slow but steady intergenerational value change towards a more inclusive society."[160] Taking Baden-Powell's approach, scouting should use its *individual power of judgment* to decide whether or not to contribute to this change. The scout movement has two means it can use to avoid becoming an institution limited to perpetuating prevailing social values with exclusionary tendency instead of shifting them toward a more inclusive vision.

The first, mentioned earlier in the book, is to commit in educating moral autonomous individuals with critical thinking on matters of importance in society—a skill that is essential for educating responsible citizens. Citizenship, which has been at the core of the movement since it was founded, requires individuals that posses their own moral framework, who are able—and willing—to make positive contributions to society as well as think critically about issues that could jeopardize free and peaceful life in common.

The second means is to do away with the view of identity as static, and accept that identities, cultures, and ways of thinking evolve, not necessarily to get worse. Recognizing plurality within a culture encourages a normative view of identity in which individuals can choose from the diverse ways of living in a culture, that is, it gives individuals more freedom to construct the world.[161] Educating in love and confidence to humankind instead of in fear of any sort of change.

3. LOCAL ROOTING, NATIONAL BELONGING, AND GLOBAL COMMITMENT

Some time ago, a former officer at the World Bureau was telling me about the changes he had observed over the years in the top leaders of these associations and of the world organization itself. He explained that, somehow, just as the role of the leader (educator) is not the determining factor in the educational activity of scouting, the role of the leaders of its associations and the organization is equally not determining. They can have a powerful influence, as we have seen, on the choice of a more open or closed model, or on the decision to take or not a more inclusive approach. But in the end, he added, you realize that the real scouting is what you see in a scout group, where the movement lives and breathes, which is often far removed from the controversies generated at the top leaders and executives level.

In the previous pages we have examined scouting's model for citizenship education, its ability to train individuals with the potential to transform society, as well as its coherence as a global movement. We have noted that citizenship education based on civic and inclusive values that promotes commitment and loyalty to the own national community can reinforce rather than debilitate the sense of global belonging and the commitment to the world community, as it happens in scouting. As a "glocal" educational movement, scouting reaches global commitment trough local action, thanks to its deep local rooting in hundreds of thousands of scout groups everywhere. That is why we could say the scout movement works both for global citizenship and national loyalty and community involvement from the local grassroots.

To understand how scouting fosters global citizenship education, in keeping with both its own principles of universal brotherhood and its practices, it is best to take a look at several examples. The concept of global citizenship is very fragile and its nature is, in essence, more descriptive and aspirational than normative: on one hand, this concept conveys the idea that citizens everywhere are affected by matters that stretch beyond the borders of our countries; on the other hand, it aspires to a republican vision of citizenship in which citizens are also aware of their responsibilities and rights on a global scale. Simply talking about "global citizenship" helps us move toward it. However, the notion of "global citizenship" does not imply that we should opt for a "global government" but rather the idea of belonging to a human community, a community that has proclaimed the Human Rights and for which we can assume some responsibilities.

If we accept the definition of "global citizen" adopted by the international NGO Oxfam, one of the most active NGOs in the area of cooperation and development education, we can see many elements that we already encountered in the definitions set down by scouting over the years: "Oxfam sees the Global Citizen as someone who: is aware of the wider world and has a sense of their own role as a world citizen; respects and values diversity; has an understanding of how the world works; is outraged by social injustice; participates in the community at a range of levels, from the local to the global; is willing to act to make the world a more equitable and sustainable place; takes responsibility for their actions."[162]

The whole definition shares characteristic traits of the scout movement: the international dimension, the involved role as citizens beyond their own country, living with and respecting diversity, interest in the functioning of society, the commitment to those weaker than ourselves, social participation at all levels, the will to leave the world better than we found it, and the assumption of responsibility.

If citizenship education in pluralist societies need to reach a consensus on which civic content to teach, even more when speaking about global citizenship education the need for a common framework of values is an imperative. According to Reimers, the best approximation to this common framework is the Universal Declaration of Human Rights.[163] It is necessary, he follows, to educate people with the skills that would make global peace and stability possible: this is the goal of global citizenship education.

The values of the scout movement and its educational methods converge in the activities undertaken as part of its educational method. Many of these activities revolve around themes of peace culture, human rights, community development, and collaboration with international organizations. Through this work, scouts are given the opportunity to develop self-esteem, confidence and life skills, while living out the scout motto, "try to leave this world a little better than you found it."

The commitment of the scout movement to congruence between its values and practices has been evident from the start, beginning in the previous century, when world scouting and the League of Nations collaborated in the 1920s.[164] Nowadays, we think nothing of an international NGO cooperating with the UN system. In the 1920s, however, when the League of Nations was a preliminary attempt to create a legitimate global framework, its interaction with world scouting was more relevant.

The League of Nations archive in Geneva's Palais des Nations contains the report of the League delegates who attended the International Scout Conference held in Denmark in 1924. Extracts from the report and the reproduction of its plenary addresses reveal the complicity between the two institutions, the League's interest in obtaining the recognition of scouting and the movement's willingness to give it.

In his speech before the scouts, Dr. Inazō Nitobe, the Japanese Vice-Secretary General of the League of Nations, explained how in 1923 the League assembly—made up of state governments—had unanimously adopted a resolution asking governments to make the conditions for scout trips between different countries easier. He also pointed out that an "Advisory Committee on Boy Scouts, Girl Guides and Youth Organisations" had been set up in the League Secretariat.

He later added: "All this shows the interest which the League of Nations is taking in the Scout movement and the brotherhood of youth. This interest will, you may be sure, increase as the points of contact between the boy scout and the League grow closer and more frequent, and perhaps the League can be of assistance to a movement which stands like yours so pre-eminently and so effectively for international co-operation, fraternity between peoples and universal peace."[165]

In the internal report for the Secretary General of the League of Nations, wrote later on by Nitobe, he noticed the positive effect of the recognition of scouting, which reinforced the cosmopolitan view of an incipient educational movement that had only been formalized as a world organization four years earlier: "There can be no doubt that the interest which the League of Nations has displayed in the Boy Scout and Girl Guide Movements has had a great effect in directing the attention of the leaders of these Movements to the importance of international fraternity. The very 'leitmotif' of this Third International Scout Conference has been international co-operation and brotherhood. Every one of the 34 national delegations seemed fully to realise that it was heir bounden duty to educate the young people committed to their charge in the ideals of international co-operation and human solidarity."[166]

Ten years later, Hitler rose to power in Germany and the nightmare of World War I was destined to seem reduced in comparison. Despite it all, scouting never lost its hope of a better world. Today, contemporary scouting maintains its firm commitment to leave the world better than it was. For instance, in the official position statement on human rights released by WAGGGS in 2007, the organization reiterates that its work "is firmly grounded in the international human rights framework that recognizes rights as inherent to all, inalienable and universal. As the voice of girls and young women, WAGGGS has identified human rights as a priority issue on which to take a stand and speak out. WAGGGS believes our rights as citizens bring with them responsibilities—to make sure that we do not allow our rights to be eroded, but also to support the rights of others."[167]

Actually, the two organizations of world scouting have done many initiatives to promote awareness on values linked with the Universal Declaration of Human Rights and the UN Convention on the Rights of the Child. These two frameworks have become the official reference for the global citizenship values shared by scouting worldwide. Nevertheless, scouting's explicit formulation of global citizenship values would be empty without the implementation of these values in projects carried out at local level by the members of the movement. This is why we grouped few of them it two blocks: peace, human rights, and community development; and legitimization of international institutions.

3.1. PEACE CULTURE, HUMAN RIGHTS, AND COMMUNITY DEVELOPMENT

Activities and projects of scouts on citizenship issues are often focused around two key areas: promoting a culture of peace and human rights (as commitment with freedom and justice), and being involved in service to society leading community development. Below, two illustrative cases of such projects are presented, including the peace project of the Great Lakes Region of Africa, and the initiative of girl guides to improve conditions for the disabled in Pakistan and Nepal.

While actions carried out at all levels of scouting are imbued with a respect for all mankind, it is useful to cite a contemporary example of how an activity can promote a culture of peace and human rights. One case of this is the peace education project launched in the Great Lakes Region of Africa, in the context of the crisis in Burundi (in October 1993), the genocide in Rwanda (1994) and the two "liberation wars" in the Democratic Republic of the Congo (formerly Zaire).[168] From the start of these events, various local scout associations from the Great Lakes region of Africa organized scout activities with children in the refugee camps, both in the country and abroad, particularly in the Democratic Republic of the Congo and Tanzania. The project organizers were the scout associations of Rwanda (ASR), Burundi (ASB), and the two provincial associations (North and South Kivu) of the Democratic Republic of the Congo.

The cooperation between the scout leaders of the different associations in this vast region, generated by the conflict, led, nearly seamlessly, to the creation of a flexible structure for cooperation between the scout associations of Rwanda (ASR), Burundi (ASB), and the two provincial associations (North and South Kivu) of the Democratic Republic of the Congo. This structure was called "Concertation Scoute des Grands Lacs" (*Scout Dialogue of the Great Lakes*).

Because of the terrible circumstances of conflict, the leaders initially dealt with emergency situations, but in time the need arose to do more and to prepare a comprehensive Plan of Action for the education of future generations, "in the spirit of peace, tolerance, understanding and reconciliation." This Plan of Action was approved at the first seminar held in 1996 in Bujumbura, where the "Peace Charter of the Scouts of the Great Lakes" was passed.

The general Plan of Action focuses, on the one hand, on the educational approach of the scouts and, on the other, on the philosophy and practice of nonviolent action. Its general aims are, first, to provide a new impetus for peace activities for young people; second, to promote exchanges between young scouts and non-scouts; and, finally, to qualitatively and quantitatively improve the management of the educators of the "Concertation Scoute des Grands Lacs" network.

The general Plan proposes the organization of national and regional seminars and workshops involving the leaders of the four scouting associations. The guidelines approved in the course of these programs are then transferred to subregional, provincial, and local levels by newly trained scouts who then further disseminate this new knowledge. In this way, thousands of young people receive the same message and are educated in the promotion of peace through the scouts' characteristic "learning by doing" method and modern educational techniques. This method and these techniques are not only used in seminars and workshops, but also in various activities directed at young people. It should also be said that the initiative uses every available opportunity to generate intercultural and interethnic contact, such as work parties to rebuild houses in Burundi that count on the participation and efforts of young people from a range of different countries working together.

Given the important social role that scout associations play in this difficult sociopolitical context, their activities have been supported by leading regional, national, and international organizations, including various town councils and the bishops of the affected dioceses, the Damien Foundation, the leprosy relief organization AHM (Munich), Save the Children, and a number of representatives from UNESCO, UNICEF, and the UNHCR. The Global Development Village organized for the nineteenth World Scout Jamboree (Chile, 1999) and the eleventh World Scout Moot (Mexico, 2000) offered a series of peace-culture workshops, hosted by regional leaders, which served as an opportunity to expand and broadly disseminate these tools and approaches.

One particular example of the scout work in this context is the Peace Project in Rwanda, which was launched in 1996. During the genocide of Rwanda and Burundi, a group of scouts led by a young scout from the Goma province buried dead bodies, distributed food and clothing, and generally formed a core of support for the international NGOs operating in the refugee camps of the area. The organizers were the scout associations of Rwanda, Burundi, and Congo, with the support of the regional WOSM office, the Belgian NGO Broederlojk Delen and the Queen Silvia Fund of the World Scout Foundation. These scouts, together with scouts from other associations in the region, secretly organized a camp for young Hutus and Tutsis, Rwandans, Congolese, and Burundis. Youths from the various associations involved also took part in two work camps to rebuild houses for people who had lost their homes during the conflict. A total of 1,194 leaders and 48,638 scouts took part in these programs. In 2002 and 2003, the participating groups diversified their actions: the preparation of leaders was increased—they were trained to teach nonviolent conflict-resolution techniques; a dissemination campaign was launched; cross-border and cross-community workshops were organized on living in peace, tolerance and interdependence, and this project was related to other themes developed by scouts in the area, such as AIDS prevention programs.

Similarly to peace culture and human rights, community development has been one of the main educational elements of the scout movement. Scouting's commitment to citizenship education has led to countless examples of involvement in communities. A project launched jointly in 1997 by the WAGGGS associations of Pakistan and Nepal to improve conditions for the disabled[169] perfectly exemplifies the scout movement's commitment to sustainable community development through collaborative projects between different countries. The Sindh Sindhuli disabilities project was a three-year development cooperation activity focused on health, in which each of the associations from the two countries worked in the other country. During the project, girl scouts from the Sindh province, of the Pakistan association, worked in the Sindhuli district of Nepal, while scouts from Nepal worked in the Sindh province of Pakistan, which lies just to the south of their country. The main objective of the joint project was to build awareness of a global community by sharing responsibility for the same problem and working together to improve the health conditions of both local communities.

The project carried out in Nepal was the Sindh-Sindhuli Handicapped Project, the purpose of which was to provide medical and orthopaedic treatment for as many disabled people in the region as possible, funds permitting. The project also included examinations and analyses and set up medical and surgical camps to provide orthopedic limbs and hearing aids. Initially, the project studied the medical history of 80 people living with poverty and disability. The first case was a 16-year-old girl who required an orthopedic bed. Her treatment began in December 1997 and she was later transferred to a school where she learnt to use the new bed and to undertake income-generating activities.

In February 1998, a medical camp was set up in Sindhuli. A team formed by a Pakistani doctor treated one thousand patients with the support of the girl scouts, who helped to organize the camp, translate, and move patients. Many patients were found to need physiotherapy, so nine scout leaders in Nepal attended a three-month course to learn the necessary skills to start a center in Sindhuli, with the support of a visiting team of professionals. The first physiotherapy center opened in March 1999 and was followed by a second, temporary center in the mountains, where two physiotherapists treated patients, mostly children. The group performed small surgical operations in Janakpur and Sindhuli, in Nepal, while more serious operations were performed in Pakistan. In 2000, another patient camp was set up, the costs of which were covered by fund-raising efforts organized by the girl scouts.

3.2. LEGITIMIZING INTERNATIONAL INSTITUTIONS

The legitimization of international institutions is one of the most important steps in fostering global citizenship. Without global institutions and frameworks, global citizenship would lack bearings and simply be a moral stance. For Bhikhu Parekh, in our time, globalization has forced us to rethink our citizenship duties, insofar as "our duties now have a political content, and our relations to human beings on other parties of the world are politically mediated. This inescapable politicisation of our universal moral duty is new to our age, and forms the central moral premise of any well-conceived theory of politics and international relations."[170]

Since world scouting was formalized in 1920, committed to the League of Nations, imitating its organizational model and maintaining close relations, it has not stopped legitimizing international institutions by recognizing and reinforcing their authority and by working in conjunction with them. Twenty-five years later, when the United Nations had been created, WOSM and WAGGGS obtained consultative status to the ECOSOC (United Nations Economic and Social Council), and since 1998 the new general consultative status. Scouting also has a presence on the advising committees of various UN organs and agencies, and cooperates on a regular basis with a dozen of its agencies, such as UNESCO, UNICEF, the WHO, the FAO, and UNHCR.

World scouting's collaboration with the UN systems is based on three challenges: first, that these relations only make sense in that they strengthen the quality of scouting's educational work, its reason for being; second, that they should enable scouting to make the voice of young people be heart in processes of national and global decision making; and third, that scouting must be able to have some influence, as an civil society organization, in the evolution of policies and structures to deal with global issues. Moreover, both world scout organizations are part of international networks of associations through which they channel positions and joint activities to influence the global political agenda on issues affecting young people.

The *Scouts of the World* project,[171] within the frame of the Millennium Development Goals of the United Nations, exemplifies the collaborative power of the scout movement with international organizations. The initiative, launched by WOSM, seeks to engage scouts in the adolescent and youth age range (15 to 26 years) in the fields of the Environment, Development and Peace, using the Millennium Development Goals of the United Nations as a framework to generate positive change in scouts' communities and internationally.

In September 2000, 189 members of the United Nations adopted the Millennium Declaration. According to the Secretary General of WOSM, this Declaration touches on universal values shared by scouting: freedom, tolerance, equality, solidarity, respect for nature and shared responsibility. The three big challenges to the world's future identified in the Millennium Declaration are: (i) Peace, security and disarmament; (ii) Development and the eradication of poverty, and (iii) Environmental protection.

Although the project covers two of WOSM's strategic priorities—youth and adolescent participation—the idea is that it will extend beyond scouting and also involve non-scouts. An open website was therefore set up to explain the Millennium Development Goals and create a network to help reach them. In this sense, the people behind the initiative would like scout organizations from the different countries to integrate the Scouts of the World program into the activities of their young branches.

Another interesting aspect of this is the network of parliament members who have been scouts who are connected through the World Scout Parliamentary Union (WSPU), created at the suggestion of the WOSM in 1991, as yet another example of scouting's contributions to the idea of global citizenship. WSPU is a nonpartisan international organization that unites national associations of parliament members who have been scouts. The WSPU's goals are to establish ties and cooperation between the parliamentary scout associations and contribute to the creation of new ones; promote friendship between members around the world; work with WOSM in areas of mutual interest, including relations with government institutions; and helping to develop scout associations in their own countries. The WSPU, which has mobilized these associations in some 20 countries, has a similar structure that the world organization. The evolution of the positions taken by successive WSPU Assemblies is interesting, in that they have become increasingly favorable to global governance beyond national sovereignty, such as the need for recognition of nonformal education in education policies, the promotion of national youth policies or a push for legislative initiatives, at the national and international level, in order to support and reinforce the scout movement.

The previous examples show means on how the scout movement ensures that citizens in every community share civic virtues that strengthen inclusive societies committed to liberty and to peace. Even though, how these values are promoted through activities varies depending on the specific context of the scout. The cases above reflect the multitude of ways in which the scout motto to "leave the world better than you found it" can be manifest through actions and activities of scouting.

Nevertheless, the scout movement remains committed to engaging in projects for the good of the world. Through scouting, young people around the globe have the opportunity to become agents of change in their local environments, as well as to develop an understanding of their potential to enact positive change in other parts of the world. This combination of awareness and action is at the root of how scouting joins its values with its practices to form globally educated citizens.

CONCLUDING REMARKS

> Establishing a lasting peace is the work of education; all politics can do is to keep us out of war.
>
> Maria Montessori

ANYONE WHO HAS BEEN FORTUNATE to participate in a World Scout Jamboree knows that national identity and religious beliefs could be used as roots to build the sentiment of global belonging, rather than as elements of exclusion. That was one of the many great intuitions of Robert Baden-Powell, the founder of scouting, when he promoted the First International Scout Jamboree in 1920, just two years after World War I. In a Jamboree, as it is in the thousands of international camps organized every year in the scout world, each one of the participant's identities are gifts to the others: symbols, languages, music, and colors, as a contribution to the diversity. One needs roots from where to become global.

In scouting, local roots and national identity are tools to generating a sense of global belonging, as global citizenship education contributes to enriching both local action and national commitment with its inclusive values of solidarity and peace. Two key elements make that possible. First, besides being accommodator of multiple identities, scouting also mitigates their excesses, through the explicit statement that national and religious identities must coexist among diversity: there is no country better than the other; there is no religion over another. And second, the unambiguous commitment of scouting toward the content of the Universal Declaration of Human Rights and the UN Convention on the Rights of the Child, makes them the world framework for the movement's shared values. On this, using a contemporary political theory approach, we could say that the scout model of citizenship combines the values of civic republicanism and liberal-democratic nationalism with the framework and duties of cosmopolitism.

Scouting is an educational movement based on the voluntary commitment of individuals, who carry out their activities at the local level through a global network of scout groups belonging to membership-based national associations –formally organized at world level. The combination of "movement" and "organization" gives scouting a particular strength, lending it the flexibility of a movement while affording it the security and consistence of an organization. Yet, the actual engine that makes scouting work is the voluntary involvement of individuals as scout leaders: because their roles are neither obligatory nor paid, it is only by the strength of the movement's purpose and shared values that their participation and commitment takes place.

The deeply intuitive nature of scouting's educational action is at the same time one of its greatest strengths and one of its worse disadvantages. Due to that intuitive character young people join scouting everywhere, looking for fun, friends, freedom, and adventure, which is what they find; through this, they develop skills and abilities for life, among them autonomy, responsibility, leadership, appreciation for diversity, and ability to deal with complexity. On the other hand, that intuitive essence makes it difficult for scouting to be perceived from outside as the power-house of education that it is. And even more, from inside the movement, its intuitive nature sometimes creates insecurity on what makes scouting *Scouting*, which may cause people to cling to traditions and symbols for fear of losing authenticity.

Certainly, the educational action of scouting cannot be seen in a picture, but rather in a film: it is a set of apparently modest elements structured into a well-defined method that generates its educational impact, arousing in young people their intrinsic desire for learning. Scouting's educational action is able to combine in balance the two continually opposing processes in character development: *initiative* ("guiding one-self"), building autonomy and reinforcing the subject's personal will; and *discipline* ("accepting guidance"), creating habits and developing responsibility. In the scout movement, young people significantly foster their competence learning through projects that are chosen by them and experienced in an environment of freedom, generating leadership, teamwork skills, and capacity to shape common goals. Scouting is indeed an experiential community where action and thinking are synergic because the learning by doing provides sense to the experience. But above all, scouting is a genuine producer of happiness, because people with capacity for altruism and service are happier. Robert Baden-Powell highlighted this when he said in his last message to scouts: "The real way to get happiness is by giving out happiness to other people. Try and leave this world a little better than you found it and when your turn comes to die, you can die happy in feeling that at any rate you have not wasted your time but have done your best."

The most important social outcome of scouting is its founding of generations of citizens who are active and responsible, morally autonomous, and have a critical thinking, becoming therefore change agents. Those millions of individuals have the inclusive values of scouting as basis to be able to define their model of society and to lead social change, both individually and collectively, for its betterment. It is true that, seemingly, the citizenship education values of scouting preserve sociopolitical stability: support for the established political order in each country, alliances with the legitimate institutions of authority, ensuring that social values and norms prevail, and not overstepping limits. Nevertheless, citizenship education in the scout movement has been a source of civil resistance against social orders deemed to be unfair: standing up to discrimination under colonization, opposing racial segregation, resisting dictatorships, overcoming armed conflicts between countries, taking a stand against the discrimination of women, and in some societies even challenging homophobia. The difference between these two realities is the difference between scouting as an organization and scouting as a movement. The values of scouting are intrinsically inclusive, non-exclusionary, but being based on volunteers in each different society, the organization can hardly escape the controversies brought by the debate over preservation or change of cultural values that societies experience. Therefore, in general, scouting as an organization does not clash with the prevailing social values and institutions, except in extreme cases. But as a voluntary movement, scouting is a source of critical individuals committed to make a change based on the inclusive values they share, even when they feel that their association is being inconsistent with those values: in scouting, young people learn through their critical thinking to extract the coherence of the values both from the example of the educator and from the official formulation by their association. It is, therefore, a true school of citizenship.

The scout movement, with all its diversity and also its consistency, has a great potential as a research subject in the social sciences. But this potential has been largely overlooked. Its delimitation through the world organizations WOSM and WAGGGS, its global dimension throughout history and today, and its vast cultural and religious diversity with the common aim of contributing to the self-development of young people as responsible individuals, as committed citizens, and as leaders of social change, make it one of the main nongovernmental agents of global citizenship education with a global focus. It is indeed a unique case among global civil society organizations, youth movements, and educational institutions. Hence, further research on many aspects of scouting shall be promoted.

Globalization has brought with it new challenges for contemporary societies. Many of these have been pointed out by the Millennium Development Goals. However, globalization has also brought an unprecedented social diversity and mobility. The reaction against diversity is strong in western societies, where the new radical right argues for "ethnopluralism" instead of multiculturalism, meaning to avoid any sort of cultural and ethnic mixing, whereas others promote religious fundamentalism with the same aim but in the opposite direction. Notwithstanding, identities, as important as they are, are human constructs and change with time. As a movement based on diversity, scouting has a very important role to play to avoid cultural clash and identity conflicts and to promote tolerance, understanding of difference, appreciation of diversity, and capacity to deal with complexity. Since wars begin in the minds of persons, it is there that the defenses of peace must be constructed. And that construction is a job for education.

A note on communication: historically, scouting as a global movement lacked means to connect its individual members, besides international camps. However, in the last years, the operations network of the scout movement has been fortunately affected by the globalization of communications, and particularly the Internet. Since scouting started in 1908 as a result of the response of British adolescents to a publication that conveyed a motivating project, relations between the local nodes of the scout network of all countries have been filtered through its national associations. Now, the emergence and development of the Internet has given the scout network its first means of global communication between individual members, which opens up new scenarios for its international fraternity and its potential coordination for common goals, as the Arab Spring has started to show.

One last remark. The model of membership-based organizations is in crisis in many countries, as traditional institutions of the industrial age are. And scouting is a movement but also a membership-based organization. If scouting is to avert this waning trend affecting associations based on stable members, it has to be able to see beyond its practices, to confirm the potential of its educational action, and to adapt it to new realities and needs, as it has done throughout its history. It should take advantage of the social adaptability of its condition of movement, particularly appealing to new generations of young people. And last but not least, it must be careful with discriminatory social tendencies, and more importantly, prevent institutions supporting (either directly or indirectly) the movement from imposing a view of society that replaces scouting's commitment to inclusive coexistence values and to the critical thinking that defines it.

If scouting can do this, it will be able to continue playing an important role in the future of many societies, just as it did throughout the twentieth century.

Rinkaby (Sweden), 22nd World Scout Jamboree
August 2011

Appendix: Countries and Territories with Associations Belonging to World Scouting (WOSM and/or WAGGGS, 2011)

1. Albania
2. Algeria
3. Angola
4. Antigua and Barbuda
5. Argentina
6. Armenia
7. Aruba
8. Australia
9. Austria
10. Azerbaijan
11. Bahamas
12. Bahrain
13. Bangladesh
14. Barbados
15. Belarus
16. Belgium
17. Belize
18. Benin
19. Bhutan
20. Bolivia
21. Bosnia and Herzegovina
22. Botswana
23. Brazil

24. Brunei Darussalam
25. Bulgaria
26. Burkina Faso
27. Burundi
28. Cameroon
29. Cambodia
30. Canada
31. Cape Verde
32. Central African Republic
33. Chad
34. Chile
35. Colombia
36. Comoros
37. Congo
38. Congo, The Democratic Republic of the
39. Cook Islands
40. Costa Rica
41. Croatia
42. Cyprus
43. Czech Republic
44. Denmark
45. Dominica
46. Dominican Republic
47. Ecuador
48. Egypt
49. El Salvador
50. Estonia
51. Ethiopia
52. Fiji
53. Finland
54. France
55. French Polynesia
56. Gabon
57. Gambia
58. Georgia
59. Germany
60. Ghana
61. Greece
62. Grenada
63. Guatemala
64. Guinea
65. Guyana

66. Haiti
67. Honduras
68. Hong Kong
69. Hungary
70. Iceland
71. India
72. Indonesia
73. Ireland
74. Israel
75. Italy
76. Ivory Coast
77. Jamaica
78. Japan
79. Jordan
80. Kazakhstan
81. Kenya
82. Kiribati
83. Korea, Republic.of
84. Kuwait
85. Latvia
86. Lebanon
87. Lesotho
88. Liberia
89. Libya
90. Liechtenstein
91. Lithuania
92. Luxembourg
93. Macau
94. Macedonia
95. Madagascar
96. Malawi
97. Malaysia
98. Maldives
99. Malta
100. Mauritania
101. Mauritius
102. Mexico
103. Moldova, Republic of
104. Monaco
105. Mongolia
106. Montenegro
107. Morocco

108. Mozambique
109. Namibia
110. Nepal
111. Netherlands
112. Netherlands Antilles
113. New Zealand
114. Nicaragua
115. Niger
116. Nigeria
117. Norway
118. Oman
119. Pakistan
120. Palestinian Authority
121. Panama
122. Papua New Guinea
123. Paraguay
124. Peru
125. Philippines
126. Poland
127. Portugal
128. Qatar
129. Romania
130. Russian Federation
131. Rwanda
132. Saint Kitts & Nevis
133. Saint Lucia
134. Saint Vincent and the Grenadines
135. San Marino
136. Saudi Arabia
137. Senegal
138. Serbia
139. Seychelles
140. Sierra Leone
141. Singapore
142. Slovak Republic
143. Slovenia
144. Solomon Islands
145. South Africa
146. Spain
147. Sri Lanka
148. Sudan
149. Surinam

150. Swaziland
151. Sweden
152. Switzerland
153. Syria
154. Taiwan
155. Tajikistan
156. Tanzania, United Republic of
157. Thailand
158. Togo
159. Tonga
160. Trinidad and Tobago
161. Tunisia
162. Turkey
163. Uganda
164. Ukraine
165. United Arab Emirates
166. United Kingdom
167. United States of America
168. Uruguay
169. Venezuela
170. Yemen
171. Zambia
172. Zimbabwe

NOTES

FOREWORD

1. LaBelle, 1981: 329.
2. Farrell, 1990; Masemann, 1990.
3. Arnove and Torres, 2007.
4. Farrell and Alexander, 1975.
5. Farrell, 1996; 1998; 2001; 2003.

CHAPTER 1

1. In 1899, the town of Mafeking was besieged by the Boers during the Boer War in what is now South Africa. The siege lasted 217 days (from October 1899 to May 1900), and though of little military importance, it was strongly echoed by the British press at a time when Great Britain was seriously lacking in national victories. When the conflict ended in a British win, Robert Baden-Powell, who commanded the defense of Mafeking, became a national hero. Springhall, 1987: 934–942.
2. Boehmer, 2004: xiii, xliv.
3. The Boy's Brigade is a paramilitary Christian youth organization (Warren, 1986a: 381–382) founded in Glasgow in 1833 with the purpose of "the advancement of Christ's kingdom among Boys and the promotion of habits of Obedience, Reverence, Discipline, Self-respect and all that tends towards a true Christian manliness" (Austin E. Birch: *The Story of the Boy's Brigade*. London: F. Muller, 1965: 101–103). The YMCA is an ecumenical Christian organization founded in London in 1844. It is now present in 117 countries and provides programs based on Christian values for young men. It is a very decentralized organization, whereby each local group controls its own operations and financing (John D. Gustav-Wrathall: *Take the Young Stranger By The Hand: Same-Sex Relations and the YMCA*. Chicago: University of Chicago Press, 1998).
4. Baden-Powell [1908] 2004: 5.
5. Warren, 1986a: 385–387.
6. *Ibid.*, 387.
7. Baden-Powell [1908] 2004: 36.
8. Baden-Powell [1908] 2004: 36

9. Baden-Powell [1908] 2004: 44–46.

10. "The scout's salute and secret sign consists in the three fingers held up (like the three points of the scout's badge) remind him of his three promises in the scout's oath." The Badge is mentioned two pages earlier: "The scout's badge is the arrow head, which shows the north on a map or on the compass. It is the badge of the scout in the Army, because he shows the way: so, too, a peace scout shows the way in doing his duty and helping others" (Baden-Powell [1908] 2004: 34, 37). The Salute and the Badge are still part of scout symbology around the world.

11. Nagy, 1967: 17.

12. Baden-Powell [1908] 2004: 5–6.

13. Nagy, 1985: 63–64; Reynolds, 1942: 150.

14. Baden-Powell, 1937.

15. Rosenthal, 1980.

16. Warren, 1986a: 388–389.

17. Rosenthal, 1986: 52; Warren, 1987: 388; Jeal, 2001: 400.

18. Colton, 1992: 4.

19. Nagy, 1985: 68. Jeal (2001: 413) adds that its adaptation to the Edwardian idea of working toward "national efficiency" was ambiguous enough to be well received by both the conservative Tories and the social democrat Fabians.

20. Nagy, 1985: 64; Jeal, 2001: 471.

21. Kerr, 1932: 11–13, 14, 29; also Nagy, 1985: 63. In the 1937 interview quoted earlier, Baden-Powell provides evidence for this view in saying that, at the Crystal Palace rally in 1909, "among the boys as they marched past, we found some groups of girls in Scout hats with staves and lanyards and haversacks, like the boys. 'Who are you?' we said. 'Oh, we are the Girl Scouts.' 'The devil you are!' 'No—Girl Scouts.' So I had eventually to write a book for them giving them the name of Guides to distinguish them from Scouts. And that is how the Girl Guides started—on their own—and they have gone on growing ever since" (Baden-Powell, 1937).

22. "Boy Scouts Scheme," a pamphlet published in 1907 by the UK Boy Scouts Association, and the "Can Girls Be Scouts?" article in *The Scout* magazine, May 1908. Both quoted in Jeal, 2001: 469.

23. Robert Baden-Powell: *Yarns for Boy Scouts*. London: C. Arthur Pearson Ltd, 1909.

24. It was published in the *Boy Scout Headquarters' Gazette* in November 1909.

25. Baden-Powell chose the name "Guides" after the well-known Corps of Guides in India; however, the term was unacceptable in the United States because it had the connotation of "Indian hunter." As a result, when the US female association was created in 1912, it adopted the name "Girl Scouts," which is now a synonym for "Girl Guides"—as shown a decade later by the name of the world association: World Association of Girl Guides and Girl Scouts (WAGGGS, 1997: 12–13).

26. Three years later the new association received official recognition by a Royal Charter of January 4, 1921, granted by George V, incorporating the Boy

Scout Association throughout the British Empire, with "the purpose of instructing boys of all classes in the principles of discipline loyalty and good citizenship."

27. Reynolds, 1942.
28. In 1912, they added a reference to parents in points 2 and 7, exceeding the limited confidence in their example at the time in England; in 1917, they added a reference to individuals "under" scouts, in response to criticisms from socialist circles; and in 1938, they changed "Officials" for "Scouters" in point 2 and rearranged the text. So points 2 and 7 ended up as: "2. A Scout is loyal to the King, his country, his Scouters, his parents, his employers and to those under him. 7. A Scout obeys orders of his parents and his patrol leader or scout master without question." Finally, in 1934, as it has already been mentioned, "country" and "creed" were added to point 4 (which came into effect in 1938), a change that would prove particularly significant later on: "4. A Scout is a friend to all and a brother to every other scout no matter what country, class or creed, the other may belong." *Policy, Organisation and Rules* document. The Boy Scouts Association, London, 1938 ("Effective from 1st October"). The eighteenth edition of *Scouting for Boys* (C. Arthur Pearson: London) still contained the old text, but in the next edition (1940), which came after the document mentioned with the new legal framework of British scouting, the text of the Scout Law had incorporated "country" and "creed" into point 4.
29. Although he concurs with the theory that Baden-Powell's original aim with scouting was to prepare a new generation of soldiers to defend the British Empire, John Springhall points out that "Baden-Powell and his Boy Scouts have also to be seen within the context of Edwardian politics and society," since "this was a period during which the children in Europe were being trained for a war which was regarded as natural and inevitable" (Springhall, 1971: 150–151).
30. Warren, 1986a: 392–393; Wonesch, 2000; and Jeal, 2001: 413–414, who also cites various documents from 1911 to 1914 in which Baden-Powell and scouting were linked to the ideas of Montessori.
31. Original text from the archives of the Scout Association UK, quoted in Jeal, 2001: 413.
32. Robert Baden-Powell: *The Wolf Cub's Handbook*. London: C. Arthur Pearson Ltd, 1916.
33. Robert Baden-Powell: *Rovering to Success*. London: Herbert Jenkins, 1922.
34. Jeal, 2001: 31, 500–501, 516.
35. Agnes Baden-Powell and Robert Baden-Powell: *How Girls can Help to Build Up the Empire: The Handbook for Girl Guides*. London: Thomas Nelson, 1912.
36. Jeal, 2001: 471–487.
37. Kerr, 1932: 90–93.
38. Jeal, 2001: 428–442.
39. Letter to the *Morning Post,* August 9, 1913; quoted in Jeal, 1989: 470.
40. Jeal, 2001: 473, 476 (469–487).

41. Robert Baden-Powell: *Girl Guiding. The Official Handbook.* London: C. Arthur Pearson Ltd, 1918.

42. As will be shown later, none of the German associations calling themselves "scouts" were given international recognition before World War II.

43. Robert Baden-Powell: *Boy Scouts Beyond the Seas.* London: C Arthur Pearson Ltd, 1913.

44. Warren, 1986a: 380; Jeal, 2001: 448; Springhall, 1987.

45. Jeal, 2001: 448–456.

46. Jeal, 2001: 449, 453.

47. Sica, 2006: 16–18.

48. Parsons, 2004: 54; Nagy, 1985: 82.

49. Quoted in Reynolds, 1942: 190–191 (the italics are mine).

50. Baden-Powell, Robert (1919): *Aids to Scoutmastership.* London: Herbert Jenkins.

51. Baden-Powell, [1919] 1949: 21.

52. Collis, Hurll and Hazlewood, 1961: 97. Quoted in Jeal, 2001: 511 (the italics are mine).

53. Archives of the Scout Association UK, Box "Co-operation-League of Nations," Chief Scout to Lord Mayor of London, September 23, 1919. Quoted in Sica, 2006: 23 (the italics are mine).

54. "And so it is in almost every problem of life; individual power of judgement is essential, whether in choice of politics, religion, profession, or sport, and half our failures and three-quarters of our only partial successes among our sons is due to the want of it. We want our men to be men, not sheep" (Baden-Powell, 1912).

55. Van Effenterre, 1963, 86–87; Jeal, 2001; WOSM, 1985: 5 (Resolution 11/26 on Jamboree competitions).

56. Nagy, 1985: 90–91; Jeal, 2001: 511–512. There are no documents listing all of the founding associations of world scouting in the archives of either the Scout Association UK or the World Scout Bureau (WOSM). Figures vary depending on the source, perhaps because it is not certain that all of the countries that attended the Jamboree in 1920 were in the new BSIB. Nagy (1985: 90) says that "8000 scouts from 21 independent countries and 12 British dependences" attended the Jamboree (making a total of 33). However, he also lists the "Founder countries of the World Scout Movement" (Nagy, 1985: 212) in an appendix without references. He cites 30: "Argentina; Austria; Belgium; Brazil; Chile; Czechoslovakia; Denmark; Ecuador; Estonia; Finland; France; Great Britain; Greece; Hungary; Italy; Japan; Latvia; Liberia; Luxembourg; Netherlands; Norway; Peru; Poland; Portugal; Romania; Sweden; Switzerland; Thailand; United States of America; Yugoslavia." He does not include the British dominions where scouting was present, such as Canada, India, South Africa, Australia, or New Zealand.

57. Until it was amended in 1977, the preamble to the WOSM Constitution read as follows: "Accredited representatives of National Scout Associations which had adopted and practised the Scout method prior to 1922,

assembled in Paris, France, in July 1922 and established the International Scout Conference for the coordination of the Scout Movement throughout the world, together with an Executive Committee and a Secretariat" (WOSM, 1973: 3).

58. There was a confusion with terms because the new world organization took the name of the "International Bureau," which was also the name adopted by the permanent secretariat of the organization.

59. "Report on the Activities of the International Bureau 1920–1922," typed document presented to the International Committee in 1922, Pg. 1. World Scout Bureau Archives (Geneva).

60. Unlike in male scouting, there was no confusion between the name of the international organization and the permanent secretariat in guiding. As I will explain later, male scouting solved this problem in the 1960s, when it changed its name from the Boy Scouts International Bureau (BSIB) to the World Organization of the Scout Movement (WOSM).

61. In the words of Robert Baden-Powell in 1928, "Of the forty countries possessing Girl Guides or Girl Scouts only ten have over five thousand members, and six of these ten are British . . . . Outside the British Empire and the United States of America, the Movement is still in an embryo state as regards strength." "Memorandum by the Founder on the Report of the World Conference," p. 2. Appendix to the "Historical Report of the Conference which took place in Hungary, May 1928." World Bureau Archives, WAGGGS.

62. "Report on the Activities of the International Bureau 1920–1922," typed document submitted to the World Committee in 1922, World Scout Bureau Archives (Geneva): p. 3. The International Peace Bureau, which still exists, was founded in 1892 and awarded the Nobel Peace Prize in 1910. In 1924, it moved its headquarters from Bern to Geneva to be closer to the League of Nations and its institutions, which it supported.

63. *The Scout,* August 14, 1920. Quoted in Sica, 2006: 24.

64. Report to the Secretary General: Report of the League Representatives to the Third International Scout Conference, Copenhagen, August 1924, p. 10. Document No. 38.191, League of Nations archive, Geneva.

65. *Jamboree: The World-wide Scout Journal,* N. 24 (October, 1926), 650: "Mr. Humbert Martin, Director of the International [Boy Scouts] Bureau, presented his report [to the 1926 Conference] as follows." Also Nagy, 1985: 102.

66. Nagy, 1985: 102.

67. See Jeal, 2001: 543–553, on relations between Baden-Powell and the BSIB and the fascist and Nazi regimes in Italy and Germany, respectively.

68. Baden-Powell, [1908] 2004: 26.

69.

'It is glorious to feel that my country is the greatest on earth; that our soldiers were in war the bravest and ever victorious against all odds; that our women are the most beautiful in the world; as also it is with our country and its scenery and climate; that in art and science, in manufacture and invention, it is the men of our nation who have led the way. And when one looks at the people of other countries, how strange and eccentric they are'. That is the kind of talk that most of us have heard; but to which nationality did the speaker belong? Was he Briton or Italian, German or American, Chinese or Swede? In truth he may have been any one of them, since people of all countries have been apt to give expression in that way to their patriotic pride. [...] The worldwide crash of war has roughly shaken us all and made us awake to the newer order of things. No longer is one nation better than another.

Published in *Jamboree*, January 1921; quoted in Sica, 1984: 156; and Sica, 2006: 19–20.

70. Nagy, 1985: 83–85; Parsons, 2004: 55–56.
71. WOSM, 1985: 3 (Resolution 14/24, "Principles of Scouting").
72. Nonetheless, as I will explain later, France has had a *laïque* scout association since 1911, recognized as such since 1920 when the BSIB was constituted, a *laïque* nature it still retains along with other scout associations.
73. As the historian Albert Balcells argues, although Baden-Powell's scouting had a religious, even Christian, background, he thought that scouting should be independent from churches as well as from political parties. Albert Balcells: "Trajectòria històrica de l'escoltisme." *Revista de Catalunya*, N. 33 (September, 1989), 56.
74. WOSM, 1985: 5 (Resolution 17/24, "Policy, International Recognition").
75. In December 1931, following the Imperial Conferences of 1926 and 1930, the British parliament passed the Statute of Westminster, thereby establishing equal status between the United Kingdom and the self-governing British dominions of the Irish Free State, the Dominion of Canada, Newfoundland (later part of Canada), the Commonwealth of Australia, the Dominion of New Zealand, and the Union of South Africa. Once the dominions had ratified the Statute, they were given their independence.
76. Tim Jeal notes that Mussolini had been praised by figures like Churchill and Edison (Jeal, 2001: 543).
77. In 1933, for example, when the Nazi regime outlawed scouting, there were 40 associations calling themselves "Scout" in Germany, though none were actually members of the international organization (Kroonenberg, 1998: 16).
78. WOSM, 1985: 3 (Res. 12/24 "Protection of Uniform, etc."), 9 (Res. 12/31 "Protection of Uniform" and Res. 12/33 "Promise and Law, Changes").
79. Charques, R.D.: "Education in the Soviet Union." *International Affairs (Royal Institute of International Affairs 1931–1939)*, Vol. 11, N. 4 (July, 1932), 493–511: 506.
80. Nagy, 1985: 94.
81. In 1936, it became compulsory to join the *Hitler-Jugend*. In his novelized memoirs of life as a young German scout at the time, Hans E. Ihle describes the situation in which he found himself that year:

The moment will come when you'll have to decide whether or not you want to join one of the branches of the Hitler-Youth organization. But that's not the worst point, as we said before. The worst moment comes when you don't even have that choice anymore; you can't borrow time by pretending to become a Nazi, similar to our German-Jewish citizens. You can't join the Hitler-Youth movement; you became unacceptable to them. Your Scout activities might have forced you to run out of choices. Then all that's left is the concentration camp.

(Ihle, 1993: 32)

82. Jeal, 2001: 543–553; Nagy, 1985: 101–103. For a comparison of the aims of USA Scouting and the Hitler Youth in the 1940s, see Lewin, 1947a; and Herbert S. Lewin: "Problems of Re-Educating Fascist Youth." *Journal of Educational Sociology,* Vol. 19, N. 7 (March, 1946), 452–458; on the differences between the British and German youth movements in the first quarter of the century, see Gillis, John R.: "Conformity and Rebellion: Contrasting Styles of English and German Youth, 1900–33." *History of Education Quarterly,* Vol. 13, N. 3 (Autumn, 1973), 249–260; for opinions on youth movements in the 1920s in the Soviet Union, see Charques, R.D.: "Education in the Soviet Union." *International Affairs (Royal Institute of International Affairs 1931–1939),* Vol. 11, N. 4 (July, 1932), 493–511: 506.

83. See the debate between Rosenthal, 1986, and Jeal, 2001, on Robert Baden-Powell's interaction with the *Balilla* and the *Hitler-Jugend.* For Rosenthal, Baden-Powell's relationship with these movements indicates that he had a positive attitude toward some fascist and Nazi ideals. Jeal, however, argues that Baden-Powell, like many of his contemporaries, was sympathetic toward some of the ideas of Hitler and Mussolini before they began to use violence, particularly in reaction to the communists, who had dissolved scouting in Russia and the whole Soviet Union. Jeal also claims that Baden-Powell maintained contact with the German and Italian youth organizations so that they were not isolated and that a recognized form of scouting could be set up there in the future. In all events, this contact was abruptly terminated following the Night of Broken Glass in October 1938 in Germany (Jeal, 2001: 544–547).

84. Kroonenberg, 1998: 17–18; also Nagy, 1967: 30.

85. Nagy, 1985: 102.

86. The word in italics, *country,* was added to the existing *class* and *creed.* Nagy, 1985: 106.

87. WOSM, 1985: 15 (Resolution 15/37, "Patriotism").

88. St George Saunders, 1948; Balcells i Samper, 1993; Cruz Orozco, José Ignacio (2003): "Entre la clandestinidad y la legalidad. El escultismo español en el primer franquismo (1939–1953)," in: Cholvy (2003), 249–263.

89. Three of its elected members could not be contacted (Nagy, 1985: 115).

90. The data on China for 1941 are for the Boy Scouts of China. Chinese scouting obtained world recognition in 1937, but it was interrupted in 1949 when the communist People's Republic of China was established and scouting was outlawed. It moved to Taiwan, where the "provisional capital" of the Republic of China had been set up, which rejected communism, and it was reestablished in 1950 as the "Boy Scouts of China." It is still a member and is an exceptional case of WOSM.

91. St George Saunders, 1949: 246–7.

92. "The paragon of the successful, self-reliant, courageous, and self-made man is a traditional American ideal. It is quite certainly the educational ideal of the Boy Scouts of America" (Lewin, 1947b: 169).

93. Nagy, 1985: 117, 119, 142–143. On research, for example, as early as December 1936, the National Director of Research of BSA described diverse research projects in the *Journal of Educational* on adolescents, adolescent leaders, juvenile delinquency, and the interests of the boys involved in BSA (Partridge, E.D.: "Research Projects Being Carried on By the Boy Scouts of America." *Journal of Educational Sociology,* Vol. 10, N. 4 (December, 1936), 220–226; see also Abt et al., 1940).

94. See Goodrich, Leland M.: "From League of Nations to United Nations." *International Organization,* Vol. 1, N. 1 (February, 1947): 3–21. The Preamble to the United Nations Charter, signed on June 26, 1945 in San Francisco (United States), asserts:

"We the Peoples of the United Nations determined

– to save succeeding generations from the scourge of war, which twice in our lifetime has brought untold sorrow to mankind, and
– to reaffirm faith in fundamental human rights, in the dignity and worth of the human person, in the equal rights of men and women and of nations large and small, and
– to establish conditions under which justice and respect for the obligations arising from treaties and other sources of international law can be maintained, and
– to promote social progress and better standards of life in larger freedom,

and for these ends,

– to practice tolerance and live together in peace with one another as good neighbours, and
– to unite our strength to maintain international peace and security, and
– to ensure, by the acceptance of principles and the institution of methods, that armed force shall not be used, save in the common interest, and
– to employ international machinery for the promotion of the economic and social advancement of all peoples,

have resolved to combine our efforts to accomplish these aims.

Accordingly, our respective Governments, through representatives assembled in the city of San Francisco, who have exhibited their full powers found to be in good and due form, have agreed to the present Charter of the United Nations and do hereby establish an international organization to be known as the United Nations." *Charter of the United Nations and its Preamble*, Department of Public Information, United Nations: http://www.un.org/aboutun/charter/.

95. Preamble, *Universal Declaration of Human Rights*: United Nations General Assembly resolution 217 A (III) of December 10, 1948 (http://www.un.org/Overview/rights.html).

96. Nagy, 1985: 123; *cf.* Kroonenberg, 1998.

97. WOSM, 1985: 25 (Res. 27/49); the French version says: "Nous nous mettons de nouveau au service des principes de la liberté et de l'indépendance des peuples et des nations ... " (p. 26).

98. WOSM, 1985: 39 (Res. 18/55).

99. Nagy, 1985: 139–140. Even so, the African member was Caucasian.

100. Parsons' thesis is that the colonial officials thought that point 2 of the Scout Law *(A Scout is loyal to the King...)* could be used to educate the young Africans. In practice, however, for the Africans, point 4 *(A Scout is ... a brother to every other Scout, no matter to what country, class or creed the other may belong)* became the key to their resistance against social discrimination (Parsons, 2004: 5–7); this last point is what Baden-Powell alluded to his 1936 article in the *Journal of the Royal African Society*, quoted earlier (Baden-Powell, 1936). See also Walton, G.: "The Scout Movement in Africa." *Journal of the Royal African Society*, Vol. 36, N. 145 (October, 1937), 477–481.

101. Parsons, 2004: especially 4–29, 61–71; also Nagy, 1967: 29–30.

102. Nagy, 1985: 139.

103. This report is quoted throughout this book as *Nagy, 1967*.

104. "Address of Dr. Jacques Moreillon, former Secretary General of WOSM, to Dr. Eduardo Missoni, WOSM Secretary General." Circular 4/2004, World Scout Bureau: March 31, 2004.

105. Nagy, 1985: 149–151.

106. As stated in the document detailing the changes made, "Further development, both as regards the specification of the age and the sex of the young people, was a matter which should be left to each National Scout Association." "Document 2: 'The Purpose, Principles and Method of the Scout Movement'. Proposed revision of present Chapter II of the World Constitution. 26th World Scout Conference" (Montreal, Canada, 1977: approved document). WOSM, Geneva, 1977: 12–13.

107. Nagy, 1985: 163.

108. Nagy makes an interesting point about the process:

> If the Movement had committed the same error as the international organizations by giving an unrestricted vote to the "mini-states", a situation could have arisen in the future when a majority of two-thirds of the member states could have voted any kind of modification to the Scout Constitution, thus changing its objectives, spirit and nature, while

still only representing less than 5% of registered and paid-up members. Theoretically, it would also be possible for the Conference to elect—as always by secret vote as required by the Constitution—a World Committee of 12 members originating from member Associations whose numbers represent no more than 0.1% of the total Scout population. It was therefore decided to grant all the privileges to these small states, which sometimes only had one Troop, but not to give them voting rights.

(Nagy, 1985: 172)

109. *The New York Times,* June 13, 1972; quoted in Björk, Tord: "The emergence of popular participation in world politics: United Nations Conference on Human Environment 1972." Stockholm: Department of Political Science, University of Stockholm, 1996: 17.
110. Kroonenberg, 1998: 65, 99–100.
111. The International Scout Conference of 1929 made two exceptions to accepting new members: the scout associations of Russia and Armenia, both formed by exiles living in France (Nagy, 1985: 94). Although the Russian association disbanded a few years later, the Armenian association in exile was recognized until the world conference recognized Armenia as a member country with full voting rights in the 1990s.
112. The two detailed studies by the Dutch writer Piet Kroonenberg include countless details about the processes in all of these countries: See Kroonenberg, 1998: 72, 101, 161–162, 236–238, 306–307, 354–358, 385–387, 389–414; Kroonenberg, 2004: 25–28, 46–50, 72–77.
113. They were Albania, Armenia, Azerbaijan, Belarus, Bosnia Herzegovina, Bulgaria, Croatia, Slovakia, Slovenia, Estonia, Georgia, Hungary, Latvia, Lithuania, Macedonia, Moldavia, Poland, Romania, Russia, Serbia and Montenegro, Republic of Tajikistan, the Czech Republic, and the Ukraine,
114. Fauvel-Rouif, 1992: 401–414.
115. YMCA: World Alliance of Young Men's Christian Associations; YWCA: World Young Women's Christian Association.
116. The International Federation of Red Cross and Red Crescent Societies.
117. Alliance of Youth CEOs, 1997, 1999, 2001, 2003, 2005.
118. The main source of information were the census archives of the World Scout Bureau in Geneva, with the help of its Statistics Unit. To eliminate peaks, when no data was available for a given year, I opted to use the data for the previous year. I have taken the world censuses of 1932–1936, which do not exist in the World Scout Bureau archives, from the annual reports of the Boy Scouts Association UK—kept in the association's archive. The only major gap in the data is from 1939 to 1946, during and just after World War II, when the world organization had minimum staff levels and the censuses were not updated. In all events, none of the data prior to 1990 had been computer processed before this research. Historical data are only for WOSM because I had no permission to access historical WAGGGS censuses.

119. For the analyses of both current and historical data, I have compared the member countries of world scouting with the independent states existing at any given time. To do so, I contrasted the data from the WOSM and WAGGGS censuses with the "Correlates of War Project," a joint initiative by the University of Illinois and Pennsylvania State University that identifies actors as member states of the international system between 1816 and 2004. Correlates of War Project. 2004. "State System Membership List, v2004.1." February 2005. Online, http://correlatesofwar.org. (Accessed July 1, 2011.)

120. United Nations: Demographic Yearbook, Historical supplement (1948–1997). Note that this division considers all countries in Central America and the Caribbean as part of the region of "North America."

121. The "World Scouting 2003 Data Set" contains (a) the number of WOSM and WAGGGS member countries in this year; (b) the number of young members of world scouting in this year, for both WOSM and WAGGGS and overall, split into three age ranges (5–9, 10–14, 15–19) and by gender; (c) the population census data of the United Nations for 2000 for the same three age groups; (d) density (the number of scouts divided by the population of the same age range, multiplied by 10,000) obtained by cross-referencing *b* with *c*.

122. The WOSM and WAGGGS censuses use different categories to classify individuals by age range in the education process. However, these age ranges are defined by each association, so the classification in the censuses is only approximate. The most clearly delimited range is the age range with which scouting began, Scouts/Guides, roughly from 11 to 15 years. It is preceded by the Senior Scouts/Senior Guides, which can range from 15 to 18 years. The Cubs/Brownies are immediately below Scouts/Guides and usually include the 8–11 age range. At the very top end, we have Rovers/Rangers for those aged 18–22, and at the very bottom, Pre-Cubs/Pre-Brownies, aged 6–8 years. However, when it comes to comparing these age ranges with the UN population census in order to calculate density, we discover that the latter divides the population into five-year age ranges, which only leaves us with two possibilities: either 5–24 years or 5–19 years. We have only used the categories of the WOSM and WAGGGS censuses that include young people and not leaders or adult support. Moreover, the most inaccurate range in the census categories is the middle one (Scouts/Guides), which is very close to the 10–14 population range. I have therefore combined the lower two (Pre-Cubs/Pre-Brownies and Cubs/Brownies) to compare them to the 5–9 years population range and I have done the same with the top two (Senior Scouts/Senior Guides and Rovers/Rangers) in order to compare them to the 15–19 years population range. This division matches that of the UN census

123. China, India, United States of America, Indonesia, Brasil, Pakistan, Russia, Bangladesh, Nigeria, Japan, Mexico, Vietnam, Philipines, Germany, and Ethiopia. United Nations, 2005a.

124. United Nations, 2005a.

125. Today, Scouting is still officially banned in five countries: People's Republic of China, North Korea, Cuba, Laos, and Myanmar. WOSM, 2006, 89.

CHAPTER 2

1. "First I had an idea. Then I saw an ideal. Now we have a Movement, and if some of you don't watch out we shall end up just an organization" (quoted in WOSM, 1998: 20).
2. Baden-Powell, [1919] 1949: 7. Notice that there he uses the term "movements" referring to organizations: historically, in scouting the two concepts have commonly been used as sort of synonyms, although their actual meaning is very different.
3. "For the general public, there [1970s] was only one form of Scouting—B.P.'s. They are fairly indifferent to the fact that boys and girls are affiliated in separate movements each having their own independent organization" (Nagy, 1985: 159).
4. "Document 2: 'The Purpose, Principles and Method of the Scout Movement'. Proposed revision of present Chapter II of the World Constitution. 26th World Scout Conference" (Montreal, Canada, 1977: approved document). WOSM, Geneva, 1977.
5. This definition is made by combining the definitions established by the two world organizations in their Constitutions (WOSM, 2008: Article 1.1; WAGGGS, 2008: Article 6).
6. "It should be noted at the outset that it is not possible to express all aspects of the Scout Movement in one independent statement" (WOSM, 1992).
7. An unreferenced quotation from Baden-Powell backs up this point: "First I had an idea. Then I saw an ideal. Now we have a Movement, and if some of you don't watch out we shall end up just an organization" (quoted in WOSM 1998: 20).
8. Nagy, 1985: 82.
9. Russell, 1917
10. Delors, 1996; WOSM, 1992: 2.
11. Alliance of Youth CEOs, 1997: 6.
12. "28 million young people are changing the world" leaflet, WOSM, 2005.
13. WOSM, 2008: Articles V–VII; WAGGGS, 2008: Articles 6–14.
14. WOSM has traditionally used the expression "non-political" as equivalent of "non-partisan": "As an educational movement, Scouting is non-political in the sense that it is not involved in the struggle for power which is the subject-matter of politics and which is usually reflected in the system of political parties" (WOSM, 1992: 2); WAGGGS is clearer when in its Constitution states that member associations should be "independent of any political organization and any political party" (WAGGGS, 2008: Article 6 e)).
15. WOSM, 1998: 28–29.

16. The expressions "children" and "young people" are unclear and sometimes interchangeable. If we take the Convention on the Rights of the Child, that understand as "child" "every human being below the age of eighteen years," we have a different perspective than taking the definition of "youth" made by the United Nations (people between 15 and 24 years old).

17. WOSM, 1998: 21.

18. WOSM, 1998: 22–23.

19. *"Policy on Involvement of Young Members in Decision-Making,"* WOSM, adopted at the 33rd World Scout Conference, 1993. *Young Women in Decision-Making,* adopted at the 90th Meeting of the WAGGGS World Board, January 1997. The 39th World Scout Conference, in January 2011, elected Karin Ahlbäck, 23 years old, as a World Scout Committee member. She has been the youngest elected member of the two world committees.

20. WOSM, 1998: 25.

21. "The Scout Movement is a voluntary non-political educational movement for young people open to all without distinction of origin, race or creed (...)" (WOSM, 2008: Article I.1). "A Member of the World Association shall be a National Organization which: (...) c) Has a membership which is: i. voluntary; ii. open to all girls and young women without distinction of creed, race, nationality, *or any other circumstance*" (WAGGGS, 2008: Article 6) (the emphasis is mine).

22. In *Scouting for Boys* (Baden-Powell, 2004 [1908]: 45), the point including nondiscrimination is found in the text of the Scout Law. This point was officially amended in 1938, when the reference to fraternity among countries was added: "A Scout is a friend to all, and a brother to every other scout, no matter to what *country*, class, or creed the other may belong" (Nagy, 1985: 106 (the emphasis is mine)).

23. Nagy, 1985: 104.

24. The 1999 World Scout Conference's stance on this issue is very explicit: "When a National Scout Association operates in a society where separate gender relationships are the norm and where coeducation is therefore excluded, the association may continue to address the male gender only or may opt for providing Scouting to both genders in single-sex settings." "Document 9: 'Policy on Girls and Boys, Women and Men Within the Scout Movement'. 35th World Scout Conference" (Durban, South Africa, 1999: adopted document), WOSM, Geneva, 1999: 4.

25. Homosexuality is legally punished in 76 countries. The case of the BSA is a different one and it will be analyzed in Chapter 3.

26. The two constitutional definitions of the purpose of the movement are as follows: in WOSM wording, "[t]he purpose of the Scout Movement is to contribute to the development of young people in achieving their full physical, intellectual, emotional, social and spiritual potentials as individuals, as responsible citizens and as members of their local, national and international communities" (WOSM, 2008: Article I.2); in WAGGGS wording, "the aim of the Girl Guide/Girl Scout Movement... is to provide girls and young women with opportunities for self-training in the development

of character, responsible citizenship and service in their own and world communities" (WAGGGS, 2008: Article 3 b)).

27. "Document 9: 'Policy on girls and boys, women and men within the Scout Movement'" (Durban, South Africa, 35th World Scout Conference). WOSM, 1999: 4.
28. WOSM, 1998: 16–17.
29. Jeal, 2001: 392–394.
30. WOSM, 2008: Article V.3, b) and g); WAGGGS, 2008: Article 6 a). Already in 1933 a resolution of the International Scout Conference established that member organizations must notify any change in the wording of the law or the promise, "or in any other regulation embodying the essential principles of Scouting" (WOSM, 1985: 9 (resolution 12/33)).
31. WOSM, 2008: article II.1: "Principles"; WAGGGS, 1997: 19–20. These three principles already figured in the first edition of *Scouting for Boys* in 1908, when explaining the scout sign: "The three fingers held up (like the three points of the scout's badge) remind him of his three promises in the scout's oath: 1. Honour God and the King; 2. Help others; 3. Obey the Scout Law" (Baden-Powell [1908] 2004: 37).
32. WOSM, 1992: 5.
33. WOSM, 1992: 5, 1998: 17.
34. A comparative document from the WAGGGS/WOSM Consultative Committee also contains a definition of the essential elements of the Promise and the Law of any WAGGGS member (very similar to the constitutional text of WOSM): "*Duty To God* ~ Acknowledgement and search for spirituality. *Duty to Country* ~ Acceptance of the concept of responsibility to the community in which we live. *To help others at all times* ~ Acceptance of the practice of helpfulness to others. *Obey the Guide Law* ~ Responsibility for self-action." "WAGGGS/WOSM Relationships. Report on the Discussion on the Fundamental Principles of WAGGGS and WOSM." Document signed by Heather Brandon and Garth Morrisson, members of the WAGGGS/WOSM Consultative Committee, summarizing the meeting held on January 14, 2001 (document not dated): 3.
35. In scouting, the French term *laïque* has been used to designate the scout associations where education in spiritual matters does not include the practice of religious beliefs by members, but an active attitude of in-depth study and understandings of the beliefs of those members. The English translation would be *secular*, but on this context the translation could lead to confusion because they strip the words of their intense educational focus on the spiritual dimension.
36. Nagy, 1967: 39.
37. WOSM, 1992: 5.
38. Russell, 1917.
39. "Document 2: 'The Purpose, Principles and Method of the Scout Movement'. Proposed revision of present Chapter II of the World Constitution. 26th World Scout Conference" (Montreal, Canada, 1977: approved document) WOSM, Geneva, 1977: p. 22.

40. As constitutionally stated in WOSM, 2008: Article II.2; and in WAGGGS, 2008: Article 2. Notice that the point 8 says "whistles" for the original male version and "sings" for the female one. The point 10 was added in 1911 to the original nine points of the 1908 *Scouting for Boys,* and it says "clean" for boys (scouts) and "pure" for girls (guides).

41. http://www5.scout.ch/en/about-us/promise-and-law (Accessed July 1, 2011). The original French wording is as following: (Promise) "Je promets, de faire tout mon possible, afin de: Me remettre sans cesse en question par rapport aux lois scoutes/Chercher le sens et les buts de ma vie/De m'intégrer dans chaque communauté dans laquelle je vie;/(avec cette confiance en Dieu) avec vous tous, j'essaie de vivre selon cette promesse". (Law) "Nous, les scouts, nous voulons: Etre vrais; Nous réjouir de ce qui est beau; Etre attentif et aider autour de nous; Choisir de notre mieux et nous engager; Ecouter et respecter les autres; Partager; Protéger la nature et respecter la vie; Affronter les difficultés avec confiance" http://www5.scout.ch/fr/le-scoutisme/traditions/loi-promesse/bases-de-la-loi-et-de-la-promesse?searchterm= loi (Accessed July 1, 2011).

42. WOSM, 1998: 8–9.

43. I have made a composition of the three relevant wordings of the components of the scout method: two constitutional and another one more comprehensible. WAGGGS Constitution lists them as: "i. Commitment through the Promise and Law; ii. Progressive Self-Development; iii. Learning by doing; iv. Teamwork through the Patrol System and training for responsible leadership; v. Active co-operation between young people and adults; vi. Service in the Community; vii. Outdoor activities; viii. Symbolism (WAGGGS, 2008: Article 6 b)). WOSM Constitution lists them as: "A promise and law. Learning by doing. Membership of small groups (for example the patrol), involving, under adult guidance, progressive discovery and acceptance of responsibility and training towards self-government directed towards the development of character, and the acquisition of competence, self-reliance, dependability and capacities both to cooperate and to lead. Progressive and stimulating programmes of varied activities based on the interests of the participants, including games, useful skills, and services to the community, taking place largely in an outdoor setting in contact with nature" (WOSM, 2008: Article 3). And the document *The Essential Characteristics of Scouting* lists them as: "A promise and law. Learning by doing. A patrol (or team) system. Symbolic framework. Personal progression. Nature. Adult support" (WOSM, 1998: 9–13). I have adopted that later one, because it includes the progressive programs (WOSM Constitution) in "Learning by doing" and the service in the community (WAGGGS Constitution) in the law and promise.

44. WOSM, 1998: 8–9.

45. Ibid.

46. On Baden-Powell's *Aids to Scoutmastership,* addressed to scout leaders ("scoutmasters"), that is, educators, he insists on this since the beginning: "The Scoutmaster has to be neither schoolmaster nor commanding officer,

nor pastor, nor instructor." "The business of the Scoutmaster is to draw out each boy and find out what is in him, and then to catch hold of the good and develop it to the exclusion of the bad.... This is education instead of instruction of the young mind" (Baden-Powell, [1919] 1949: 19–20).

47. Ibid.: 8.
48. "Meaning and Relevance of the World Organization of the Scout Movement. Address by Dr. Jacques Moreillon, Secretary General of WOSM, to the Summit Meeting of the 20th Inter-American Scout Conference" Guadalajara, Mexico, March 21, 1998.
49. The local scout group doesn't exist in all countries: at least I know the exception of BSA, where instead of *scout groups* the nuclear subjects are the "units" of each age group.
50. "Document 7: 'Governance of WOSM'. 37th World Scout Conference" (Yasmine Hammamet, Tunisia, 2005: adopted as a reference document). WOSM, Geneva, 2005: 4.
51. "The components of the network are both autonomous and dependent vis-à-vis the network, and may be a part of other networks, and therefore of other systems of means aimed at other goals. The performance of a given network will then depend on two fundamental attributes of the network: its connectedness, that is its structural ability to facilitate noise-free communication between its components; its consistency, that is the extent to which there is sharing of interests between the network's goals and the goals of its components" (Castells, 2000: 171).
52. "Actions that speak louder...," issue of "The Bottom Line," World Scout Foundation, June 2002. http://scout.org/en/content/download/3241/30663/file/20bl_wosmstrat_e.pdf (Accessed July 1, 2011).
53. Ibid.
54. Hall, Edward T. (1986): "Unstated Features of the Cultural Context of Learning," in Thomas, A. and Ploman, E. W. (eds.): *Learning and Development: A Global perspective*. Toronto: OISE Press, 157–176 (p. 159). Quoted in Farrell, 2011.
55. Olson, 2003: ix; Farrell, 2011.
56. Baden-Powell, [1923] 2007: 8. The idea refers both to boys and girls, as a bit later he adds: "Much of the open-air life with its nature study, camping, exploration, mapping, sketching, etc., appeals with equal force and with equal advantage to girls. Thus, the whole youth of the world appears to be ready."
57. Dewey, 1897; Nelson Block notices it in Block and Proctor, 2009: 9.
58. Russell, 1917.
59. Arnove and Torres, 2007: 8. In social sciences this bias has been called *methodological nationalism* (Smith, Anthony D. (1979): *Nationalism in the Twentieth Century*. Oxford: Martin Robertson and Co., 191).
60. Arnove and Torres, 2007: 133.
61. Tra Bach, Huberman and Sulser, 1995.

62. Ibid.: 63.
63. Nagy, 1967: 59–62
64. Nagy, 1985: 119.
65. Tra Bach, Huberman and Sulser, 1995: 208–215.
66. Holmes, 1921: 122–123.
67. Ibid., 123. Holmes concludes adding that "In other words, in the Boy Scout philosophy of education the balance between the claims of the individual and of the communal self is steadily maintained, and the way is thus opened for the ideal or universal self to come to the birth, and for the highest of all causes to make its appeal to the heart. To achieve and maintain this balance should be the primary aim of all who are interested in education: and in no branch of education is the need for the realization of this aim more urgent than in that which deals with adolescence."
68. Tra Bach, Huberman and Sulser, 1995: 109–110.
69. Quoted in Jeal, 2001: 413.
70. Proctor, 2009b: xxvii.
71. Russell, 1917.
72. James M. Burns: *Leadership*. New York: Harper & Row, 1978.
73. Delors, 1996.
74. Alliance of Youth CEO, 1997: 6.
75. Miquel A. Essomba, 'Educar en el temps lliure: Simplement educar?', *Barcelona Educació*, 77 (June 2011), 12–15.
76. Farrell, 2011.
77. "Comments of Dr. Jacques Moreillon, former Secretary General of WOSM (1988–2004), on the PhD thesis of Eduard Vallory Subirà 'Global Citizenship education.' " Barcelona, December 20, 2007.
78. Farrell, 1997.
79. Farrell, 2011.
80. FCEG, 2003: 79.
81. "Document 7: 'Governance of WOSM' . . . ," WOSM, Geneva, 2005: 4–6.
82. Nevertheless, democratic systems are continuosly expanding: in 2000, of 147 where data were available, 121 (68% of world population) had some or all the elements of a formal democracy, in comparison with the only 54 countries (46% of world population) in 1980. UNDP, 2002: 14–15.
83. "It should be necessary to add formally to the conditions for NSOs [National Scout Organizations] to be recognized and to maintain their membership, the establishment and development of democratic structures and democratic decision-making processes" ("Document 7: 'Governance of WOSM' . . . " WOSM, Geneva, 2005); and "WAGGGS' Policy on Structure and Management of Associations." Adopted by the World Board, WAGGGS, October 1998. London: World Bureau, WAGGGS.
84. Alliance of Youth CEOs, 2005: 4.
85. "Document 7: 'Governance of WOSM' . . . ," WOSM, Geneva, 2005: 4. This definition of 'scout group' does not apply to the case of the BSA, where the chartered organizations system explained in Chapter 3 entitle

external institutions to sponsor separately the age groups: a cub scouts pack, a boy scouts troop, a Varsity scouts team, or a Venturing crew, with separate administrative approvals by the BSA.

86. Ibid.: 4.

87. The two world organizations understand as "national organization" the scout organization of a "politically independent country," and establish that in each of them only one organization (association or federation of associations) can be recognized. (WOSM, 2008: art. V.2; WAGGGS, 2008: Article 9 b)).

88. "Document 7: 'Governance of WOSM' . . . ," WOSM, Geneva, 2005: 5.

89. Ibid.: 7.

90. Although the two WOSM-member Irish associations (the Catholic one and the open one) merged in 2004, in WAGGGS there is still an Irish open association and a Catholic one, federated as the Council of Irish Girl Guides Associations.

91. In 1990, moreover, Spanish and Arabic became "working languages" of the world scout conferences with translation, and later on Russian was also added in the same category.

92. At the world scout conference (WOSM), each national member organization has six votes (Article 10, WOSM Constitution), and at the world conference, WAGGGS, each national member organization has one vote (Article 6, Section 3, WAGGGS Constitution).

93. It is called the *World Scout Committee* by WOSM and the *World Board* by WAGGGS.

94. These individuals must have originally belonged to a national member organization, which must have nominated them.

95. Nagy, 1985: 113.

96. "World Scout Committee Triennial Report, 2002–2005," World Scout Bureau, 2005. "Report & Financial Statements for the year ended December 31, 2006," World Board, WAGGGS, 2007. The Beresford study revealed that the approximate budgets in pounds sterling for 1998/99 amounted to almost £2 million for WAGGGS and close to £3 million for WOSM, of which the income from member fees totaled £1.3 million (65%) for WAGGGS and £2 million (66%) for WOSM. "Fact-finding Study (WOSM/WAGGGS)," document submitted by John Beresford, Chair of the Constitutions Committee of the WOSM, to the World Scout Committee, October 7, 2000, 20–22.

97. These are the Inter-American/West Hemisphere region (1946), the Asia-Pacific region (1956), the Arab region (1956), the European region (1961), the African region (1967) and, since 1996, for WOSM only, there is also the Eurasian region (former USSR). The date in brackets is the date the regions were founded in the WOSM.

98. For WOSM, membership of a national scout organization to its corresponding region is voluntary (WOSM, 2008: Article XIX.1).

99. The Chairs of the regional WAGGGS committees are members with voting rights on the World Board (WAGGGS, 2008: Article 22); Chairs of the

regional WOSM committees became ex-officio (non-voting) members of the World Scout Committee in 2008 (WOSM, 2008: art. XII.2).

100. Both the WOSM Constitution (Article XXI) and the WAGGGS Constitution (Article 38), establish that the regulations (Constitution and Statutes) of the regions must be approved by the World Committee/Board and that, in the event of conflict between regional and world regulations, the world regulations will prevail. (WOSM, 2008; WAGGGS, 2008).

101. The regional directors are employed by the World Bureau, the body that appoints them after consulting with their respective regional committees (WOSM, 2008: Article XIX.2 c)).

102. Proctor, 2009b: xxxv.

103. The WAGGGS mission was adopted as a resolution of its World Conference in 1996.

104. "A Strategy for Scouting: Understanding the Mission Statement." WOSM, Geneva: 2000. The WOSM mission was approved by the World Scout Conference in 1999 (Resolution 3/1999), and the full text adds that "This [mission] is achieved by: involving them throughout their formative years in a non-formal educational process; using a specific method that makes each individual the principal agent of his or her development as a self-reliant, supportive, responsible and committed person; assisting them to establish a value system based upon spiritual, social and personal principles as expressed in the Promise and Law."

105. The WAGGGS/WOSM Consultative Committee is a joint working sub-group of members of the executive governing bodies of WAGGGS (World Board) and WOSM (World Scout Committee), created to allow the two organizations to work together on common issues and explore a possible shared vision for the future. It began operation in January 2001.

106. "We do not see a clash in the stated missions of the two world organizations—they are about the realisation of the potential in everyone—male or female—within their influence". "The determination to express in words the need for a focus on the needs of girls and young women is a perfectly understandable recognition of a reality in the world in which we live—generations of hard experience demonstrate that, without that focus, the needs of women are subordinated to those of men" "WAGGGS/WOSM Relationships. Missions of the World Organizations." Document signed by Garth Morrisson and Heather Brandon, members of the WAGGGS/WOSM Consultative Committee, April 2, 2001: B-2.

107. Nielsen, 2003: 161.

108. Ibid.

109. I find appealing on that sense the narrative of the merged and mixed association of scouting in India, with a reference of what "the leaders of the nation wished": "In 1950 the Boy Scout Association in India and the Hindusthan Scout Association merged under the name of Bharat Scouts and Guides. The Girl Guide Association of India merged on 15th August,1951, thus completing the merger of the Boy Scout Association and the Girl Guide Association as wished by Pandit Jawaharlal Nehru, Maulana

Abul Kalam Asad and other leaders of the nation, to form the present day Bharat Scouts and Guides thus adding one more milestone to the world History of Scouting and providing scope for unified organization which will lead the young to their future" http://www.scouting4peace.org/group/bharatscoutsandguidesindia (Accessed July 1, 2011).

110. In the same way, Proctor states: "The litigious battles between Boy Scouts and Girl Scouts in the United States, not only divided the two movements, but it set them on paths apart from other nations and from each other in the future" (Proctor, 2009b: xxxi).

111. Report to the Secretary General: Report of the League Representatives to the Third International Scout Conference, Copenhagen, August 1924, pp. 5 and 10. Document No. 38.191, League of Nations archive, Geneva.

112. "Justice: Les trous de mémoire de l'abbé Cottard au procès de la noyade des scouts." Article published in *Le Monde*, October 20, 1999.

113. "Une association proche de l'extrême droite." Article published in *Le Monde*, July 25, 1998.

114. "Les fichiers baladeurs des Guides et Scouts d'Europe. Le mouvement scout tente de remettre de l'ordre dans ses rangs." Article published in *Le Monde*, April 25, 1999.

115. "Une association proche de l'extrême droite." Article published in *Le Monde*, July 25, 1998.

116. The complete reference says: "We must from the outset avoid making our International Conference a "Parliament"—that is, a meeting of *representatives* of different countries. If we allow the spirit of national interests to come in to conflict with our one interest, "the girl," we are going to miss the essential spirit that should inspire us. The work of delegates [at the International Conference] is to bring their experiences from all parts of the world to bear upon and help the better training of *the girl*. It is not to watch the interests of their particular country as against those of other countries. Unless and until we are not assured of the right spirit it would be better that we should not attempt to start an International organization." "Memorandum: By the Founder on the Report of the World Conference," July 19, 1928, p. 4. Document annex to the "Historical Report of the Conference which took place in Hungary, May 1928," signed by Katharine Furse, Secretary of the Conference, on July 22, 1928. Archive of the World Bureau, WAGGGS.

117. Nagy, 1985: 103.

118. The analysis of these three axes is based on resolutions of world scout conferences, which have all been published. Despite my requests to the WAGGGS World Bureau, archive problems have meant that it was not possible to access the resolutions approved by the WAGGGS world conferences since it was established.

119. Parsons, 2004: xi.

120. Robert Baden-Powell moral authority, and even the title of "Chief Scout of the World" that he received by acclamation at the London Jamboree of 1920, were democratically established by the new world organism in

the following International Scout Conference (París, 1922), the first one in which resolutions were adopted. Thus, Resolution 3/22 establishes that "The Conference re-affirms its recognition of Sir Robert Baden-Powell as the Chief Scout of the World and asserts its belief that the ideals as set forth in *Scouting for Boys* are so fundamentals as to transcend the limit of race and country. They place on record their appreciation of the immense obligation under which the world lies for the system which his genius has evolved and the distribution of that system to all nations to which his personality has materially contributed" (WOSM, 1985: 1).

121. WOSM, 2001: 51.
122. More specifically, the new institution was called "International Union of European Guides and Scouts," adopted through Decree 1130/03/AIC of the Vatican's Pontifical Council for the Laity.
123. Article 1.2.13: "The youth's full religious development requires that their chiefs should belong to the same Church or Community as theirs, should profess the same doctrine, should take part in the same liturgical and sacramental life."

Article 1.2.14: "Some non Christian young people may be exceptionally admitted within the units, on condition that their parents have previously accepted to recognise the confessional character of the Group. No one may pronounce his Scout or Guide promise if he is not baptised. However, a Scout or a Guide may be admitted to pronounce his Promise if he is involved in the catechumenate."

Bylaws of the International Union of European Guides and Scouts-European Scouting Federation, 2003. English version: http://www.uigse.org/statuto_en.asp; French version: http://www.uigse.org/statuto_fr.asp (Accessed July 1, 2011).
124. "To his [Baden-Powell's] distress, some of the pacifists set up a splinter group, the National Peace Scouts, while some of the militaristically inclined people established the British Boy Scouts and the Empire Scouts as an answer to his un-compromising stand against including military drill in his scheme" (Hillcourt, 1964: 296). See also Nagy, 1985: 67.
125. Kergomard and François, 1983: 38.
126. Macleod, 1983: 157.
127. "Fact-finding Study (WOSM/WAGGGS)," document submitted by John Beresford, Chair of the Constitutions Committee of the WOSM, to the World Scout Committee, October 7, 2000, p. 9.
128. "A National Organization which has been part of the World Association through a Member Organization may, on the attainment of political independence by its country, apply direct for Membership of the World Association. In a country where the formalities of political independence are in process but not fully completed the National Organization in that country may submit an application for Membership of the World Association. Subject to recommendation by the World Board the application may be submitted to Full Members meeting at a World Conference, for approval. The World Conference may authorize the World Board to

send, at its discretion, the official acceptance as a Member of the World Association and the Certificate of Membership; this to be either when the formalities of the country's independence are completed or, in special circumstances, at a time considered more appropriate by the World Board . . . ." WAGGGS Bylaws: Bylaw I, section 4 (WAGGGS, 2008).

129. Sunder, 2001: 500–501.

130. Nagy (1967: 43–44) mention the case of the split association "All India Boy Scout Association," which he says it had more than 145,000 members, and that among the causes of the split "also touches the application of scout methods": whereas the internationally recognized scout association had introduced methodological changes and have started coeducation and mixed groups, the split one wanted to maintain the traditional systems imported from British and keep boys and girls separated.

131. http://www.wfis-europe.org/ (Accessed July 1, 2011).

132. WFIS website: http://www.wfis-worldwide.org (Accessed July 1, 2011).

133. "The election will be held, and votes able to be cast, between the dates of March 17th 2007 to March 31st 2007. Votes should be sent to wfis.election@gmail.com." WFIS website: http://www.wfis-worldwide.org/election.html (Accessed November 2, 2006).

134. "If an attempt were to be made to put oneself in the shoes of the innocent boy who needs scouting, and not in those of the adult who is generally responsible for the quarrels, one would become more tolerant towards the 'lost sheep' " (Nagy, 1967, 49).

135. "We therefore recommend that the new rules setting out the principles of recognition be stricter about educational conditions, but not quite so hard about ideological-political criteria which are, by definition, extra-scout matters" (Nagy, 1967, 49).

CHAPTER 3

1. Hanna Arendt: *Crisis of the Republic*. New York: Harcourt, Brace, Jovanovich, 1972.

2. Crick, 1999: 343 onward.

3. Kymlicka, 1999: 85–88.

4. Putnam, 2000. Warburton and Smith make also an interesting criticism of the Australian government's introduction of compulsory volunteer schemes, a direct consequence of the argument that a country with more volunteers—even if it is compulsory!—is a country with more democratic values (Jennifer Warburton and Jennifer Smith: "Out of the Generosity of Your Heart: Are We Creating Active Citizens through Compulsory Volunteer Programmes for Young People in Australia?" *Social Policy and Administration*, 37:7 (Dec. 2003), 772–786). We have also dealt with this issue in Vallory and Pérez, 2001.

5. Skocpol, 2003.

6. Kymlicka, 1999: 88. Joseph P. Farrell has also explained how democratic citizenship values can be acquired through scouting (Farrell, 2001: 131–132).

7. Russell, 1917.

8. As WOSM states it, "The mission of Scouting is to contribute to the education of young people (. . .) to help build a better world where people are self-fulfilled as individuals and play a constructive role in society."

9. "The legitimacy of regime institutions is one contributing factor which helps promote voluntary compliance with the law, and therefore an effective public policy-making process, but strengthening human rights and civil liberties in transitional democracies may be even more important" (Norris, 1999: 264).

10. John M. Mackenzie (ed.): *Imperialism and Popular Culture*. Manchester & Dover, NH: Manchester University Press, 1986, 3.

11. There are five premises underpinning the theory of progress: 1. Belief in the value of the past; 2. The conviction that western civilization is noble and thus superior to others; 3. Acceptance of the worth of economic and technological growth; 4. Faith in reason and the scientific and scholarly knowledge obtained through it, and 5. Belief in the intrinsic importance and the ineffable worth of life on earth (Robert A. Nisbet: *History of the idea of progress*. New Brunswick NJ: Transaction Publishers, 1998, 317).

12. "The aim of Scouting training is to improve the standard of our future citizenhood, especially in Character and Health; to replace Self with Service, to make the lads individually efficient, morally and physically, with the object of using that efficiency for service for their fellow-men" (Baden-Powell, [1919] 1949: 33–34).

13. WOSM, 1990.

14. "In the 1920's the Committee included such members as the Earl of Meath, head of the Duty and Discipline movement and founder of the Empire Day; the Earl was determined to oppose any internationalist leanings within the Movement that went beyond some harmless phraseology. In the beginning this conservative faction even criticised the idea of a world Jamboree. (. . .) In particular, they opposed ties with the British League of Nations Union, on the grounds that it was a 'political organisation' " (Sica, 2006: 24–25).

15. "Probably a local branch [of the *League of Nations Union*] exists in your town; if so, you should ask the secretary if you can help him in any way, such as distributing handbills for meetings." *The Scout*, "August 14, 1920. Quoted in Sica, 2006: 24.

16. The quote comes from BP's influential *Aids to Scoutmastership*, written for adult educators (Baden-Powell ([1919] 1949: 88)). The reference to citizenship is also explicit: "Citizenship has been defined briefly as "active loyalty to the community." In a free country it is easy, and not unusual, to consider oneself a good citizen by being a law-abiding man, doing your work and expressing your choice in politics, sports, or activities, "leaving it to George" to worry about the nation's welfare. This is passive citizenship. But *passive* citizenship is not enough to uphold in the world the virtues of freedom,

justice and honour. Only *active* citizenship will do" (Baden-Powell, [1919] 1949: 34).

17. Jeal, 2001: 413.
18. Baden-Powell, [1908] 2004: 298.
19. "Document 7: 'Governance of WOSM'. 37th World Scout Conference" (Yasmine Hammamet, Tunisia, 2005: adopted as a reference document). WOSM, Geneva, 2005, 13.
20. Parsons, 2004: 256.
21. Jeal, 2001: 545.
22. Parsons, 2004: 5, 7.
23. WOSM, 1985: 9 (resolution 9/31).
24. Saint George Saunders, 1948.
25. Baden-Powell, [1908] 2004: 45.
26. Parsons, 2004: 6.
27. Nagy, 1967: 29–30.
28. The constitutions of the two world organizations reproduce the original wording: "A Scout obeys orders of his parents, Patrol Leader or Scoutmaster without question" (WOSM, 2008: Article II.2); "A Guide obeys orders" (WAGGGS, 2008: Article 2).
29. Robert Baden-Powell: "What Scouts Can Do," 1921: 15; quoted in Sica, 1984: 61–62.
30. Russell, 1917. He adds: "These two forces are but the two sides of the same shield, opposed yet essentially one in the course of education."
31. The article conclude saying that "one cannot help looking forward and hoping that this comradeship of the Scout and Guide movement will contribute to an improved mutual relationship between the different elements in the population and so tend to bring about the unity necessary for making an united South African people in the future" (Baden-Powell, 1936: 368, 370, 371). An example of the achievement of this vision is found in the example of Isabella Direko, who in 1999 became Premier of the Free State province in South Africa. She stressed to WAGGGS that during the apartheid, while black people were being controlled and repressed, girl guides encouraged and helped her to be strong and assertive and gave her the courage to overcome all obstacles to triumph in the end.
32. See Parsons, 2004, on anti-colonialism and civil rights; Ihle, 1993, on self-styled scout German youth and their struggle against the Nazi dictatorship; Balcells and Samper, 1993, on the opposition of Catalan Scouting to Franco's Spanish regime; Kroonenberg, 1998, on resistance to the prohibition of Scouting in Soviet regimes; Verga and Cagnoni, 2002, on Italian Scouting's resistance in Lombardy prior to 1945; and Mechling, 2001: 207–235, 2009; Sunder, 2001; and Applebome, 2003: 234–252, on the BSA's discrimination policy against homosexuals and atheists and also on the nonconformism of some of its members.
33. Balcells and Samper, 1993: 137–138.
34. "Los Scouts de Argentina (..) adherimos a la conmemoración del trigésimo aniversario del último golpe de estado, que quebrantó las instituciones de la

República e instaló en nuestro país la dictadura más sangrienta de la historia nacional, mediante la aplicación sistemática del terror estatal y de brutales métodos de exterminio y proscripción, que necesitan un claro pronunciamiento de la Justicia para terminar con la impunidad de los victimarios. Dictadura que implementó, además, un proyecto económico, político y social atentatorio contra la democracia y contra los intereses fundamentales de la Nación y del pueblo argentinos. Proyecto cuyas gravísimas consecuencias aún hoy seguimos padeciendo, con altísimos niveles de desocupación, con más de la mitad de la población bajo la línea de la pobreza, con generaciones de argentinos con deficiencias de desarrollo intelectual y físico por la pobreza estructural (. . .)." "A 30 años del último golpe de Estado," Statement of the Consejo Directivo de Scouts de Argentina, March 24, 2006.

35. Warren, 2009: xviii.
36. "The Marrakech Charter," WOSM, 2005.
37. "It is our challenge to take up the task and prepare our young people to be involved citizens, whether in their local, national or international communities. This requires a vision which is deeply rooted in their immediate environment but which goes far beyond." "Community Involvement Resource Pack," The Europe Office, WAGGGS, and the European Scout Region-World Scout Bureau, 1989: 2–3.
38. Jacques Moreillon, Secretary General of WOSM (1988–2004); Lesley Bulman, Chief Executive of WAGGGS (1997–2006).
39. Alliance of Youth CEOs, 1997, 1999, 2001, 2003, 2005. Most documents could be downloaded from: http://scout.org/en/about_scouting/partners/youth_platforms/alliance_of_youth_ceos/joint_publications   (Accessed July 1, 2011)
40. Skocpol, 2003: 142–144.
41. " 'Together We can Change Our World'—A Toolkit on Advocacy: Supporting and encouraging young people to speak out, educate, and take action." Europe Region, WAGGGS: 2008. http://www.wagggsworld.org/en/grab/3384/1/1advocacyENG.pdf (Accessed July 1, 2011).
42. "Why advocacy?" Lesley Bulman's speech to the WAGGGS Working Group in Advocacy, London, May 2006. Archive of the Chief Executive of WAGGGS.
43. Document *Advocacy Guidelines*, WAGGGS, 2007.
44. Circular 33/2004, World Scout Bureau, November 2004.
45. Circular 4/2005, World Scout Bureau, January 2005.
46. "Scouting's Social Impact: 28 million young people are changing the world." Presspack, doc n. 3, version 31.05.2006. WOSM Document of Communication: World Scout Bureau.
47. http://www.wagggsworld.org/en/take_action/gat (Accessed July 1, 2011); also "Report, 33rd World Conference, WAGGGS. South Africa, 2008." London: WAGGGS.
48. Robertson, 1995: 40. Along the same lines, Beck gives the example of large multinational corporations that see their production strategies in terms of

"global localization": their executives are convinced that globalization does not mean building factories everywhere, but becoming a living part of each respective culture (Ulrich Beck, *What Is Globalization?* Cambridge: Polity Press, 2000: 46).

49. Baden-Powell, [1908] 2004: 5.

50. Kunz, 1969: 666.

51. Jordan, 2005.

52. It is also worth noting that WAGGGS has set a maximum limit so that the financial contribution from any one association does not make up more than 50 percent of all fees. "Fact-finding Study (WOSM/WAGGGS)," document presented by John Beresford, Chairman of WOSM Constitutions Committee, to the World Scout Committee, October 7, 2000: 21.

53. Followed by Japan (12.5%) and Germany (8.0%) (Source: United Nations data, 2011).

54. The Young Men's Christian Association has existed in the United States since 1851, seven years after it was founded in the United Kingdom.

55. MacLeod, 1983.

56. "The purpose of this corporation shall be to promote, through organization and cooperation with other agencies, the ability of boys to do things for themselves and others, to train them in Scoutcraft, and to teach them patriotism, courage, self-reliance, and kindred virtues, using the methods which are now in common use by Boy Scouts." *United States Code. Title 36: Patriotic and national Observances, Ceremonies and organizations. Subtitle II: Patriotic and National Organizations. Part B: Organizations. 309: Boy Scouts of America.* http://uscode.house.gov/download/pls/36C309.txt (Accessed July 1, 2011).

57. Macleod, 2009: 25.

58. *United States Code. Title 36: Patriotic and national Observances, Ceremonies and organizations. Subtitle II: Patriotic and National Organizations. Part B: Organizations. 803: Girl Scouts of the United States of America.* http://uscode.house.gov/download/pls/36C25.txt (Accessed July 1, 2011).

59. Miller, 2009: 28–29.

60. Arneil, 2010: 56.

61. The BSA allowed girls to join its Exploring program in 1969. Although they are still barred from joining the traditional Cub or Scout programs for younger children, at the time of writing there are more girls in this age group (Venturer, 14–20 years old) in BSA than in GSUSA.

62. Arneil, 2010: 62–63.

63. Mechling, 2001: 37.

64. The "don't ask, don't tell" American policy on sexual orientation has even lead to many lesbian came out of the closet in girl scouting, as it is explained in: Nancy Manahan (ed.): *On My Honor: Lesbians Reflect on Their Scouting Experience.* Northboro MA: Madwoman Press, Inc., 1997.

65. Mechling, 2001: 189–93.

66. Within each chartered organization, there may be one or more "units," meaning a group of youth and adults which are collectively designated

as a Cub Scout pack, Boy Scout troop, Varsity Scout team, or Venturing crew/Sea Scout ship.

67. Nagy, 1985: 117–118.
68. Mechling, 2001: 35. In a document of 2000 in favor of the BSA policy on discrimination of homosexuals, the Mormons Church declared to group 400,000 BSA members and the Catholic Church to group 355,000 BSA members. "Brief of Amicus Curiae, National Catholic Committee On Scouting, General Commission on United Methodist Men of the United Methodist Church, the Church of Jesus Christ of Latter-Day Saints, the Lutheran Church-Missouri Synod, and the National Council of Young Israel", Boy Scouts of America v. Dale, 530 US 640, 657 (2000) [February 28, 2000].
69. Applebone, 2003: 310–311.
70. Mechling, 2001, 36.
71. *Salt Lake Tribune,* August 3, 1974.
72. "Scouting for the 11-Year-Old," The Church of Jesus Christ of Latter-day Saints website: http://lds.org/pa/display/0,17884,4834-1,00. html (Accessed July 1, 2011).
73. "Guidebook for Parents and Leaders of Youth." Intellectual Reserve, Inc., 2001. The Church of Jesus Christ of Latter-day Saints website: http://www. lds.org/youthresources/pdf/GuideParLead36415.pdf (Accessed July 1, 2006).
74. The coexistence with racist practices in society had created tensions in BSA and scouting in general. For instance, "during the 1929 World Jamboree, the publisher of the *Chicago Defender*, Robert S. Abbott, sent a cablegram to the assembled scout leaders. He wished to bring to their attention "the atrocious practice of lynching and burning alive of human beings in the United States." He asked that they not "accept in your august body Boy Scouts from those cities and states where lynchings are permitted and who at the same time have witnessed lynchings without protests as well as those who believe in this barbarous practice of taking human life without due process of law." Abbott entreated the international scouting community to abolish "color segregation in your ranks by seeing that all boys in the southern and other states be permitted to join the same brigades as is done in the North." E-mail to the author from David L. Peavy, July 30, 2011.
75. Kunz, 1969: 674–675.
76. Mechling, 2001, 35–36.
77. Boy Scouts of America v. Dale (99–699) 530 U.S. 640, 665 (2000).
78. "Brief of Amicus Curiae, The General Board of Church and Society of the United Methodist Church, the United Church Board for Homeland Ministries, The Religious Action Center of Reform Judaism, The Diocesan Council of the Episcopal Diocese of Newark, and the Unitarian Association." Boy Scouts of America v. Dale, 530 US 640, 657 (2000) [March 29, 2000]; Mechling, 2001, 225.
79. Resolution proposal: "BSA Statement regarding Matters of Sexuality." Document signed by Dick DeWolfe, President, Boston Minuteman

Council; Rick Gables, President, West Los Angeles County Council; Lew Greenblatt, President, Chicago Area Council; John Harbison, President, Los Angeles Council; Mike Harrison, Past Chairman of the Board, Orange County Council, California; Tom Lynch, Chairman of the Board, Cradle of Liberty Council, Philadelphia; John McGillicuddy, President, Greater New York Councils; Wayne Moon, President, San Francisco Bay Area Council; Tom Morgan, President, Viking Council, Minneapolis. April 27, 2001.

80. Resolution 05/2001, European Scout Conference; resolution G11 (sexual discrimination), Europe Regional Conference, WAGGGS.

81. Many of these data are compiled by young conservative Hans Zeiger on a book defending the exclusionary policy of BSA executives (Zeiger, 2005, 23).

82. "It is common knowledge that the BSA prohibits homosexuals, atheists and females. Around the country, the Boy Scouts are under increasing pressure to become politically correct, watered-down, feminized, and secularized. Inevitably, these changes would come at the expense of such virtues as duty to God, moral cleanliness, bravery, and reverence" (Zeiger, 2005, 13).

83. "Duty to God is not a mere ideal for those choosing to associate with the Boy Scouts of America; it is an obligation".... "Homosexual conduct is inconsistent with the traditional values espoused in the Scout Oath and Law and that an avowed homosexual cannot serve as a role model for the values of the Oath and Law." "Resolution of the National Executive Board of Boy Scouts of America," February 2002. http://www.scouting.org/media/press/2002/020206/resolution.html (Accessed November 2, 2006, not available anymore; a reproduction of the Resolution could be found here: http://www.bsa-discrimination.org/html/bsa-0202-resolution.html; also quoted in Zeiger, 2005: 66).

84. Boyle, 1994.

85. Mechling, 2001: 223.

86. Ibid.: 213, 215–216.

87. Ibid.: 44.

88. Mechling, 2009: 185; James Davison Hunter: *Culture Wars: The Struggle to Define America*. New York: Basic Books, 1991.

89. Mechling, 2001: 44.

90. Sunder, 2001: 500–502, 529–531.

91. Weinberg, 1997.

92. Mechling, 2001: 214.

93. Mechling, 2009: 177.

94. Applebome, 2003.

95. Background notes for the presentation of Dr. Jacques Moreillon, World Scout Bureau, Geneva: 1994.

96. Warren, 2009: xv.

97. WOSM, 1992: 5.

98. WOSM, 1998: 17.

99. "WAGGGS/WOSM Relationships. Report on the Discussion on the Fundamental Principles of WAGGGS and WOSM." Document signed by Heather Brandon and Garth Morrisson, members of the WAGGGS/WOSM Consultative Committee, summarizing the meeting held on January 14, 2001 (document not dated): 3.

100. Nagy, 1967: 27.

101. Sica, 2006: 70.

102. Adroher, 1998: 51–55.

103. Nagy, 1985: 100.

104. The French Law of 1905 established the religious neutrality of the State and its lack of authority in religious matters, in stark contrast to the situation in Britain, where the 1534 Act of Supremacy, inspired by King Henry VIII and passed by Parliament, made the monarch head of the Church of England—"Supreme Governor"—which has been the case since 1559.

105. In Scouting, the French term *laïque* has been used to designate the scout associations where education in spiritual matters does not include the practice of religious beliefs by members, but an active attitude of in-depth study and understandings of the beliefs of those members. The English translation would be *secular,* but on this context the translation could lead to confusion because they strip the words of their intense educational focus on the spiritual dimension.

106. Kergomard and François, 1983: 34.

107. Pope Benedict XV "did not admire the scout movement and doid not hide his feelings." It was not until Pope Pius XI, in 1922, that Catholic scouting found a firm supporter. Domenico Sorrentino: *A History of the International Catholic Conference of Scouting.* Rome: Nuova Fiordaliso, 2004, 17–28.

108. Nagy, 1985: 100.

109. Nagy, 1967: 46; WOSM Secretary General Monthly Report, August/ September 1996, 3–5.

110. WOSM Secretary General Monthly Report, March 1995, August/ September 1996, March 1998.

111. Nagy, 1985: 94. "It was a question that remained highly controversial until 1977 when the Constitution was amended under which the status quo was more or less respected but strong emphasis was placed on the spiritual dimensions of Scout education."

112. WOSM, 1985: 3 (Res. 14/24); see also "From Conference to Conference," article by the Director of the Boy Scouts International Bureau in *Jamboree: Journal of Boy Scouting,* May 1947 (Vol. II): 147.

113. Kergomard and François, 1983: 345–346.

114. "For information of the Committee of the Council for meeting of 28th September, 1949. Twelfth International Scout Conference. August 8–10, 1949, at Elvesaeter, Norway." Report signed by J.F. Colquhoun, [UK Scouting] Commissioner at Headquarters, September 8, 1949: page 3 (World Scout Bureau Archives).

115. Kergomard and François, 1983: 346.

116. "For information of the Committee of the Council for meeting of 28th September, 1949. Twelfth International Scout Conference. August 8–10, 1949, at Elvesaeter, Norway." Report signed by J.F. Colquhoun, [UK Scouting] Commissioner at Headquarters, September 8, 1949: page 4 (World Scout Bureau Archives).

117. "The active pluralism of Scouts Pluralistes is what sets it apart from other youth organizations. It is a key focus of our education action with children and young people. Hence, our local groups take in all youths regardless of their background, beliefs, philosophy, or culture. Muslims, Catholics, Protestants, Jews, laïques, agnostics, etc., all have a place in the pluralist scouting. We choose to mix our social backgrounds and multiple spiritual values, sources of wealth and tolerance, in a bid for openness and the right to difference." "Qui sommes-nous?," section of the website of the Scouts et Guides Pluralistes de Belgique: http://www.sgp.be/modules/icontent/index.php?page= 10 (Accessed July 1, 2011).

118. The founding associations of UIPL were from Belgium (both the Flemish and the French-speaking ones), Cameroon, Catalonia, Central Africa, France, Gabon, Italy, Ivory Coast, Luxembourg, Madagascar, and Togo.

119. WOSM, 2001: 45.

120. "Report of the Common Working Group on the Spiritual Dimension in Scouting and Guiding," European Guide and Scout Conference, Ofir (Portugal), April 12–18, 1986. Quoted in Adroher, 1998: 67–69.

121. Nagy, 1967: 39.

122. Mechling, 2009: 189.

123. Robert Baden-Powell, " 'Religion in the Boy Scout and Girl Guide Movement': an address by the Chief Scout to the Joint Conference of Commissioners of Scouting and Guiding at High Leigh, July 2, 1926" (quoted in WOSM, 2001: 29).

124. WOSM, 2001: 42.

125. Dominique Bénard, "Spiritual Development in Scouting," working document, March 2000, p. 1. Quoted in WOSM, 2001: 45.

126. WOSM, 2006: 78–79.

127. To use Parsons' (2004: 25) words when speaking about British colonial Africa, "Scouting was thus both an instrument of social control and equally potent expression of social protest."

128. Robert Baden-Powell, ' "Religion in the Boy Scout and Girl Guide Movement": an address by the Chief Scout to the Joint Conference of Commissioners of Scouting and Guiding at High Leigh, July 2, 1926" (quoted in WOSM, 2001: 1).

129. "What is it about the national boundary that magically converts people toward whom we are both incurious and indifferent into people to whom we have duties of mutual respect?" (Marta Nussbaum: "Patriotism and Cosmopolitanism," in Cohen, 1996: 14).

130. "My complaint about identity politics is not meant to question, in any way, the contributions that the sense of identity of deprived groups can make in changing the predicament of those groups. Gender or class or caste can be

taken up from the perspective of deprivation and can then be an important part of resisting inequality and injustice. Part of my unease with identity politics lies in the use that is made of the bonds of identity by privileged groups to act against the interest of others. Identity is invoked not only by impoverished groups seeking redress, but also by privileged groups that try to suppress and terrorize the others" (Sen, 2003: 328).

131. Sica, 2006: 23; Collis, Hurll and Hazlewood, 1961: 97 (quoted in Jeal, 2001: 511).

132. "Try to leave this world a little better than you find it," extract from Robert Baden-Powell's last message, quoted in Hillcourt, 1964: 445.

133. Reimers, 2007: 2.

134. WOSM, 1985: 3 (resolution 14/24, "Principles of Scouting").

135. "Statement from the World Scout Committee on Human Rights Issues," March 2010 (Circular 3/2010, World Scout Bureau).

136. Diederik A. Stapel and Siegwart Lindenberg: "Coping with Chaos: How Disordered Contexts Promote Stereotyping and Discrimination." *Science*, April 8, 2011: Vol. 332, no. 6026, pp. 251–253.

137. WOSM Secretary General Monthly Report, March 1992.

138. UNDP, 1995.

139. Inglehart and Norris, 2003.

140. Inglehart and Welzel, 2005, 2010. The first dimension reflects the contrast between societies in which religion is very important and those in which it is not. Societies near the traditional pole emphasize the importance of parent-child ties and deference to authority, along with absolute standards and traditional family values, and reject divorce, abortion, euthanasia, and suicide. The second dimension is linked with the transition from industrial society to post-industrial societies: the unprecedented wealth that has accumulated in advanced societies during the past generation means that an increasing share of the population has grown up taking survival for granted. Thus, on those societies priorities have shifted from an overwhelming emphasis on economic and physical security toward an increasing emphasis on subjective well-being, self-expression and quality of life, giving high priority to environmental protection, tolerance of diversity and rising demands for participation in decision making in economic and political life. These values also reflect mass polarization over tolerance of outgroups, including foreigners, gays and lesbians and gender equality.

141. Inglehart and Welzel, 2005: 24–25, 48–76, 94–114, 115–134.

142. "To accept the topic of homosexuality as one of the possible sexual behaviors is not acceptable from the point of view of an educational proposal that has a precise vision of what men and women are. Therefore, even agreeing with the need to avoid any sort of exclusion of people, the ethical relativism cannot be accepted (one should be demanding on the principles and tolerant only on their implementation): the reason to not exclude is on the dignity of human beings, not on the acceptability of the behavior" ["L'affrontare il tema dell'omosessualità come uno dei possibili comportamenti sessuali non è accettabile nell'ottica di una proposta educativa che

ha una precisa visione dell'uomo e della donna. Quindi pur concordando sulla necessità di evitare qualsiasi tipo di emarginazione verso le persone, non si può accettare il relativismo etico (si deve essere esigenti sui principi e tolleranti solo sulla loro applicazione): la ragione per non emarginare sta nella dignità delle persone, non nella accettabilità dei comportamenti"]. Letter asking the withdrawal of the workshop on homophobia at the Roverway 2006 signed by the Presidents of the National Committee of AGESCI, the Catholic Scout/Guide Italian association, June 15, 2006.

143. Ironically, a survey on that Roverway participants carried out by the Institute of the Innocents, an Italian government-backed body which conducts research into children and families, shown that one quarter of the girls and 12 percent of the boys would consider a same-sex experience, and that 9 out of 10 expected to have sex before they got married. http://www.telegraph.co.uk/news/worldnews/1581970/Nine-in-10-Scouts-favour-sex-before-marriage.html.

144. "The National Study of Youth and Religion" a research project directed by Christian Smith and Lisa Pearce (http://www.youthandreligion.org/), quoted in Mechling, 2009: 186–187.

145. Inglehart and Welzel, 2005: 31, 134.

146. According to the research, in 2001 the ten countries with less than 49 percent of population disapproving homosexuality were the Netherlands (22%); Sweden (26%); Iceland (32%); Denmark (41%); Switzerland (43%); Germany(45%); Spain (47%); Canada (49%); and Luxembourg (49%). The research shows the particularity of the US case, because being tolerant on many other issues, on this one it still had a 60 percent of rejection. Inglehart and Welzel, 2005: 40–41, 127–128. However, since then and just in the last decade same-sex marriage has been legalized in ten countries: Netherlands (2001), Belgium (2003), Spain (2004), Canada (2005), South Africa (2006), Norway and Sweden (2009), and Argentina, Iceland, and Portugal(2010). In the US, Massachusetts was the first state to legalize same-sex marriage in 2004, later on followed by Connecticut, DC, Iowa, New Hampshire, New York, and Vermont. Mexico city did the same in 2010.

147. Inglehart and Welzel, 2005: 128. They add that "with considerable effort" they found the following percentages saying that homosexuality is never justifiable: Bangladesh 99%; Egypt 99%; Jordan 98%; Pakistan 96%; Indonesia 95%; Iran 94%; Algeria 93%; Azerbaijan 89%; Turkey 84%; and Albania 68%.

148. Ibid.: 129.

149. Sen, 2006: 23–29, 156–160.

150. Tra Bach, Huberman and Sulser, 1995: 209–212.

151. Ibid.: 209, 213.

152. Ibid.: 213–214.

153. Parsons, 2004: xiv, xii.

154. Russell, 1917.

155. Inglehart and Welzel, 2005: 145.

156. Baden-Powell, 1912, 162.

157. Ibid. (our emphasis).

158. Tra Bach, Huberman and Sulser, 1995, 215.

159. Lewin, 1947: 226–227.

160. Inglehart and Welzel, 2005: 43.

161. Sunder, 2001; Sen, 2006.

162. Oxfam, 2006.

163. Reimers, 2007: 11.

164. "Report to the Secretary General: Report of the League representatives to the Third International Scout Conference, Copenhaguen, August 1924." Document No. 38.191, League of Nations archive, Geneva.

165. Ibid.: 3.

166. Ibid.: 15.

167. "Building World Citizenship. 1996–2002 Summary." London: World Bureau, WAGGGS, 2003.

168. Sources: WOSM, 2002: 37; "Promising Practices. Scout Sub-Regional Peace Education Programme in the Great Lakes Region of Africa" (World Scout Bureau, WOSM: Geneva, 2003); "The Bottom Line. Scouting and Peace 'We were too late last time' (Rwanda)." (World Scout Foundation: Geneva, 2002).

169. Sources: "Building World Citizenship Projects Summary" (World Bureau, WAGGGS: London, 2003); e-mail to the author from Lydia Mutare, WAGGGS, April 10, 2007.

170. Parekh, 2003: 11.

171. Sources: "Circular N. 33/2004, November 2004. Scouts of the World/Youth of the World" (World Scout Bureau, WOSM: Geneva, 2004); *The Scouts of the World Award Guidelines* (World Scout Bureau, WOSM: 2006). My gratitude to Richard Amalvy and to Arturo Romboli.

BIBLIOGRAPHY

Abt, Lawrence E., Paul Mendenhall, and E.D. Partridge (1940): "The Interests of Scouts and Non-Scouts." *Journal of Educational Sociology*, 14:3 (Nov.), 178–182.

Adroher, Raül (1998): *La laïcitat a l'escoltisme/Laicity in Scouting/Guiding*. Barcelona: Fundació Escolta Josep Carol.

—— Elena Jiménez and Eduard Vallory (2005): *Escoltisme laic i transformació social: L'experiència d'Escoltes Catalans*. Vic: Eumo Editorial (Universitat de Vic).

Alliance of Youth CEOs (1997): "The Education of Young People: A Statement at the Dawn of the 21st Century." IAA, IFRCS, WAGGGS, WOSM, YMCA, YWCA.

—— (1999): "National Youth Policies: Towards an Autonomous, Supportive, Responsible and Committed Youth." IAA, IFRCS, WAGGGS, WOSM, YMCA, YWCA.

—— (2001): "Girls and Young Women in the 21st Century: Recommendations for Action." IAA, IFRCS, IYF, WAGGGS, WOSM, YMCA, YWCA.

—— (2003): "The Empowering Africa's Young People Initiative: A Holistic Approach to Countering the HICV/AIDS Pandemic." IAA, IFRCS, IYF, WAGGGS, WOSM, YMCA, YWCA

—— (2005): "Children and Young People: Participating in Decision-Making. A Call for Action." IAA, IFRCS, IYF, WAGGGS, WOSM, YMCA, YWCA and UNICEF.

Arneil, Barbara (2010): "Gender, Diversity, and Organizational Change: The Boy Scouts vs. Girl Scouts of America." *Perspectives on Politics* 8:1, 53–68.

Arnove, Robert F. and Carlos A. Torres (eds.) (2007): *Comparative Education: The Dialectic of the Global and the Local* (3rd edition). Lanham, MD: Rowman and Littlefield Publishers.

Anheier, Helmut, Marlies Glasius, and Mary Kaldor (eds.) (2001): *Global Civil Society 2001*. Oxford: Oxford University Press.

Applebome, Peter (2003): *Scout's Honor: A Father's Unlikely Foray into the Woods*. New York: Harvest Book/Harcourt.

Archibugi, Daniel, David Held, and Martin Köhler (1998): *Re-imagining Political Community: Studies in Cosmopolitan Democracy*. Cambridge: Polity Press.

Baden-Powell, Olave (1917): *Training Girls as Guides*. London: C. Arthur Pearson.

Baden-Powell, Robert S.S. ([1908] 2004): *Scouting for Boys* (Elleke Boehmer, ed.). Oxford: Oxford University Press.

—— (1912): "The Other Fellow's Point of View." *Headquarters Gazette*: June.

—— ([1919] 1949): *Aids to Scoutmastership* (World Brotherhood Edition). London: Herbert Jenkins Limited.

—— (1922): *Rovering to Success*. London: Herbert Jenkins Limited.

—— ([1923] 2007): "Education in Love Instead of Fear (Re-edition of the report presented to the 3rd International Congress of Moral Education. Geneva, 1st of August 1922). Geneva: World Scout Bureau [Originally published in *Jamboree: The World-Wide Journal*, n. 9 (Jan. 1923)], http://scout.org/en/content/download/17187/158436/file/Education%20In%20Love.pdf (Accessed July 1, 2011).

—— (1936): "A New Development in the Scout Movement in South Africa." *Journal of the Royal African Society*, 35:141 (Oct.), 368–371.

—— (1937): "Be Prepared" (interview). *The Listener*, British Broadcasting Corporation (Jan.).

—— (2006): *Citizens of the World: Selected Writings on International Peace* (compiled and edited by Mario Sica). Roma: Fiordaliso.

—— (2007): *Playing the Game: A Baden-Powell Compendium* (edited by Mario Sica). London: Macmillan.

Balcells, Albert and Genís Samper (1993): *L'escoltisme català (1911–1978)*. Barcelona: Barcanova.

Baubérot, Arnaud and Nathalie Duval (eds.) (2006): *Le scoutisme entre guerre et paix au XXe siècle*. Paris: Éditions L'Harmattan.

Bertrand, Jean-Luc (compiler) (2004): "Panafrican Youth Forum on AIDS: Dakar, March 2004. General Report." IAA, IFRCS, IYF, WAGGGS, WOSM, YMCA, YWCA.

Benhabib, Seyla (2006): *Another Cosmopolitanism*. Oxford: Oxford University Press.

Block, Nelson and Tammy Proctor (eds.) (2009): *Scouting Frontiers: Youth and Scout Movement's First Century*. Cambridge: Cambridge Scholars Publishing.

Boehmer, Elleke (2004): "Introduction," in Baden-Powell ([1908] 2004), xi–xxxix.

Boix, Carles and Daniel N. Posner (1998): "Social Capital: Explaining Its Origins and Effects on Government Performance." *British Journal of Political Science*, 28:4 (Oct.), 686–693.

Boy Scouts Association [UK], The (1951): *A Challenge to Scouting. The Menace of Communism*. London: Staple Printers, 1951.

—— (1966): *The Advance Party Report (Popular Edition): Being the Recommendation of the Chief Scout's Advance Party, 1966*. London.

Boy Scouts International Bureau, The (1954): *Boy Scouts in Five Continents*. London.

Boyle, Patrick (1994): *Scout's Honor: Sexual Abuse in America's Most Trusted Institution*. Rocklin, CA: Prima Publishing.

Bulman-Lever, Lesley (2010): *One Billion Girls: The Lives of Girls Around the World*. London: Marylebone Publishing Ltd.

Brélivet, Alain (2004): *Scouts sans frontières. Le Scoutisme dans sa dimension internationale.* Paris: L'Harmattan.

Brogan, Hugh (1987): *Mowgli's Sons: Kipling and Baden-Powell's Scouts.* London: Jonathan Cape.

Callan, Eamonn (1997): *Creating Citizens: Political Education and Liberal Democracy.* Oxford: Oxford University Press.

Castells, Manuel (2000): *The Information Age: Economy, Society and Culture. Vol. I: The Rise of the Network Society* (2nd edition). Malden MA and Oxford: Blackwell.

—— (2004): *The Information Age: Economy, Society and Culture. Vol. II: The Power of Identity* (2nd edition). Malden MA and Oxford: Blackwell.

Cholvy, Gérard (ed.) (2003): *Le Scoutisme: Un Mouvement d'Éducation au XXe Siècle. Dimensions Internationales.* Actes du Colloque international tenu à l'Université Paul-Valéry, Montpellier III (September 21–23, 2000). Montpellier: Université Paul-Valéry.

Cohen, Joshua (ed.) (1996): *For Love of Country: Debating the Limits of Patriotism* (Martha Nussbaum with respondents). Boston: Beacon Press.

Coleman, Andrea, Mary Ehrenworth, and Nancy Lesko (2004): "*Scout's Honor*: Duty, Citizenship, and the Homoerotic in the Boy Scouts of America," in Rasmussen, Mary Louise, Eric Rofes, and Susan Talburt (eds.), *Youth and Sexualities: Pleasure, Subversion, and Insubordination In and Out of Schools.* New York: Palgrave Macmillan, 153–176.

Collis, H., F. Hurll, and R. Hazlewood (1961): *BP's Scouts: An Official Story of the Boy Scouts Association.* London: Collins.

Colton, Joël (1992): "Definition of Youth and Youth Movements. Youth and Peace," in Fauvel-Rouif, 3–13.

Crick, Bernard (1999): "The Presuppositions of Citizenship Education." *Journal of Philosophy of Education,* 33:3, 337–352.

Delors, Jacques et al. (1996): *Learning: The Treasure Within. Report to UNESCO of the International Commission on Education for the Twenty-first Century.* Paris: UNESCO.

Dewey, John (1897): "My Pedagogic Creed," *School Journal,* 54 (Jan.), 77–80.

—— ([1916] 1997): *Democracy and Education.* New York: The Free Press, Simon & Schuster.

Dower, Nigel and John Williams (2002): *Global Citizenship: A Critical Reader.* Edinburgh: Edinburgh University Press.

Farrell, Joseph P. (1990): "And the Boys Took It Up for Themselves: Scouting as an Example of International Institutional Transfer." Paper presented at the annual meeting of the Comparative and International Education Society. Anaheim, CA.

—— (1996): "Narratives of Identity: the Voices of Youth." *Curriculum Inquiry,* 26:3, 235–243.

—— (1998): "Democracy and Education: Who Gets to Speak and Who Is Listened To?." *Curriculum Inquiry,* 28:1, 1–7.

—— (2001): "On Learning Civic Virtue: Can Schooling Really Play a Role?" *Curriculum Inquiry,* 31:2, 125–135.

—— (2003): "'Hey Joe....?' Moral Education, Moral Learning, and How Could We Ever Know If and When the First Produces the Second?" *Curriculum Inquiry*, 33:2, 105–115.

—— (2011): "'And the Boys Took It Up for Themselves.' Scouting: Successful Cross-Cultural Transfer of Global Citizenship and Spiritual Values." Paper presented at the international conference "Education and Global Cultural Dialogue" (May 2011). Toronto: Ontario Institute for Studies in Education (University of Toronto).

—— and Alexander, William (1975): *The Individualized System: Student Participation in Decision-Making*. Toronto: OISE Press.

Faure, Edgar et al. (1972): *Learning To Be: The World of Education Today and Tomorrow*. Report of the International Commission on the Development of Education. Paris-London: UNESCO-Harrap.

Fauvel-Rouif, Denise (ed.) (1992): *La jeunesse et ses mouvements: Influence sur l'évolution des sociétés aux xixe et xxe siècles*. Commission Internationale d'Histoire des Mouvements Sociaux et des Structures Sociaux. Paris: Éditions du CNRS.

FCEG (2003): *Acte de Commemoració dels 75 anys d'escoltisme català/Ceremony Commemorating the 75th Anniversary of Catalan Scouting and Guiding*. Barcelona: Federació Catalana d'Escoltisme i Guiatge. http://www.escoltes. org/fceg/22feb.htm (Accessed July 1, 2011).

González-Agàpito, Josep (ed.) (2009): *Escoltisme, autoformació i ciutadania activa. Un balanç de cara al futur*. Lleida: Pagès editors and Institut d'Estudis Catalans.

Gustav-Wrathall, John Donald (1998): *Take the Young Stranger by the Hand: Same-Sex Relations and the YMCA*. Chicago: University of Chicago Press.

Gutmann, Amy (1999): *Democratic Education*. Princeton: Princeton University Press.

Habermas, Jürgen (1999): *The Inclusion of the Other: Studies on Political Philosophy*. Cambridge: Polity Press.

Held, David (1995): *Democracy and the Global Order: From the Modern State to Cosmopolitan Governance*. Cambridge: Polity Press.

Hillcourt, William (with Olave Baden-Powell) (1964): *Baden-Powell: The Two Lives of a Hero*. New York: The Gilwellian Press.

Holmes, Edmond (1921): *Give Me the Young*. London: Constable & Co. Ltd.

Inglehart, Ronald and Pippa Norris (2003): *Rising Tide: Gender Equality and Cultural Change Around the World*. Cambridge: Cambridge University Press.

Inglehart, Ronald and Christian Welzel (2005): *Modernization, Cultural Change, and Democracy: The Human Development Sequence*. Cambridge: Cambridge University Press.

—— (2010): "Changing Mass Priorities: The Link between Modernization and Democracy." *Perspectives on Politics*, 8:2 (June): 551–567.

Ihle, Hans E. (1993): *Hitler's Boy Scouts Dictator-Fighters (Along the razor's edge)*. Lanham MD and London: University Press of America.

Jeal, Tim (1989): *Baden Powell, Founder of the Boy Scouts*. London: Hutchinson.

—— (2001): *Baden-Powell, Founder of the Boy Scouts.* New Haven CT: Yale University Press.

Jordan, Ben (2005): "Inculcating Character and Good Citizenship: The Boy Scouts of America and the Divisions of Gender, Age, and Race, 1910–1930." Paper presented at the 2005 Society for the History of Children and Youth conference "Children's Worlds, Children in the World." Marquette University (Milwaukee, WI), August 4–7, 2005.

—— (2010): " 'Conservation of Boyhood': Boy Scouting's Modest Manliness and Natural Resource Conservation, 1910–1930." *Environmental History*, 15:4, 612–642.

Jover, Mateo (ed.) (1994): "Trends. Trends in the World Today: How They Affect Young People. Questions and Challenges for Scouting." Geneva: WOSM.

Kant, Immanuel ([1795] 1991): "Perpetual Peace," in *Kant: Political Writings* (ed. and intro. Hans Reiss). Cambridge: Cambridge University Press, 93–130.

—— ([1803] 2003): *On Education.* Mineola NY: Dover Publications Inc. (reproduction of the 1899 English edition, London: Kegan Paul & Co).

Kergomard, Pierre and Pierre François (1983): *Histoire des Éclaireurs de France de 1911 à 1951.* Paris: Éclaireuses et Éclaireurs de France.

Kerr, Rose (1932): *The Story of the Girl Guides 1908–1932.* London: Girl Guides Association.

Kroonenberg, Piet J. (1998): *The Undaunted: Keeping the Scouting Spirit Alive. The Survival and Revival of Scouting in Central and Eastern Europe.* Geneva: Oriole International Publications.

—— (2004): "The Undaunted II: Keeping the Scouting Spirit Alive. The Survival and Revival of Scouting in Eastern Europe and Southeast Asia." Las Vegas, NV: Las Vegas International Scouting Museum.

Kunz, Phillip R. (1969): "Sponsorship and Organizational Stability: Boy Scout Troops." *The American Journal of Sociology*, 74:6 (May), 666–675.

Kymlicka, Will (1995): *Multicultural Citizenship: A Liberal Theory of Minority Rights.* Oxford: Oxford University Press.

—— (1999): "Education for Citizenship," in Mark Halstead and Terence McLaughlin (eds.), *Education in Morality.* London: Routledge, 79–102.

—— and Wayne Norman (1994): "Return of the Citizen: A Survey of Recent Work on Citizenship Theory." *Ethics*, 104:2 (Jan.), 352–381.

—— and Cristine Straehle (1999): "Cosmopolitanism, Nation-States, and Minority Nationalism: A Critical Review of Recent Literature." *European Journal of Philosophy*, 7:1 (April), 65–88.

LaBelle, Thomas J. (1981): "An Introduction to the Nonformal Education of Children and Youth." *Comparative Education Review*, 25:3, 313–329.

Lewin, Herbert S. (1947a): "Hitler Youth and the Boy Scouts of America: A Comparison of Aims." *Human Relations*, 1:2, 202–227.

—— (1947b): "The Way of the Boy Scouts: An Evaluation of an American Youth Organization." *Journal of Educational Sociology*, 21:3 (Nov.), 169–176.

MacDonald, Robert H. (1993): *Sons of the Empire: The Frontier and the Boy Scout Movement 1890–1918.* Toronto: University of Toronto Press.

MacLeod, David I. (1982): "Act Your Age: Boyhood, Adolescence, and the Rise of the Boy Scouts of America." *Journal of Social History*, 16:2 (Winter), 3–20.

—— (1983): *Building Character in the American Boy: The Boy Scouts, YMCA, and Their Forerunners, 1870–1920*. Madison, WI: University of Wisconsin Press.

—— (2009): "Original Intent: Establishing the Creed and Control of Boy Scouting in the United States," in Block and Proctor, 13–27.

Masemann, Vandra (1990): "The Culture of Scouting: Institutional Transfer in Short Pants." Paper presented at the annual meeting of the Comparative and International Education Society. Anaheim, CA.

Mechling, Jay (2001): *On My Honor: Boy Scouts and the Making of American Youth*. Chicago: University of Chicago Press.

—— (2009): "God and 'Whatever' in the Boy Scouts of America," in Block and Proctor, 175–189.

Miller, Susan A. (2009): "Trademark: Scout," in Block and Proctor, 28–41.

Mills, Sarah (2009): "Youth Citizenship and Religious Difference: Muslim Scouting in United Kingdom," in Block and Proctor, 190–206.

—— (2011) "Scouting for Girls? Gender and the Scout Movement in Britain." *Gender, Place and Culture: A Journal of Feminist Geography*, 18:4, 537–556.

Moreillon, Jacques (2004): "Secretary General Monthly Reports (1988–2004)." Geneva: WOSM. (Cyclostiled).

Nagy, Laszlo (1967): "Report on World Scouting/Etude sur le Scoutisme Mondial." Geneva: Graduate Institute of International Studies/Institut Universitaire de Hautes Études Internationales (Cyclostyled).

—— (1985): *250 Million Scouts*. London: Dartnell.

—— (1992): "Scouting Action in Peace Education," in Fauvel-Rouif, 401–414.

Ndene, Pascal (2007): *Un scout sénégalais: L'aventure citoyenne*. Paris: L'Harmattan.

Nielsen, Harriet Bjerrum (2003): *One of the Boys? Doing Gender in Scouting*. Geneva: WOSM, http://www.scout.org/en/content/download/3411/31932/ file/Gender_complete.pdf (Accessed July 1, 2011).

Norris, Pippa (ed.) (1999): *Critical Citizens: Global Support for Democratic Governance*. Oxford: Oxford University Press.

Olson, David R. (2003): *Psychological Theory and Educational Reform: How School Remakes Mind and Society*. Cambridge: Cambridge University Press.

Oxfam (2006): *Education for Global Citizenship: A Guide for Schools*. Oxfam Development Education Programme. Oxford: Oxfam.

Parekh, Bhikhu (2003): "Cosmopolitanism and Global Citizenship," *Review of International Studies*, 29, 3–17.

Parsons, Timothy H. (2004): *Race, Resistance and the Boy Scout Movement in British Colonial Africa*. Athens OH: Ohio University Press.

Pryke, Sam (1998): "The Popularity of Nationalism in the Early British Boy Scout Movement." *Social History* 23:3, 309–324.

—— (2001): "The Boy Scouts and the 'Girl Question.' " *Sexualities*, 4:2, 191–210.

Proctor, Tammy M. (1998): "(Uni)forming Youth: Girl Guides and Boy Scouts in Britain, 1908–1939." *History Workshop Journal*, 45, 103–134.

—— (2000): "'A Separate Path': Scouting and Guiding in Interwar South Africa." *Comparative Studies in Society and History*, 42:3 (July): 605–631.

—— (2009a): *Scouting for Girls: A Century of Girl Guides and Girl Scouts*. Santa Barbara CA: Praeger.

—— (2009b): "Introduction: Building and Empire of Youth," in Block and Proctor, xxvi–xxxviii.

Putnam, Robert D. (2000): *Bowling Alone: The Collapse and Revival of American Community*. New York: Simon and Schuster.

Reuben, Julie A. (1997): "Beyond Politics: Community Civics and the Redefinition of Citizenship in the Progressive Era." *History of Education Quarterly*, 37:4 (Winter), 399–420.

Reimers, Fernando (2007): "Developing Global Citizenship: Contemporary Challenges and Opportunities for the World Scout Movement." *World Scientific Congress: Education and Scout Movement*. Geneva: World Scout Bureau.

Reynolds, Ernest E. (1942): *Baden-Powell: A Biography of Lord Baden-Powell of Gilwell*. London: Oxford University Press.

—— (1950): *The Scout Movement*. London: Oxford University Press.

Robertson, Roland (1995): "Glocalization: Time-Space and Homogeneity-Heterogeneity," in Featherstone, Mike, Scott Lash, and Roland Robertson (eds.), *Global Modernities*. London: SAGE, 25–44.

Rosenthal, Michael (1980): "Knights and Retainers: The Earliest Version of Baden-Powell's Boy Scout Scheme." *Journal of Contemporary History*, 15:4 (Oct.), 603–617.

—— (1986): *The Character Factory: Baden-Powell's Boy Scouts and the Imperatives of Empire*. New York: Pantheon Books.

Rothschild, Mary Aickin (1981): "To Scout or to Guide? The Girl Scout-Boy Scout Controversy, 1912–1941." *Frontiers, A Journal of Women Studies*, 6:3 (Autumn), 115–121.

Russell, James E. (1917): "Scouting Education." *Teachers College Record*, 18:1, 1–14.

Saint George Saunders, Hilary (1948): *The Left Handshake. The Boy Scout Movement during the War 1939–1945*. London: Collins.

Scaillet, Thierry, and Françoise Rosart (eds.) (2004): *Scoutisme et guidisme en Belgique et en France: Regards croisés sur l'histoire d'un mouvement de jeunesse*. Louvain-la-Neuve: Academia-Bruylant.

Scaillet, Thierry, Sophie Wittemans, and Françoise Rosart (2007): *Guidisme, scoutisme et coéducation. Pour une histoire de la mixité dans les mouvements de jeunesse*. Louvain-la-Neuve: Academia-Bruylant.

Scheidlinger, Saul (1948): "A Comparative Study of the Boy Scout Movement in Different National and Social Groups." *American Sociological Review*, 13:6 (Dec.), 739–750.

Schnapper, Dominique (2000): *Qu'est-ce que la citoyenneté?* Paris: Gallimard.

Scout Association, The (2007): *An Official History of Scouting*. Foreword by Lord Baden-Powell. London: Hamlyn.

Sen, Amartya (2001): *Development as Freedom*. Oxford: Oxford University Press.

—— (2003) "Continuing the Conversation." *Feminist Economics,* 9 (2–3), 319–332.

—— (2006): *Identity and Violence: The Illusion of Destiny.* New York NY: W.W. Norton.

Seton, Ernest T. (1911): *The Official Handbook for Boys*. New York: Boy Scouts of America.

Sica, Mario (ed.) (1984): *Footsteps of the Founder. About 650 Quotations Drawn from the Writings of Lord Robert Baden-Powell.* Second enlarged edition. Milan: Editrice Àncora Milano.

—— (2006): "Baden-Powell and International Peace: An Introduction," in Baden-Powell, 9–38.

Skocpol, Theda (2003): *Diminished Democracy: From Membership to Management in American Civic Life*. Norman OK: University of Oklahoma Press.

Springhall, John (1971): "The Boy Scouts, Class, and Militarism in Relation to British Youth Movements, 1908–1930." *International Review of Social History*, 16, 125–158.

—— (1987): "Baden-Powell and the Scout Movement before 1920: Citizen Training or Soldiers of the Future?." *The English Historical Review*, 102:405 (Oct.), 934–942.

Sunder, Madhavi (2001): "Cultural Dissent." *Stanford Law Review*, 54: 495 (Dec.), 495–567.

Tedesco, Laureen (1998): "Making a Girl into a Scout: Americanizing Scouting for Girls," in Inness, Sherrie A. (ed.), *Delinquents & Debutantes: Twentieth-Century American Girls' Cultures*. New York: New York University Press, 19–39.

Tra Bach, Mai, Laurie Huberman and Françoise Sulser (1995): "The Educational Impact of Scouting: Three Case Studies on Adolescence." Geneva: WOSM, http://www.scout.org/en/content/download/3415/31949/file/edimpact_e.pdf (Accessed July 1, 2011).

United Nations (UN) (2000): "Millennium Declaration" (A/RES/55/2, 18 September). New York.

—— (2005a): *World Population Prospects: The 2004 Revision.* New York: United Nations Secretariat, Department of Economic and Social Affairs, Population Division.

—— (2005b): *The Millennium Development Goals Report 2005.* New York: United Nations Secretariat, Department of Public Information.

United Nations Development Program (UNDP) (1995): *Human Development Report: Gender and Human Development.* Oxford: Oxford University Press.

—— (2002): *Human Development Report: Deepening Democracy in a Fragmented World.* Oxford: Oxford University Press.

Vallory, Eduard (ed.) (2003): *Educar en la política: Dotze raons per a la participació en la vida pública*. Barcelona: Pòrtic.

—— (2004): "Paradiplomacy in Associations: Recognition of National Minorities in International Civil Society Organizations." Master's thesis, the University of Chicago, Division of the Social Sciences.

—— (2007): "Global Citizenship Education: Study of the Ideological Bases, Historical Development, International Dimension, and Values and Practices of World Scouting" (PhD dissertation). Barcelona: Universitat Pompeu Fabra, http://www.escoltes.cat/research (Accessed July 1, 2011).

—— (2009): "Status Quo Keeper or Social Change Promoter? The Double Side of World Scouting's Citizenship Education," in Block and Proctor, 205–220.

—— (2010): *L'escoltisme mundial. La discreta remor d'un bosc que creix*. Barcelona: Proa.

—— and David Pérez (2003): *La participació associativa genera implicació política/Participation in Associations Leads to Political Involvement*. Barcelona: Fundació Escolta Josep Carol.

Van Effenterre, Henri (1961): *Histoire du scoutisme*. Paris: Presses Universitaires de France (*Que sais-je?*, 254).

Verga, Carlo and Vittorio Cagnoni (2002): *Le Aquile Randagie: Scautismo clandestino Lombardo nel periodo '28–'45*. Roma: Nuova Fiordaliso.

Voeltz, Richard A. (1992): "The Antidote to 'Khaki Fever'? The Expansion of the British Girl Guides during the First World War." *Journal of Contemporary History*, 27:4 (Oct.), 627–638.

Watt, Carey A. (2005): *Serving the Nation: Cultures of Service, Association, and Citizenship in Colonial India*. Oxford: Oxford University Press.

—— (1999): "The Promise of 'Character' and the Spectre of Sedition: The Boy Scout Movement and Colonial Consternation in India, 1908–1921." *South Asia*, 22:2 (Dec.), 37–62.

Warren, Allen (1986a): "Sir Robert Baden-Powell, the Scout Movement and Citizen Training in Great Britain, 1900–1920." *The English Historical Review*, 101:399 (Apr.), 376–398.

—— (1986b): "Citizens of the Empire: Baden-Powell, Scouts, Guides and an Imperial Ideal, 1900–1940," in Mackenzie, 232–256.

—— (1987): "Baden-Powell: A Final Comment." *The English Historical Review*, 102:405 (Oct.), 948–940.

—— (1990): " 'Mothers of the Empire'? The Girl Guides Association in Britain, 1909-1939," in Mangan, J.A. (ed.), *Making Imperial Mentalities: Socialisation, and British Imperialism*. Manchester: Manchester University Press, 96–109.

—— (2009): "Understanding Scouting and Guiding after a Hundred Years," in Block and Proctor, xi–xxii.

Weinberg, Micah (1997): "Boy Scouts and Non-Believers." *Princeton University Law Journal*, I:1 (Spring), http://www.princeton.edu/~lawjourn/Spring97/weinberg.html (Accessed July 1, 2011).

Wilson, John S. (1959): *Scouting Round the World*. London: Blandford Press.

Wonesch, Margarete (2000): "Montessori-Pädagogik und Pfadfindererziehung: Gemeinsame Aspekte zweier reformpädagogischer Erziehungsmodelle," *Montessori–Zeitschrift für Montessori-Pädagogik*, 3, 108–132.

WAGGGS (World Association of Girl Guides and Girl Scouts) (1997): *Girl Guiding/Girl Scouting: A Challenging Movement*. London: World Bureau, WAGGGS.

—— (2003): *International Education*. London: World Bureau, WAGGGS.

—— (2008): "Constitution and By-Laws" (in force). London: World Bureau, WAGGGS.

WOSM (World Organization of the Scout Movement) (1973): "Constitution and By-Laws" (not in force). Geneva: World Scout Bureau.

—— (1985): "Resolutions of the World Scout Conference 1922–1985." Geneva: World Scout Bureau.

—— (1990): *Scouting 'Round the World*. Geneva: World Scout Bureau.

—— (1992): "Fundamental Principles." Geneva: World Scout Bureau.

—— (1998): "The Essential Characteristics of Scouting." Geneva: World Scout Bureau.

—— (2001): "Scouting and Spiritual Development." Geneva: World Scout Bureau.

—— (2002): "Scouting and Peace." Geneva: World Scout Bureau.

—— (2006): "World Scouting Report 2006: Youth, a Force for Development." Geneva: World Scout Bureau, http://www.scout.org/es/content/download/4159/44250/file/WSR2006_EN.pdf (Accessed July 1, 2011).

—— (2008): "Constitution and By-Laws" (in force). Geneva: World Scout Bureau.

Young, Iris M. (2000): *Inclusion and Democracy*. Oxford: Oxford University Press.

Zeiger, Hans (2005): *Get Off My Honor: The Assault on the Boy Scouts of America*. Nashville, TN: Broadman & Holman Publishers.

Index

Note: The letter 'n' following the locators refer to notes in the text.